Theory and Interpretation of Narrative
James Phelan, Peter J. Rabinowitz, and Robyn Warhol, Series Editors

Narrative Middles

Navigating the Nineteenth-Century British Novel

EDITED BY

Caroline Levine
AND **Mario Ortiz-Robles**

Copyright © 2011 by The Ohio State University.
All rights reserved.
Library of Congress Cataloging-in-Publication Data
Narrative middles : navigating the nineteenth-century British novel / Edited by Caroline Levine and Mario Ortiz-Robles.
  p. cm. — (Theory and interpretation of narrative)
Includes bibliographical references and index.
ISBN-13: 978-0-8142-1173-1 (cloth : alk. paper)
ISBN-10: 0-8142-1173-9 (cloth : alk. paper)
ISBN-13: 978-0-8142-9272-3 (cd)
  1. English literature—19th century—History and criticism. 2. Narration (Rhetoric)—History—19th century. I. Levine, Caroline, 1970– II. Ortiz-Robles, Mario, 1964– III. Series: Theory and interpretation of narrative series.
PR468.N29N37 2011
823'.809—dc23

2011018774

This book is available in the following editions:
Cloth (ISBN 978-0-8142-1173-1)
CD-ROM (ISBN 978-0-8142-9272-3)

Cover design by Greg Betza
Type set in Adobe Garamond Pro
Text design by Juliet Williams

♾ The paper used in this publication meets the minimum requirements of the American National Standard for Information Sciences—Permanence of Paper for Printed Library Materials. ANSI Z39.48-1992.

9 8 7 6 5 4 3 2 1

*For Eli, Paloma,
and Joe, who came along in the middle*

CONTENTS

Introduction
        CAROLINE LEVINE and MARIO ORTIZ-ROBLES   1

PART I. CENTERS

Chapter 1 Character Insecurity in *Sense and Sensibility*
        ALEX WOLOCH   25

Chapter 2 The Make-Believe of a Middle: On (Not) Knowing Where You Are in *Daniel Deronda*
        HILARY M. SCHOR   47

Chapter 3 Before and Afterwardsness in Henry James
        KENT PUCKETT   75

PART II. REPETITIONS

Chapter 4 Everyday Life in Anne Brontë
        AMANDA CLAYBAUGH   109

Chapter 5 The Clerk's Tale: Characterizing the Middle in *Dombey and Son*
        SUZANNE DALY   128

Chapter 6 *Pendennis*'s Stasis and Journalism's Work
        AMANPAL GARCHA   142

PART III. SUSPENSIONS

Chapter 7 Dilatory Description and the Pleasures of Accumulation: Toward a History of Novelistic Length
AMY M. KING   161

Chapter 8 An Anatomy of Suspense: The Pleasurable, Critical, Ethical, Erotic Middle of *The Woman in White*
CAROLINE LEVINE   195

Chapter 9 The Latent Middle in Morris's *News from Nowhere*
MARIO ORTIZ-ROBLES   215

Select Bibliography   249
Contributors   251
Index   253

INTRODUCTION

CAROLINE LEVINE
and MARIO ORTIZ-ROBLES

Let me tell you why I'm no fan of the middle class. Nothing "middle" is all that great. Middle class, Middle Ages, Middle East—they're trouble, all of them. . . . Upper class, lower class: pick a side. You get in the middle: crush like grape.
—Stephen Colbert, The Colbert Report, Jan. 24, 2007

Not long ago, within the literary academy and without, beginnings and endings were attracting a lot of attention. The very idea of beginning pulled together vexed ideas about origins and originality, birth, precedence, intention, and revolution. Political battles were waged between two ways of imagining beginnings: on the one hand, the quest for origins, the desire to ground the political world in essential truths; on the other, the desire to break from the past in a total way, as in the French revolutionaries' attempt to start again in the "year zero." Jacques Derrida pointed to the necessary violence involved in founding institutions and systems of law, while Edward Said affirmed beginnings as the activity of "making or producing difference."[1] And while beginnings evoked both deep conservatism and exciting innovation, endings seemed inextricable from anxiety and ideology, calling up death and *telos*, culmination and apocalypse. Frank Kermode understood endings as necessary—but always fictional—consolations for "men in the middest," while Francis Fukuyama famously announced that we had almost reached the end of history, a point where everyone would agree that liberal democracy was the best and most rational form of government for all.[2]

Critical or triumphant, all of those who wrote about beginnings and endings recognized their immense and mythical power. The Bible begins, "In the beginning . . . ," and ends with the end of the world. Another long Western tradition associates beginnings and endings with the pull of home: Odysseus struggles to reach the end of his journey, which is also his point of departure, and so his journey is an attempt to complete a circle. And the Hollywood happy ending, to return to our present, claims narrative priority in a culture for which last frontiers offer endless possibility and closure provides a gratifying correlate to its manifest destiny. In narratives high and low, then, beginnings and endings allow cultures to reflect on birth and death, departure and belonging, origin and fruition, mythic pasts and apocalyptic futures, revolutionary politics and divine eschatology.

The drama of these extremes is clear and inescapable. And yet, in our postmillennial moment, there seems to be a strong sense among academics in the humanities that arguments over origins and culminations have played themselves out, and for the most part we scholars are agreed that beginnings and endings are neither true nor foundational: as fictions fraught with meaning, they play crucial cultural roles, but they no longer seem to be a terribly useful heuristics for those eager to debate politics, philosophy, and the future of the humanities.[3] To be sure, for plenty of voices outside the university, beginnings and endings continue to exert an intense attraction—from debates over intelligent design and Darwin's *On the Origin of Species* to warnings over irreversible climate change, the extinction of species, and the end of fossil fuels, to religious extremists determined to usher in the end of the secular world. But in the day-to-day work of philosophical theory and cultural and historical scholarship, the heated debates over origin and *telos* that raged for several decades are no longer seen as equal to the task of teasing out and coming to terms with the more troubling implications of the millenarian politics and cultural malaise characteristic of the post–Cold War period. Instead, subtler, more fine-grained and gradualist accounts of political and cultural experience are needed in order to address critically the discourse of "crisis" we all too often leave unexamined as a "passing" moment or a "glitch" in our matrix.

If it seems tricky to pinpoint the origins of the end of a debate about endings and origins, this book plans to renounce the task altogether—and on principle. That is, we intend to accept both beginnings and endings as shadowy and overheated and to settle ourselves down instead to the bewildering, massive, deliberately undramatic enterprise of coming to terms with middles. The middle is of course notoriously impossible to sustain—undecided, transitional, vacillating, even cowardly. And yet, the middle is also precisely what we cannot escape, as Frank Kermode makes clear: it is because we live in the "middest," Kermode claims, because we are born *in medias res* and die *in mediis rebus*, that we need the consolatory fictions of endings. J. Hillis Miller argues that beginnings and endings always, in the end, turn out to be middles after all—citations and repetitions rather than innovations and culminations.[4] And indeed, in the past three decades theorists have actually given us ample reason to turn to the middle: from poststructuralist emphases on undecidability, iterability, and rhizome and trace structures to post-Marxist models of Left politics, the middle, it turns out, has been there all along. Maybe it has been just too vast, omnipresent, and crucial to be recognized as such.

It might seem politically worrying to embrace the middle, since it so clearly lacks drama and conviction—calling to mind such humdrum states as the middle-of-the-road, the middle class, middling quality, and the jadedness of midlife. But could there be such a thing as a radical middle? A liberatory, expansive, ethical middle? A middle filled with significance, energy, vitality, power? Is it possible to mine the idea of the middle for values that go beyond mediocrity and indecision? The middle, after all, gestures to a rich and various range of meanings, including *continuity, development, center, hub, digression, transition, deviation, disjunction, rupture, crisis, turning point, crossing, intersection, node, meantime, error, wandering,* and *interruption.* The middle points us to such crucial phenomena as changes and processes, ebbs and flows, hubs and breaks. And, most of all, it points us to the tough, imperfect, anxious, exciting experience of having decidedly left our beginnings behind, while never quite knowing what will happen to us in the end.

For literary critics, middles raise questions of both form and content. The novel, in particular, engages both the formal middle—the bulk of its narrative space—and the problem of middlingness—the middle class, the unheroic, the ordinary. In recent years, the form of the novel has been by and large less interesting to critics than its social content—its engagement of the city and the nation, and its participation in ideologies of empire, class, gender, race, and sexuality. And yet, growing signs of a renewed interest in formalist criticism have been appearing recently. This new wave of formalists are not simply looking backward, trying just to warm over the New Criticism: instead, they aim to show how literary forms matter in the social world, and thus they seek to combine a subtle attentiveness to the workings of aesthetic form with the political and historical impulses of cultural studies.

Broadly speaking, recent work that brings together formalist readings of the novel with sociopolitical history falls into three camps. The first group has the longest tradition of linking aesthetic forms to social content, and that is the Marxist model of form as ideology. From as far back as Georg Lukács to recent works by Fredric Jameson, Franco Moretti, and Garrett Stewart, Marxist-formalist critics have read the forms of literature as struggling to contain or suppress social clashes and contradictions.[5] Ultimately, these struggles always fail, which means that the novel form is best understood as an attempt to impose a false and impossible coherence on the materials of the social world. This model of reading tends to understand the middle as the site of revealing textual eruptions, conflicts, absences, and fissures, while endings then close down such contradictory energies in favor of strained ideological conclusions. One brilliantly innovative Marxist mode of reading the novel's middle can be found in Elaine Freedgood's *Ideas in Things,* which focuses on the objects that appear, without much attention, in the bulky interior of the Victorian triple-decker. These things matter not because the novel privileges them, but precisely because they had real histories of production, circulation, and consumption beyond the pages of the text. This is "not the history that the novel narrates, but the history that the novel secretes: the history it hides and emits." Thus the object, though only mentioned in passing in the novel's middle, can be read as a site where the realist novel "stockpiles" historical information, compressing into a single thing a vast and terrifying story of world trade, genocide, and enslavement.[6]

Where the Marxist tradition has apprehended form as a strategy for containing political instabilities, a second group of critics has been inclined to understand literary forms as more straightforward indexes—manifestations or enactments—of sociocultural realities.[7] For example, in their groundbreaking book *The Victorian Serial,* Linda K. Hughes and Michael Lund argue that the serial publication of the novel—with its extended length and multiple interruptions—embodied certain basic values at the heart of nineteenth-century British culture. "The assumption of continuing growth and the confidence that an investment (whether in time or money) in the present would reap greater rewards in the future were shared features of middle-class capitalism and serial reading."[8] Here the forms of the middle reflect and convey the beliefs of a dominant culture. Two other influential scholars of print culture, Leah Price and John Plotz, have focused on portable pieces of the novelistic middle—the extract and the quotation—as bearers of cultural values outside of the context of the novel proper.[9] And in quite a different example, Ronald R. Thomas argues that detective fiction adopted devices for isolating identities that reflected the anxieties and aspirations of new, modern, bureaucratic societies "preoccupied with systematically bringing under control the potentially anarchic forces unleashed by democratic reform, urban growth, national expansion, and imperial engagement." It is no accident, Thomas argues, that a genre consumed with finding clues to pinning down identity comes into being at the same moment as the modern English police force and the science of criminology.[10] For this second group of scholars, then, the forms of the novel's middle are capable of revealing the intellectual, social, and political dynamics of its cultures.

These first two cohorts have recently come under fire from a third and increasingly vocal collection of scholars. In the eyes of these critics, the notion that literary forms unconsciously reveal political and social struggle has come to seem condescending and untrue: they urge us instead to see writers as *deliberately* deploying literary forms to engage in self-conscious political and social projects. Susan J. Wolfson led the way in 1999 when she argued that Romantic writers were hardly unconscious purveyors of a "romantic ideology" that masked political struggle in unified "organic forms": instead, they were themselves fully aware of the constructedness of literary unities and deliberately drew on formal strategies to investigate problems of "subjectivity, cultural ideology, and social circumstance." Thus their works "reflect on rather than conceal their constructedness (not only aesthetic, but social and ideological)." As for Foucauldian readings, which "see all aesthetic form as only subordinate to an all-determining social form," these, Wolfson argued, overlook the ways that literary forms "may resist, revise, or reform a prevailing social context."[11] Similarly, in *Disorienting Fiction*, James Buzard argues that the shift in the novel "from a loosely assembled entertainment" to a genre in the middle of the nineteenth century that had "aspirations to total formal integration" was not so much the sign of a middle class trying to repress conflicts and contradictions as it was a "self-conscious questioning" by writers eager to capture and convey their nation as a "culture."[12] Likewise intent on moving away from critical assumptions about the naïveté of literary writers, John Kucich makes the case that Victorian realism was a "complex, highly self-conscious" project that "made a sophisticated awareness of scientific epistemology the basis for formal ordering."[13] The scholarly object for this third group is to understand nineteenth-century writers less as dupes or instruments of political and social formations than as thinkers aware of the ways that aesthetic forms can mold and intervene in the social world. The form of the novelistic middle, in this third model, is poised to emerge less as a process of repression or reflection than as a matter of conscious engagement.

While the contributors to this volume draw from all three of these socially conscious formalisms, it seems telling that they are all quite vigorous about emphasizing the notion of form as a deliberate and self-conscious enterprise. The middle emerges, throughout this volume, as a responsive and knowing formal engagement with the social world. It is this third model, then, that is found most clearly at the heart of this volume, and it is the one that may well represent the most powerful version of "neoformalism" in novel studies today.

In turning to the vast and sprawling middle of the nineteenth-century novel, in particular, this volume has two principal objectives. The first is to contribute to a long-standing gap in narrative theory. Theorists of narrative have made much of beginnings and endings, but it is in the vast, bulky middle of the nineteenth-century multiplot novel that narrative theory is inclined to let us down. It is not that theorists have overlooked the middle: it is that they have too often cast the middle in functionalist terms, as *on the way* to an ending that will bestow it, retrospectively, with meaning. In *S/Z*, Roland Barthes makes the famous case that the classic nineteenth-century novel manipulates us into a desire for ideological endings by mobilizing "an organized set of stoppages" on the way to an inevitable closure, one that resolves contradictions and represses possibilities.[14] Peter Brooks, in a more psychoanalytic vein, argues that "we would do best to speak of the *anticipation of retrospection* as our chief tool in making sense of narrative, the master trope of its strange logic. We have no doubt foregone eternal narrative ends . . . yet we still read in a spirit of confidence, and also a state of dependence, that what remains to be read will restructure provisional meanings of the already read."[15] And it is not only Marxist and psychoanalytic traditions of reading narrative that have tended to stress endings as the ultimate sites of narrative significance, the points where the text has been heading all along. D. A. Miller's remarkable Foucauldian analysis of the Victorian novel suggests that the novel's linear, cumulative time disciplines dispersals and deviations in order to bring every detail into line with its own ultimate evaluative judgments: "The moral lesson George Eliot seeks to impose," for example, "depends on our ability to correlate the end of a character's career with what was there in germ at the beginning."[16] Even narratology, which has offered so many refined instruments for the analysis of the middle of novels—from modes of focalization and diegesis to duration and anachrony—has rarely turned its attention to the middle *as such*, to middleness itself as a quality of narrative.[17] In her study of closure, Marianna Torgovnick suggests that sheer length is a problem for the middle: it is too massive and full to remain in the memory beyond the most climactic events.[18] But Catherine Gallagher points out that length is itself a formal element—"one of the most prominent generic features of the novel"—and yet one to which neither narratology nor other formalist accounts of literature have paid any sustained attention.[19] Nicholas Dames argues that this is a mistake indeed, since nineteenth-century theories of the novel form treated it less as an *object* than as a temporal *process:* they imagined "novelistic form as produced by reading in time, by rhythms of attention and inattention, slow comprehension and rapid skipping-ahead, buildups and discharges of affect."[20] Henry James and Percy Lubbock would later come to reject this theorization of the novel, redefining the very critical category of form as spatial design, and privileging such formal devices as "point of view" and the symmetry of parts. The Jamesian conception of form has prevailed ever since, but Dames argues that understanding the novel as a static artifact has prompted critics to neglect the time-bound activity of reading that was so important to nineteenth-century thinkers. This volume proposes, then, that nineteenth-century novelists, dwelling lengthily and lovingly on the middle, were absorbed in the experience of middleness *per se*. Spending hundreds of pages *in medias res*, absorbed in complex processes of *Bildung* and characterization, carefully deploying suspenseful cliffhangers and ironic interruptions, managing mistakes and crises, interludes, digressions, and transitions, the nineteenth-century novel offers narrative theory the opportunity to theorize the middle.

Our second objective is methodological in a broader sense. If for too long the techniques of formalist analysis have remained separate from the sociopolitical approaches that are the mainstay of cultural studies, this volume suggests that narrative middles are an ideal site for the convergence of formalist and historicist methods. The middle of the nineteenth-century novel, after all, has long seemed poor in form—a large, loose, baggy monster—but exceptionally rich in content, conveying political and social conflicts and norms, from ideologies of gender, race, and sexuality to institutional reform and imperial expansion. By attending to the middle of the nineteenth-century novel in terms of *both* form and content, we hope to challenge and to nuance the traditional categories we employ in reading narrative and to bridge the gap between intrinsic and extrinsic criticism, historicist and formalist models of reading. All of the contributions collected here address relations between the operations of the narrative middle, on the one hand, and sociocultural events and processes, on the other—including capitalism, middle-class identity, subject formation, gender norms, labor practices, scientific knowledge, and revolutionary terrorism. And all suggest that the workings of narrative form are bound up with the workings of the social, just as the social comes to be articulated and known through the practices of narrative form.

But why, if the goal is to generate a new set of theoretical, generalizable understandings of narrative middles, should this collection restrict its focus specifically to the nineteenth-century British novel? The most important reason lies precisely in our desire to capture the difficulty—and the interest—of joining sociohistorical and formal concerns. The world of nineteenth-century Britain focuses our attention on three crucial *social* middles: first, the middle class, which achieved political hegemony through industrial capitalism rather than revolutionary action; second, the centrist reform program pursued through institutional mediation in a purposefully ongoing process that stubbornly held to the middle, refusing both dramatic beginnings and resolved endings; and third, the hub of empire, as London marked the metropolitan center of an empire that stretched across the world. The novel's form, an aesthetic compromise between imaginative vision and historical discourse (Lukács famously called it the "epic of a world abandoned by God"), accords in its British variant a corresponding priority to the middleness of the world it inhabits by avoiding rhetorical excess and dramatic extremes.

For Franco Moretti, the nineteenth-century English novel is a terrible disappointment compared with its Continental counterparts: "the awful Victorian plot" is also "the worst novel of the West," because, Moretti insists, its middle involves no real possibility of change. Its heroes are always already innocent, and the narrative offers no searching uncertainties about value or social stability, always ending on the side of a naïve justice.[21] He prefers the willingness of the Continental novel to face up to the question of failure—the inevitable loss of illusions, the inability to realize a resolution between the free self and the demands of socialization—confronting the contradictions of modernity rather than evading or misrepresenting them. For Moretti, that is, the problem with the English novel is that nothing really unsettles the middle: no tension, no insecurity, no possibility of the radically new. In an essay called "Serious Century," Moretti goes so far as to claim that the middle of the nineteenth-century novel is little but "filler." We tend to associate narrative progress with a logic of "turning points," but he claims that these turn out to be surprisingly infrequent in the nineteenth-century novel, which follows instead the rhythms of everyday life and the value it places on repetitive patterns of conduct such as manners that provide a blueprint for a programmatically uneventful sense of normalcy. The nineteenth-century novel, Moretti argues, has collapsed adventure into everyday banality, the better to represent a social world in which work has given a new regularity to bourgeois life and impersonal style has become the mark of its seriousness of purpose. The middle, in other words, is the cultural repository of a serious century for which the reality principle has become a cultural value about which beginnings and endings have little to teach us.[22]

And yet, Moretti exposes something particular about the English novel's middle that engages the attention of our own volume. Moretti's favored Continental narratives are precisely those that avoid the marriage plot. Balzac and Stendhal give us heroes who refuse to marry willingly and for love because such a reconciliation with the social would imply an unshaken faith in the normalizing values of bourgeois society. They must reject marriage as an illusion, a ruse, a trap, a loss of the mobile energy of youth—an attempt to compel the hero to sacrifice his freedom to the engulfing and deadening processes of socialization. For the novel to stay faithful to modernity's contradictions, according to Moretti, two poles—self-determination and socialization—must remain opposed, straining against one another. But if the hero represents self-determination, it is the marriageable woman who stands in for the normalizing forces of socialization. Implicitly, in other words, to attach oneself to a wife is to lose one's freedom and energy. Women must be kept at bay for the sake of the historical dialectic. But it is in precisely this context that the English novel might begin to look more interesting than Moretti gives it credit for. By persistently intertwining marriage and *Bildung*, the British novel makes the question of femininity crucial to the question of modern subjectivity. Far from imagining the solitary, questing, masculine self as the prototype of modernity, the British novel puts at its center two people, to be precise, two *different* people, whose difference depends precisely on the binary division of gender. And while it may be true that the British novel tends to opt for happy endings, unlike its Continental cousins, and while it is all too obvious that the marriage plot adopts a heteronormativity that brings with it a trail of pernicious political consequences, it is one achievement of the British novel that it *never* forgets femininity—and never lets us forget it. Indeed, the middle of the nineteenth-century English novel works hard to theorize the gender of modernity—and it does so with an eye to its failures as well as its successes.

In our attempt to fulfill these theoretical and methodological objectives, we have grouped the essays in this collection under three conceptual rubrics: centers, repetitions, and suspensions. These categories pertain not only to salient formal characteristics of narrative middles; they are also, in keeping with the general aims of the volume, discursive patterns that help us to situate the social and cultural importance of middles. The first major question that gathers together the essays in this volume, then, is the question of the novel's center. Is there a midpoint, a heart of the novel, that holds everything together? The novelistic center appears as a site of interrogation or negotiation where the very centrality of the center is simultaneously foresworn and recuperated by formal strategies that make visible, in its absence or its problematization, the enduring importance of the center to nineteenth-century culture. When W. B. Yeats famously describes radical change as coming at a moment when the "center cannot hold," he is referring to the classic notion that "things" (order, life, totality) are held in place as though balanced on a central support. But one need not have the image of a gyre in mind to understand that meaning tends to gather around the center, whether this be on account of the cyclical nature of the seasons, an established human history of centrally governed social formations, or the body's tendency to position itself in the world following the dictates of the central nervous system. Writing during a period of cultural upheaval and political uncertainly, Yeats might well have felt that things were falling apart all around him, but the displacement of the center, or, rather, of centrality, as the fundamental organizing principle of thought was already underway in British culture in the nineteenth century. Darwin's theory of evolution and Marx's conceptualization of historical materialism are two mid-century instances of a more general tendency that was pushing human agency away from the center of explanation. It is not the case that the nineteenth-century novel stages a Copernican revolution in displacing centrality as much as it makes visible centrality's waning power as well as the strategies devised to come to terms with its diminishing returns.

On a formal level, the postponement of semantic clarity towards the moment of novelistic closure is very often accompanied by false or partial resolutions that, by appearing at the very center of the action, anticipate the end and, in so doing, retrospectively reaffirm the importance of centrality. John Harmon's soliloquy in the middle of Dickens's *Our Mutual Friend* or the interrupted wedding scene in Charlotte Brontë's *Jane Eyre* suggest themselves as explanatory centers that yet have to be rehearsed, repeated, or recovered before they attain their full narrative value. Then there is free indirect discourse, the realist novel's greatest contribution to mimetic representation, which charts a moving center of novelistic consciousness as the perspective shifts from one character to the next without thereby privileging a disembodied narrator that would come to occupy the absent center. The plasticity of free indirect discourse comes to symbolize this displacement as it itself becomes the most active site or vehicle of stylistic experimentation in the realist novel. The use of multiple narrators in Wilkie Collins, the hybrid form Dickens adopts in *Bleak House,* narrative interruptions in George Eliot, and Thackeray's meddling narrators are all formal innovations that, for all their inventiveness, also illustrate the centrifugal forces at work in the middle as narrative authority is multiplied, curtailed, and undermined by experiments in focalization.

Part I opens with Alex Woloch's essay on *Sense and Sensibility.* In a novel that centers on two co-protagonists—Elinor and Marianne—Austen questions the possibility of character centrality itself: who can be said to occupy the center of a double plot? Woloch's response is that Austen carefully crafts a "character structure" in which identities emerge only through comparisons and juxtapositions. (Of the two sisters, Marianne has "the advantage of height," but as Woloch asks, "how tall does that make either sister?") And this is not only a formal structuring principle for the narrative: it is a brilliant enactment of a specific *social condition*—the condition of being middle-class. The middle class, after all, "does not have an intrinsic social, or circumstantial, identity, but emerges only contingently, in negative relation to both the landed aristocracy and the unpropertied working class." In a world where social identity emerges only through comparison, Austen stages the insecure social status of her characters by deliberately choosing a character-pair, rather than a single protagonist, to organize her novel. "Locked together in continual juxtaposition, Marianne and Elinor embody the essentially contingent identity of those many individuals—then or now—who are unable to define themselves through a fixed or stable economic ground." And thus Austen joins narrative form to economic conditions in a way that never simply objectifies social relations: "Both the responses to and the condition of socioeconomic insecurity emerge only in relation to the narrative form."

Sense and Sensibility is not, of course, the only nineteenth-century plot organized around two main characters. Hilary Schor's essay shows that George Eliot deliberately troubles all settled sense of middles and centers through her famous double-plot structure in *Daniel Deronda*. She asks not only: who is at the center of the story? But also: where is its temporal middle? What is the central crisis of the narrative? Schor organizes her essay around a startling variety of meanings for middles—from meantime to mixture to meddling to crossing to disruption—and shows us how Eliot self-consciously engages them all, and all in the interest of affirming the humbling, interesting, disorienting experience of living in the middle. The question of the middle, Schor argues, is a question of knowledge. As the two plots meet and cross, and as the novel moves forward and backward to fill in two asymmetrical backstories and to project two different but intertwining futures, both readers and characters struggle to piece together the middle in disrupted and fragmentary moments, our grasp of narrative chronology always pointedly mixed-up and crisscrossed. Schor argues that this disorienting middle has ethical, epistemological, and political implications. To grasp their own roles in the midst of events, the characters must recognize the limits of their knowledge. What is it, then, to learn to live in the middle? It is an awe-inspiring experience, an experience of humbling ignorance. Indeed, as Gwendolyn recognizes the limits of her knowledge, she also comes to apprehend her own marginality, her movement away from the center: to know oneself in the narrative middle is to know that one is not at the center of the plot. Readers, trained by conventional novels, might well prefer the masterful and knowing satisfactions of closural endings and new beginnings. But Eliot deliberately deprives her heroine of both: what Gwendolyn discovers in the middle is her own ignorance and what she looks forward to, at the end, is no choice, no culmination, no new beginning, but only the "continuing middle." It may be a mistake to think of this as an unhappy ending, Schor suggests, if we think of marriage for women as typically coming too soon and repentance too late: the chance for women to live in the continuing middle is a chance to catch up with the knowledge permitted to them.

While Austen and Eliot deliberately unsettle the work of locating the novelistic center, Henry James makes the remarkable decision to drop it out altogether. Writing self-consciously in response to the English novel, James has been included as often in the British tradition as in the American one. Kent Puckett concentrates on the fact that the crucial, central event of *The Princess Casamassima*—Hyacinth Robinson's vow to participate in revolutionary violence, which precisely bisects his life—takes place in the unrepresented time *between* the two volumes of the New York Edition of the novel. Puckett argues that James had long been troubled by the problem of crafting a balanced novelistic whole, where the hermeneutic center—the novel's center of consciousness—would converge with the material center—the literal formal middle of the novel. Characters in James, as in *Daniel Deronda,* typically come to their knowledge either too early or too late, and the novel often reaches its own central crisis equally lopsidedly, leaving both the content and the form of the novel off-kilter. But in *The Princess Casamassima,* James purposefully took on the task of joining the formal, temporal middle with the psychic center of consciousness, inviting us to read always in two directions—backward from the vow to Hyacinth's childhood and complex social past, and forward to the fulfillment of the promise he makes to commit revolutionary violence. The vow in the missing middle of the novel precisely marks the point between the two, the moment that bisects the before and the after and makes it possible to read backward to causes and forward to effects. And so, Puckett argues, James dramatizes what Freud would come to call *Nachträglichkeit*—"afterwardsness"—"a position where if we would read for significance we would need to decide but cannot finally decide between reading forward or backward, from trauma to symptom or from symptom to trauma." It is this movement both backward and forward that makes psychoanalysis possible at all: "the fact that present and past are understood as parts of a greater analyzable whole." It is the same movement that allows James to construct his novel as an "organic whole," organized around a central point. And thus it is the middle, and emphatically *not* the end, that permits both novelistic form and meaning itself to take shape.

If centers organize the novelistic middle, creating coherence and order, repetitions might seem to act as a drag on narrative, unnecessarily elongating the text—making too much of the middle. And yet, narrative cannot do without repetition. Narrative theory has insisted on this point at least since Gotthold Ephraim Lessing, who argued that there can be no narrative without a subject who appears again and again, marking the passage of time for us through successive appearances. And the nineteenth-century English novel allows us to reconceptualize this property of narrative not only as a formal fact but also as a fact of social life. Repetition allows Victorian writers to reflect, and reflect on, the problem of mundane contemporary existence: such as the ordinary sameness that characterizes daily life, or the recurrent habits and manners that allow us to identify distinct social groups, or the dreary mechanical routines of factory labor. But how can the novel, in particular, embrace repetition without losing its energy, its excitement, its readability? It is "the essential nature of work to be perpetual, repetitive, habitual," writes Elaine Scarry, and this is crucially at odds with narrative's reliance on action, adventure, event.[23] The monotony of modern labor may seem impossible to capture in the novel without succumbing to a tedium that threatens to eradicate narrative interest altogether. Indeed, Elizabeth Gaskell's *North and South* never actually allows us inside the factory to see the workers at the machines, and Victorian poetry—Elizabeth Barrett Browning's "Cry of the Children," or Thomas Hood's "Song of the Shirt"—seems far more intent on capturing the monotony of industrial work, and far more capable than the novel, too, given its formal properties of rhythm and rhyme. And yet, Victorian novelists often embraced repetition, sometimes even purposefully stalling narrative flow, and found that this was no barrier to popularity with audiences. Thackeray, for example, chooses to represent journalistic work not as the breathless quest for change and novelty that it so often seemed in a rapidly modernizing social landscape, but rather as routinized, habitual hackwork that could emerge for readers as a reassuringly familiar, unchanging, and stable fact of life. Similarly, Dickens and Trollope show characters comfortably repeating a recognizable set of virtues, manners, and behaviors, thereby signaling class identity as legible, stable, and predictable both on and off the page. And most intriguingly, the nineteenth-century British novel often critically engages the intrinsic repetitiveness of the narrative middle—making use of it, displaying it, amplifying it—in order to focus readers' attention on the structures and meanings of repetition in the social world.

The three essays in Part II examine the repetition of formal and cultural motifs in the middle of narrative as one of its constituent characteristics. Amanda Claybaugh reads the extraordinarily insistent repetition of Anne Brontë's narratives as part of a project to represent precisely the dreary repetitiveness of humdrum life: the realities of both governessing and marriage. Everyday life for women is a monotonous round of sameness. And yet, in order to bring the hard truths of women's lives into the domain of fiction, Anne Brontë twice comes to a narrative impasse: both of her novels—*Agnes Grey* and *The Tenant of Wildfell Hall*—reach points where they simply cannot move forward unless they break from the representation of unremitting repetitiveness. In order to resolve her narrative difficulties, Brontë imports conventional plots into the middles of both of her novels: the courtship plot in *Agnes Grey* and the temperance plot in *Tenant*. It is true, Claybaugh argues, that these plots are familiar templates associated with dominant nineteenth-century ideologies." But, she argues, novelists sometimes used imported plots less as ways to support certain social projects than as formal resources, modes of emplotment necessary to narrative itself. Form, that is, might trump ideology. "What Anne Brontë's middles suggest, then, is that plots need to be understood as recognizable forms, ones that can be emptied of their substantive content and replaced with content of a quite different kind."

In her reading of *Dombey and Son,* Suzanne Daly focuses on a sector of the labor force in which repetition is the very essence of the form of labor performed: the clerks whose task is to copy documents. Starting from the observation that it is specifically two clerks who move closely around the plotted and the moral centers of the novel—the good Walter and the sinister Carker—Daly asks why clerks matter so much to the novel's middle, and why one must withdraw altogether. Turning to contextual evidence, Daly shows that Victorian culture was anxious about the class of clerks, understanding them as social climbers and interlopers, aspiring above their station. Clerks in Dickens—we might think not only of Carker but also of Uriah Heep—are typically tainted by sly ambition, deceit, and corruption. In order to allow Walter *both* to climb the social and the financial ladder *and* to remain a wholesome moral center for the novel, Dickens seems to have no choice but to drop him out of the middle of the novel, to allow his social ascent to take place in an unrepresented elsewhere. "To be dead to the world for thirty chapters is in this context to be cleansed of the taint of clerkship and social climbing that would otherwise cling to the character." Daly suggests that the narrative middle and the middle class exist in a strained relationship that is bound up with the relationship between plot and character: the plotted middle depends on the unruly and immoral actions of the slick and slippery Carker for its dynamic interest, while the middle class, in order to emerge as a reliable moral and social center, must be repetitive and predictable, like the static, and mostly absent, character Walter. Class, it turns out in Daly's reading, is precisely an effect of the repetition of certain recognizable attributes. Using the stable repetition of character to redeem the instability of plot, Dickens offers up an eventful novelistic middle with the redemptive hero nowhere to be found.

Amanpal Garcha considers the repetitive routines of journalistic work in his reading of Thackeray's *Pendennis.* On the surface, journalism would seem to be opposed to humdrum repetition, since it prizes the sensationalist novelty of the "news." And yet, according to Garcha, Thackeray describes journalism in long dilatory passages to still narrative flow, emphasizing stasis, repetition, and generality, appealing in worldly, sophisticated tones to the reader's knowledge of the world. Garcha shows how Thackeray pits the content of Pen's writing against the form of his career, the humdrum, tedious experience of the hack writer, who is forced to churn out the impression of constant change while caught in precisely the opposite—a repetitive cycle of sameness. Curiously, the novel privileges the dreary repetitiveness over the excitement of journalism, and Garcha argues that this is no accident: in a capitalist context characterized by bewilderingly rapid change, "routine implies a reassuring, if dull, repetition of acts and consistency of identity." Purposefully destroying narrative desire "secure[s] the narrator's melancholy identity as a man whose experience provides him with a clear, unaffected view of otherwise exciting and emotionally rich events," and thus the novel's antiplot middle achieves an effect of truthfulness precisely by distancing the narrator from the eventful world represented. Despite its baggy, repetitive digressiveness, *Pendennis* was popular with Victorian readers, and this essay suggests that the pleasures that these passages afforded had everything to do with the increasingly alienated nature of middle-class labor: "The large amount of plotless text . . . allowed readers to indulge in a . . . potent and immediate fantasy of escaping such alienating labor altogether and sharing the Thackerayan narrator's position beyond work, experience, and desire."

Just as repetitions threaten to quell narrative excitement, so too do pauses and delays, moments where the novel suspends its action. Here, too, the Victorian novel, surprisingly, seems to have embraced rather than avoided such suspensions. Chapter seventeen of *Adam Bede* is a classic example: "In which the story pauses a little." And as *Adam Bede* suggests, such stoppages may be crucial to the act of reflecting on narrative action, and thus may be essential to the ethical project of the novel. For at least the past three decades, it has been common critical practice to suggest that the nineteenth-century novel educates, instructs, or disciplines its readers by providing models of conduct or coercive strategies of containment that produce responsible citizens and well-adapted subjects. Often premised on a representational logic of outcomes, these models forget, or fail to account for, the crucial importance of the middle to the work of formation, such as it is, that the novel, by its own admission, performs. Emma Bovary, to be sure, never paid close attention to the ending of the novels she avidly read, or, if she did, she must have taken it as the price to be paid for what really mattered to her, which was all in breaking the monotony of provincial life, of suspending the natural order of narrative progression. This negative example (and a French one, at that) shows that the cultural work of the novel often takes place through an engagement with the amorphous middle. Critical thinking, spiritual inspiration, and political action result not from dramatic resolutions nor game-changing events; they are the product of narrative suspensions where readers are left to ponder the implications of the forces acting on characters or in situations that remain unformed, suspended in the very process of becoming. Latency and dilation, delays and protraction, suspense itself as the formalization of the lingering middle, contribute to a readerly musing or deliberation that is productive of ethical thought. Narrative suspensions are difficult to quantify, or even isolate, insofar as they signify an absence of form as such, or suggest form as incomplete or interminable, and therefore demand an active engagement that is also a necessary suspension of judgment. The suspended middle, whether composed of endlessly detailed descriptions of the natural world, rapidly accelerating sensations, or dense historical reconstructions, creates the conditions of possibility for the production of active subjects rather than the passive subjects of a discipline perhaps too rapidly associated with novelistic mechanisms of visibility that are, in any case, inoperative or suspended in the stops and starts constitutive of the middle. The state of uncertainty or undecidability to which the suspended middle gives rise thus calls for an ethics of accountability that turns less on decisive events than on what Eliot calls the "incalculably diffusive" effects of the "unhistoric acts" performed in everyday life.

The final section of this volume considers the ethics of narrative suspensions. Amy King points out that narrative theory tends to overlook long descriptive passages as inconsequential obstructions that impede the forward-moving patterns of plotted unfolding. And yet, King argues, protracted descriptions of natural and social environments had a significant theological value in the early nineteenth century, and they became crucial to the novelistic realism that would dominate the Victorian period. Drawing from the tradition of natural theology, which understood God's work as perceptible in the smallest details of the natural world, writers such as Gilbert White and Mary Russell Mitford wrote extensive descriptions of their local environments as acts of reverence. Enormously popular and influential, these writers tapped into a readerly pleasure that favored the accumulation of detail rather than the teleological momentum of plot. Lingering lovingly on the most minute observations, they also presumed an ethical value in the dilation and protraction of stilled observation, which refuses to subordinate "insignificant" details to larger patterns of meaning and value. Nineteenth-century realist novels clearly drew on this tradition of protracted local detail and description, and took for granted that their readers took as much pleasure in the accumulation of minute description as they did in the forward movement of plot. And so it may be necessary, King argues, to think of realism not as a secular enterprise, but as an ethical, ecological project that respected the local detail and extended description of the novelistic middle as a worthy end in itself.

If some nineteenth-century novelists engaged in a deliberate resistance to the headlong, future-oriented pleasures of plotted narrative, others seemed to thrive on it. Suspense was a staple of the nineteenth-century novel, and it has long been understood to depend on long-deferred endings. But the next essay in the volume suggests that the anxious and exciting delays of the suspenseful middle were actually far more important to the ethics of nineteenth-century novels than their endings. Focusing on Wilkie Collins's *The Woman in White*, Caroline Levine argues that for nineteenth-century novelists, the suspensions of the narrative middle enjoyed a power and meaning of their own. In *The Woman in White*, characters respond in a range of widely different ways to the text's suspenseful delays and withholdings—some are passionately engaged in the pursuit of truth, others completely indifferent to the emergence of a mystery. By modeling an array of reactions to suspenseful delays, Collins makes suspense the *content* as well as the form of the narrative. The charming central characters of the text—Walter and especially Marian—suggest that the most appealing response to suspense is a range of active and affectively intense responses, "including hope, desire, skepticism, distrust, suspicion, anxiety, longing, superstition, dread, uneasiness, tension, prediction, calculation, speculation, curiosity, and conjecture." Unlike the Fairlie clan, who find mysteries unbearable, uninteresting, or just plain inconvenient, Walter and Marian teach us to take the experience of the uncertain middle seriously not only as pleasurable and epistemologically productive but also as ethically responsible. And Collins is not the only nineteenth-century novelist to value the suspenseful middle. *The Woman in White*, Levine argues, is "one particularly self-conscious and brilliant instance among many of Victorian narrative middles that are more inclined to invite an active, engaged, critical thinking than a helpless, thoughtless submission."

Bringing us to the *fin de siècle*, Mario Ortiz-Robles addresses the curious latency of the middle in Victorian utopian novels, a genre that enjoyed a remarkable popularity at the end of the nineteenth century. Unlike early modern utopian fictions, which are premised on the accidental discovery of a previously unknown, geographically remote society, late Victorian utopian fiction usually involves time travel into the future and an evolved version of contemporary society. This creates a narrative paradox: on the one hand, the middle in these utopian novels is suspended between a future that is fully realized and an unpromising present for which the future remains uncertain; that is, there is no middle. On the other, the structural suspension of the middle accounts for a characteristic feature of the genre: long expository passages that describe the functioning of the new society and provide, in retrospect, a historical account of how it came to pass; that is, there is nothing but middle. Through a reading of William Morris's *News from Nowhere*, this essay examines the narrative temporality of late Victorian utopian fiction in the context of the radical reconceptualization of time that resulted from the cultural assimilation of Marx's historical materialism as a new science of history and Darwin's theory of evolution by natural selection as a new scale of human temporality. The latency of the middle in late-Victorian utopian fiction allows Ortiz-Robles to consider the extent to which utopia's promise of ethical and political transformation is enacted when the reader is enjoined to actively create a middle that the narrative does not openly provide.

When teaching the middle of the bulky nineteenth-century novel, many scholars these days turn to the great mountain of historical information to fill the middle lectures. But important though it is, contextual material may also mask some problems of specifically *narrative* interest: what exactly is the middle of the sprawling nineteenth-century novel *for*? How does it work? And are we missing something important when we suggest to our classes that the world outside of the text was filled with excitement, while the novel simply bided its time, waiting to come to a proper and satisfying end? Read together, these essays gesture to a new set of classroom questions that go well beyond the texts under examination here: that is, to a pedagogy of the middle. Woloch, Schor, and Daly, for example, invite us to think about the temporal middle—midway through the *story*, midway through the *plot*—and its relation to the characterological middle: which person or persons are at the center of the novel's consciousness, its heart? Or to put this another way, how should we think about the relationship between the "center" and the "middle"? Claybaugh and Garcha ask us how the realist novel, with its insistence on representing the ordinary experience of the everyday, incorporated work into narrative. How does the middle of the novel convey the repetitive routines of modern labor? Similarly interested in the intersection of social pressures and narrative forms, Woloch and Daly suggest that narrative middles were crucial places for nineteenth-century Britain to work out questions of class: always a relational term, class requires contrast to take shape, and where better than in the middle of the story, where multiple characters vie for power and centrality? Garcha, King, and Ortiz-Robles all contend that Victorian readers enjoyed a leisurely, dilatory, plotless middle much more than we have ever recognized, and that the growing audience for the novel did not actually demand the forward-looking pleasures of suspense. Garcha and Ortiz-Robles argue that the slow middle was a reassuring suspension of lived experience, whereas King suggests that the novel's long descriptive pauses registered a profound reverence for the things of the world. Together, they ask what unacknowledged pleasures and values the long middle offered its first readers. By contrast, Levine asks whether the more conventional readerly pleasures of suspense offered something more serious than scholars have typically recognized, and her essay and King's converge in a sense that the middle—whether plotless or plotted—was a site of ethical and epistemological value. What does one appreciate in the middle? What are the functions of delays, gaps, and interruptions in plotted unfolding? How can we talk about length as an experience of reading, of time, of continuity? Schor and Levine examine the ways that readers and characters yearn for knowledge in the middle of the novel: what kind of knowledge do we learn to seek, and what can we know *in medias res*? And Puckett and Ortiz-Robles turn our attention to the problem of promising: how should we think about the middle as a space of anticipation or latency, where the past informs a future that has not yet come to pass? What and how does the middle ask us to look forward? Does the middle inform both the before and the after? The essays that follow show just how fruitful such questions can be. Indeed, the various contributions to *Narrative Middles* perform exemplary readings that, in their scope as well as their specificity, offer models of interpretive practice and interrogation for the classroom.

If beginnings and endings matter because they establish and enact hierarchies, this volume invites critical attention to the more commonplace processes of the middle: these are more ordinary, yes, bulkier and more humdrum, but valuable and always necessary—indeed, inescapable. By merging formalist analysis with an attention to the social, political, and cultural problems of the British nineteenth century, the essays collected here allow the middle to take shape, perhaps for the first time, as a genuine sociopolitical and literary event worthy of both historical and narratological attention. And by bringing formalist and historicist methods together, this volume suggests a new direction for nineteenth-century literary studies—a direction that might occupy us for a long while in the dilatory, baggy, bewildering, and ongoing scholarly middle.

Notes

1. Jacques Derrida, "Force of Law: The 'Mystical Foundation of Authority,'" trans. Mary Quaintance, in *Deconstruction and the Possibility of Justice,* eds. Drucilla Cornell, Michael Rosenfeld, and David Gray Carlson (New York and London: Routledge, 1992), 3–67; Edward Said, *Beginnings: Intention and Method* (Baltimore and London: Johns Hopkins University Press, 1978), xiii.

2. Frank Kermode, *The Sense of an Ending: Studies in the Theory of Fiction* (Oxford: Oxford University Press, 1967), 8; Francis Fukuyama, *The End of History and the Last Man* (New York: Avon Books, 1992).

3. One important exception is Brian Richardson, who, in a fascinating recent collection of essays, argues that although critics have repeatedly acknowledged the importance of narrative beginnings, few have actually paid attention to their complexity and richness. The articles included here focus especially on fictions of beginning. *Narrative Beginnings: Theories and Practices* (Lincoln and London: University of Nebraska Press, 2008).

4. Kermode, 7. J. Hillis Miller, *Reading Narrative* (Norman: University of Oklahoma Press, 1998). See especially the chapter called "Middles," 61–77.

5. See Georg Lukacs, *The Theory of the Novel*, trans. Anna Bostock (Cambridge, MA: MIT Press, 1971); Fredric Jameson, *The Political Unconscious: Narrative as a Socially Symbolic Act* (Ithaca: Cornell University Press, 1981); Franco Moretti, *The Way of the World: The Bildungsroman in European Culture* (London and New York: Verso, 1987); and Garrett Stewart, "The Foreign Offices of British Fiction," *Modern Language Quarterly* 61 (2000): 1–206.

6. Elaine Freedgood, *The Ideas in Things: Fugitive Meaning in the Victorian Novel* (Princeton: Princeton University Press, 2006), 36.

7. D. A. Miller famously argues, too, that the sheer quantity of paper that makes up the massive form of *Bleak House*, as well as insistence that we move backward and forward, linking events and characters, "train us . . . in the sensibility for inhabiting the new bureaucratic, administrative structures." *The Novel and the Police* (Berkeley: University of California Press, 1988), 88–89.

8. Furthermore, dramatically changing conceptions of time ushered in by rapid industrialization and new theories of geological formation and evolution found their narrative manifestation in the "contraction and expansion of reading time" fostered by serialized publication. Linda K. Hughes and Michael Lund, *The Victorian Serial* (Charlottesville: University Press of Virginia, 1991), 4, 5.

9. See Leah Price, *The Anthology and the Rise of the Novel* (Cambridge: Cambridge University Press, 2000); and John Plotz, *Portable Property: Victorian Culture on the Move* (Princeton: Princeton University Press, 2008).

10. Ronald R. Thomas, *Detective Fiction and the Rise of Forensic Science* (Cambridge: Cambridge University Press, 2001), 4.

11. Susan J. Wolfson, *Formal Charges: The Shaping of Poetry in British Romanticism* (Stanford: Stanford University Press, 1999), 19, 14, 231. Wolfson has led the charge to rethink formalist approaches not only in her own book, but also in a co-edited special issue on form in 2000: *Reading for Form*, eds. Susan J. Wolfson and Marshall Brown, *Modern Language Quarterly* 61, no. 1 (March 2000).

12. James Buzard, *Disorienting Fiction: The Autoethnographic Work of Nineteenth-Century British Novels* (Princeton: Princeton University Press, 2005).

13. John Kucich, "Intellectual Debate in the Victorian Novel," in *The Cambridge Companion to the Victorian Novel*, ed. Dierdre David (Cambridge: Cambridge University Press, 2001), 219.

14. Roland Barthes, *S/Z*, trans. Richard Miller (New York: Hill and Wang, 1974), 76.

15. Peter Brooks, *Reading for the Plot: Design and Intention in Narrative* (Cambridge, MA, and London: Harvard University Press, 1984), 23.

16. Miller, *The Novel and the Police*, 26.

17. Brian Richardson's collection, *Narrative Dynamics*, was part of the inspiration for this volume. While Richardson does not articulate his concerns in terms specifically of the "narrative middle," he suggests that new accounts of temporality have been emerging, and his notion of narrative dynamics differentiates the beginning and the end from the "movement and shaping of the plot"—and so seems to invite an attention to the middle. *Narrative Dynamics: Essays on Time, Plot, Closure, and Frame* (Columbus: The Ohio State University Press, 2002), 2.

18. "It is difficult to recall *all* of a work after a completed reading, but climactic moments, dramatic scenes, and beginnings and endings remain in the memory and decisively shape our sense of the novel as a whole." Marianna Torgovnick, *Closure in the Novel* (Princeton: Princeton University Press, 1981), 3–4.

19. Catherine Gallagher, "Formalism and Time," *Modern Language Quarterly* 61, no. 1 (March 2000): 229.

20. Nicholas Dames, *The Physiology of the Novel: Reading, Neural Science, and the Form of Victorian Fiction* (Oxford: Oxford University Press, 2007), 11.

21. Moretti, *The Way of the World*, 201, 214.

22. Franco Moretti, "Serious Century," in *The Novel*, vol. 1, ed. Franco Moretti (Princeton: Princeton University Press, 2006), 364–400.

23. Elaine Scarry, *Resisting Representation* (Oxford: Oxford University Press, 1994), 65.

PART I

Centers

ONE

Character Insecurity in *Sense and Sensibility*

ALEX WOLOCH

Marianne and Elinor. Elinor and Marianne.

The two sisters in *Sense and Sensibility* are stuck with each other as only fictional persons can be. At the core of this novel's character-system we don't find a single center but rather an uneasy middle: not a defined protagonist who might organize and anchor the surrounding fictional totality (the normative model for the nineteenth- and twentieth-century novel), but two co-protagonists in dynamic, shifting relation to one another. I want to pursue the nature and implications of this kind of narrative "middle": one that is grounded in a simple structural choice (two main characters instead of one) but that can have profound and often intricate consequences across different registers of a novel. In these terms, the narrative center constitutes an arena of privilege—that privilege which attaches, *discursively,* to any protagonist and that might be intertwined with or set against the elaboration of the implied person in the story itself. (We can think immediately of Emma Woodhouse and Fanny Price for two radicalized examples of this.) The narrative middle, on the contrary, constitutes an arena of contestation—an intrinsically uncertain space made up of co-protagonists who, in contingent relationship with one another, are always vulnerable to repositioning, transformation, reevaluation. This middle space, at its most realized, is a structurally curious one. It can unfold characters who are simultaneously privileged and imperiled, torn between background and foreground, just as, in *Sense and Sensibility* itself, Marianne and Elinor both seem so confident *and* so anxious, looming between wealth and disinheritance, and marked, above all, by those rich, memorable "personalities" that, even in their very distinctness, are forged so clearly out of a troubled, comparative matrix.

To put this in different terms, Austen's novel emphatically blends a formal condition—that state of contingent centrality which can attach to co-protagonists—with a social and psychological one: the sibling rivalry that marks both Dashwood sisters across the narrative. Like so many actual siblings, but *also* like other character-pairs (Don Quixote and Sancho Panza; Rastignac and Goriot; Huck and Jim; Carrie and Hurstwood), these two sisters depend on each other, even when they stand out in relief against one another. The very active pressure of their disagreement can blur the lines between them—as when (to pick one simple example) Elinor imagines and then rejects her sister's thoughts, clarifying her own thoughts only by thinking about the thoughts she putatively *wouldn't* think: "As it was, it required but a slight effort of fancy to connect [Colonel Brandon's] emotion with the tender recollection of past regard. Elinor attempted no more. But Marianne, in her place, would not have done so little. The whole story would have been speedily formed under her active imagination; and everything established in the most melancholy order of disastrous love."[1] This kind of strong relationship between two interlocked characters can be both psychological and structural. The characters are closely linked as fictional persons in the imagined world of the story but also as juxtaposed elements within the narrative discourse. The two sisters *share* the form, and emerge, as represented individuals, only through the way that the text inflects each of them (imperfectly) within the narrative totality.

The narrative "middle" constituted by these two co-protagonists is thus legible only at the intersection of story and discourse, as Austen's novel develops a complex relationship between the very configuration of the two characters, as formal elements within the narrative structure, and their social and psychological elaboration. How do you represent two persons in a single structure? Consider this late, idiosyncratic painting by Pieter Bruegel, *Peasant and Bird Nester* (fig. 1), which narrows down his usually multicentered compositions to the starkest dimension: two figures, locked in a strangely precarious—and imbalanced—relationship, that Bruegel seems to have frozen at its most unstable point. On the one hand, we can't look at the central figure without soon looking away *from* him, toward the scene at which he so emphatically points. On the other hand, this secondary figure toward whom our attention is called—with his contorted limbs and obscured face—can't be comprehended directly, but only through the intervention of the very person

FIGURE 1. Pieter Bruegel the Elder, *Peasant and Bird Nester* (1568)

who subordinates him. Each figure, across the axis of center and periphery, works to displace the other. Crucially, Bruegel draws this lack of secure place into the referenced world itself: we belatedly discover the thief in the tree only to see, at once, the hat that suggests his own impending fall, just as the central figure, as though through the very act of pointing us into the background that displaces him, stumbles unwittingly on the water's edge. It is a pointedly unstable compositional—and referential—moment: it can't hold for one second longer (as background and foreground begin to trade places) and yet it is impossible to see, in this confusion, exactly what we would see next. Both figures are about to fall.[2] And the suspended play between background and foreground seems to produce—or perhaps is motivated by—this insecure physical vulnerability, as though such insecurity were intrinsic to the character-pair as such.

I want to offer a reading of Austen's novel that also hinges on the way in which the referenced and formal vulnerability of two characters (lodged within the middle of a single structure) are profoundly intertwined. Like Bruegel's painting, this novel presents an extremely insecure, unsettled world, more anxious, arguably, than any of Austen's other works. Such insecurity is grounded in the uncertain positions of its two main characters both as unmarried, unpropertied women within the plot and *as* co-protagonists in the unfolding composition. In George Perec's 1969 *La Disparation*, famously written without the letter "e," characters feel a vague sense that something is missing from their world, without ever being able, of course, to understand or articulate an absence that is unfolding strictly on the level of form. In a similar way, an anxiety or unsettling that originates in the formal division of *Sense and Sensibility* between co-protagonists manifests itself continually as a profound problem, situation, or condition within the story world. As with Bruegel's painting, Austen draws the fundamental compositional premise of the discourse—that splitting between Marianne and Elinor—into the world of the story itself.

In this reading, one of the key accomplishments of *Sense and Sensibility* is the way that different registers of the narrative—plot, theme, tempo, voice— are saturated with that charged "middleness" that derives from the underlying, formal division of the two co-protagonists. Let me begin with a very minor (but to my mind striking) example, the short description of the two sisters' entrance into a "crowded" party that they are brought to, by Lady Middleton, when they first arrive in London in volume two: "[T]hey were permitted to mingle in the croud, and take their share of the heat and inconvenience, to which their arrival must necessarily add" (175). There's a disquieting, almost clenched force to this sentence, which rests on the final modifying clause and above all on that unforced (even redundant) addition of "necessarily." Here the unwelcome conditions that people encounter in a structure—in this case the "heat" and "inconvenience" of the gathering—are, without any choice, changed and worsened by their own participation within the structure. In this anxious world, identity no sooner asserts itself in a social framework than it endangers, or risks displacing, itself. It's unlikely, I think, that this sentence would appear in a different Austen novel, as it ultimately draws its charged resonance from the formal structure particular to *Sense and Sensibility*. Like so many events, relationships, and circumstances in this novel, this brief but stark description is both intertwined with, and motivated by, that division between the two co-protagonists which is engrained into the narrative fabric, the axiomatic principle of the novel and its construction. And if the apposition of the novel's title presents such a division in its most idealized form we might hold onto the countervailing, material phrase *Heat and Inconvenience*— as it suggests a condition of being far more general than simply this London party—to foreground the socioformal processes that necessarily underlie these more abstract terms.

The opposition between the two sisters has, of course, always been the ground for interpretations of the novel. Indeed, we can almost equate the exercise of comparative evaluation with the history of this novel's critical comprehension. As Marilyn Butler writes, "the reader's developing knowledge of the sisters is based on a substructure which demands that he adjudicate between them."[3] Rereading *Sense and Sensibility* tends to revolve around a reevaluation of the two main characters: the reader comes away, *this* time, with a higher or lower opinion of someone—or other. And critical arguments over the novel also center, often implicitly, on more elaborated versions of such character-criticism, like an endless court of appeals overturning previous verdicts. But critics have offered few interpretations of, or turned their full attention towards, the structural premise that generates all these different comparisons.[4] I want to delay making another comparison between Marianne and Elinor and instead put this process of comparison itself at the center of interpretation. In an unusual way, this narrative catches the very conceptual mechanisms through which we inevitably interpret it—juxtaposition, comparison, discrimination—and grounds them in the represented, social world of the novel itself. *Sense and Sensibility* is thus a work of art in which the frame and the object are ingeniously, disconcertingly intertwined.

Even as we derive a set of consequential differences out of our varied juxtapositions of Marianne and Elinor we need also to focus on the rather unforgiving way in which *Sense and Sensibility* suggests that identity—and analysis itself—emerges only through juxtaposition. It would be difficult to overestimate the importance of comparison in *Sense and Sensibility:* both as an activity within the story itself and as a mode of apprehension central to the novel's own heuristics and narrative structure. Evaluation and analysis, both by the narrator and within the narrative, seem to be impossible without comparison. An object does not possess intrinsic qualities that are directly discernible to consciousness, but only emerges as an object—with specific, defining characteristics—in negative relation to others. Words, ideas, people, values, and social categories *all* only take shape through comparison, juxtaposition, and contrast. Nothing stands absolutely. This decline of intrinsic value is rooted in much larger sociohistorical developments. Like Hegel's *Phenomenology of Mind*, a text written almost contemporaneously with *Sense and Sensibility*, Austen's work bears witness to a world in which absolute value no longer inheres within objects themselves but only emerges as the individual object or individual person is placed in radically contingent relationship to other, equally unstable, objects or persons. Austen's novel, like Hegel's *Phenomenology*, tells the story of this collapse of absolute value, and the struggles of different individuals to accommodate themselves, in various ways, to such a collapse.

It's a collapse that's registered above all, as I have been suggesting, in the comparative interlocking of the two co-protagonists that underlies the character-system. It is of course possible to represent a sibling relationship without having this manifest itself as a significant character relationship within the narrative discourse itself. "A brother is as easily forgotten as an umbrella," Joyce writes in *Ulysses*,[5] and we need look only so far as *Emma* to see Austen very deliberately inscribing a sister into the story only to crowd her out within the narrative discourse. Emma might be a younger sister within the referenced world of the novel but she is certainly a great "only child" in the history of narrative *structure*. In a similar fashion, *Sense and Sensibility* itself—as though to urge us against naturalizing the comparative structure that radiates through the novel—includes (only to find various ways of diminishing) a third sister, Margaret, who has very little character-space at all.[6] Margaret's function, indeed, might be to remind us how precarious character-space in Austen can always be: how easily a person can fall out of (or get lost within) a novel; or, perhaps more disturbingly, by getting integrated *into* a narrative—through functionalization, abstraction, distortion—fall out of personhood itself. The structured relationship between characters gains particular charge in Jane Austen's novels, which, perhaps more rigorously and relentlessly than any previous British fiction, create tightly organized narrative frameworks within which multiple characters are placed in intricate thematic and narrative juxtaposition.[7] The close juxtaposition between Marianne and Elinor is only the most evident example of a process that informs the essential structure of characterization in all of Austen's novels: each character is quite precisely inflected into the narrative form as a whole, and *any* Austen character only emerges in-and-through a complicated network of intersecting but differentiated character-representations and plotlines.

Compare these two passages. First, from *Emma*: "Mr Woodhouse considered eight persons at dinner together as the utmost that his nerves could bear—and here would be a ninth" (292). And, from Austen's letters, in one of her famously rare comments about her own work: "3 or 4 Families in a Country Village is the very thing to work on."[8] This aphorism is almost always taken to imply Austen's investment in a *small* enough group of persons that the narrative can be precise. The delimited social scale might thus be collapsed into the more strictly formal delimitation signaled in Austen's other well-known depiction of her novels as "the little bit (two Inches wide) of Ivory on which I work with so fine a brush."[9] But there's an odd lack of specificity in this phrase that seems to work in another direction: "3 or 4 Families," Austen writes, as though this were the number of families in which the narrative *wouldn't* be able to remain so precise but would begin to lose its own ability to keep count. And if "three" or "four" seems much less than Woodhouse's "eight" or "nine," we need to remember that it's not the three or four families that would cause this blur—but rather the several persons *within* each of these families, persons not even mentioned in Austen's statement except insofar as they clearly motivate the ambiguity. Austen's comment thus suggests that she is interested not merely in radically delimiting narrative scope but, simultaneously, in placing more *persons* within this delimited frame than it can comfortably comprehend.

In this sense, the framework of the novelistic character-system in Austen might remind us of a crucial space within the fictional world of *Sense and Sensibility*: the rented cottage in which the Dashwoods are situated after their expulsion from Norland Park. It's a space that never seems quite big enough, with its two "sixteen feet square" sitting rooms (28), "dark narrow stairs" (72) and "crooked" ceiling (108) for the persons—or the aspirations of the persons—lodged within it. A key location in the plot, the Barton cottage also catalyzes numerous descriptions of insufficient space:

> "[H]ow snug they might live in such another cottage as yours—or a little bigger." (260)
>
> "And so you are most comfortably settled in your little cottage and want for nothing!" (222)
>
> "The smallness of the house," said [Mrs. Jennings], "I cannot imagine any inconvenience to them, for it will be in proportion to their family and income." (284)
>
> "There is not a room in this cottage that will hold ten couple, and where can the supper be?" (252)

Not enough room in the cottage; not enough room in the novel. The interlocking of Marianne and Elinor determines both their emergence as characters, within the narrative discourse, and their actions and struggles as individuals within the story itself. "Marianne entreated [Elinor], with all the eagerness of the most nervous irritability, not to speak to her for the world. In such circumstances, it was better for both that they should not be long together" (180). Such negativity, which compels the sisters frequently to avoid, elude, mislead, or pull away from one another, cannot be disentangled from their very proximity to and intimacy with one another. On the contrary, the negation here is merely the residual consequence of "be[ing] long together," and, more specifically, of defining their own identities—and often formulating their own thoughts—in relation to the other.

"Such behaviour as this," thinks Elinor, "so exactly the reverse of her own, appeared no more meritorious to Marianne, than her own had seemed faulty to her" (104). This statement, in its perfect equality and pronominal confusion, emphasizes the comparative structure that underlies—and potentially subsumes—the sisters' different personalities. Merit and fault don't reside in actions themselves, but emerge relatively through juxtaposition. "Elinor's happiness was not so great. Her heart was not so much at ease, nor her satisfaction in their amusements so pure" (54). This passage gives us *no* actual information about Elinor's unease or dissatisfaction: the only benchmark of these qualities in Elinor is Marianne, whose precise level of ease and satisfaction is also left unspecified. Even physical attributes emerge in this comparative matrix: Marianne, we learn, "[has] the advantage of height" (46), but how tall does that make either sister?

Both characters are often conscious of this process—each one knows that her sibling might come to an emotion or thought simply in negative relation to herself: "Elinor thought it wisest to touch that point no more. She knew her sister's temper. Opposition on so tender a subject would only attach her the more to her own opinion" (50). The sisters need to disagree with each other—in order to take on any cognitive personality at all. As though in the grip of this comparative instability, the narrative itself proliferates double negatives, sentences tautly balanced between dominant and subordinate clause, and a sustained series of paired, internally juxtaposed adjectives. In six pages alone (pages that concern precisely the move to the Barton cottage), we have "comfortable and compact" (23), "poor and small" (24), "cultivated and woody" (24), "frankness and warmth" (26), "tall and striking" (26), "large and handsome" (27), "hospitality and elegance" (27), "talent and taste" (27), "silent and grave" (29). It's in this way that the very process of signification in *Sense and Sensibility*—what Lionel Trilling calls "the hum and buzz of implication" in Austen's narratives—connects so viscerally to the novel's social field.

The comparisons that Marianne and Elinor make, as we have seen, don't arise out of a simple case of sibling rivalry. Rather, they are at the center of a much larger process: the continual struggle of each sister both to discern and to distinguish herself within the world that surrounds her. Both individual judgment and social position are radically contingent in *Sense and Sensibility:* neither sister can make a cognitive determination (about the value, beauty, or character of a person, action, or object) or comprehend her *own* social identity except through juxtaposition, placing herself in continual (negative) relationship to the objects or persons she discerns. "Her manners were by no means so elegant as her sister's, but they were much more prepossessing" (106). If we had to guess what Austen novel contains this passage we might correctly pick *Sense and Sensibility:* with its syntax of "not so; much more" applied to two siblings. This description, however, does not refer to Elinor and Marianne but to the daughters of Mrs. Jennings—both now married themselves: Mrs. Middleton and Mrs. Palmer. The co-protagonists are implicated in this sentence only insofar as Elinor is *making* the comparison; deriving and applying these contingently related categories of "elegance" and "prepossession" through which to define "manners." This comparison, in other words, is part of a network of distinctions both embraced by and imposed upon nearly all the characters who enter the narrative. In this case, Mrs. Palmer and her husband have literally *just* entered—both the novel and the cottage at Barton—and the observation is embedded in a sequence of distinctions that Elinor makes as she views the guests for the first time.[10]

In fact, Marianne and Elinor engage in such comparative analysis all the time, even as both of them are refracted, differentially, through the character-system as a whole. Caught in the middle rather than at the center of the narrative form, each observation or judgment by Marianne or Elinor also, simultaneously, distinguishes her as an agent of observation and judgment. "'She has great discernment. I know nobody who distinguishes characters better'" (198). These two sentences from *Mansfield Park* comprehend this process most economically: here Mary Crawford's own character gets distinguished by *her* relative skill in distinguishing character; even as Edmund, who makes this comment, indulges in the same act that he valorizes. As with comparative judgments, the sense of distinction is always relative: to feel "distinguished" is to deny any intrinsic value, to get entangled in the structure of commonality one seems to negate. "[T]he performers themselves were, *as usual,* in their own estimation, and that of their immediate friends, the first private performers in England" (250; emphasis added). Without an organized and constrained system of valuation, it is necessary and commonplace for each person to consider him- or herself "first" or distinguished. While Mr. and Mrs. Palmer continually argue over whether all "all infants [are] alike" or whether their baby is "the finest child in the world" (248), the narrative suggests that these two claims are interdependent: not just because, like the performers, *all* parents think that their children are "the finest," but because the gesture of distinction itself takes place only in a structure that implicates it in the common. "It was the desire to be appearing superior to other people. The motive was too common to be wondered at" (112).

Once again, we need to note how *Sense and Sensibility* substantializes this thematic dialectic between distinction and commonality within the narrative form itself. The impulse of this sociological vision—like the topography of the rented cottage (which has few parallels in Austen's fiction)—is elaborated in the ironic positioning, and continually effected displacements, of Marianne and Elinor as potentially central characters. With each evaluation they make, Marianne and Elinor are not only positioning themselves in the world—but being positioned in the novel. There's a cumulative pathos that results from all these comparisons—a pathos that is discernible only at the intersection of the story and the form, in the subtle relationship between the two sisters' development as individuals within the imagined world of the novel and their development as contingent, precariously emergent characters within the narrative structure itself. In fact, *Sense and Sensibility* establishes a dynamic correspondence between the psychological vulnerability of these characters (as quite competitive, close, and yet often uneasy siblings); the social uncertainty that each sister faces as part of a disinherited (or newly unpropertied) family; and the insecurity that Austen draws out of the most essential—and formal—processes of literary characterization itself.

As I have suggested, one way to understand *Sense and Sensibility* is within a larger history focused on the inflection or coordination of two main characters within a single narrative structure. We can make an important distinction here: while dyads such as Sancho and Quixote in *Don Quixote* or Gogo and Didi in *Waiting for Godot* travel and work together throughout a plot, other pairs—think of Anna Karenina and Levin perhaps most dramatically—are conjoined almost entirely on the level of *discourse,* and not in the story itself. The distinction, we can see, is largely one of form: in an open novelistic structure such as *Don Quixote,* the kind of discursive balance that holds between Anna Karenina and Levin would have little meaning. Oscillating between his two central figures (as, say, with Lydgate and Dorothea in *Middlemarch*), Tolstoy confirms the closed integrity of the narrative form itself—and mediates the characters' interaction *through* form. In *Sense and Sensibility,* Austen blurs the line between these two kinds of pairing. It's rare that a relationship which has been so motivated on the level of story (psychologically, sociologically, referentially) is rigorously worked through, simultaneously, on the level of discourse itself. The precise division and comparisons between Marianne and Elinor; the subtle, increased intertwining of Elinor's perspective with the narrative voice itself; the placement and elaboration of each scene in relation to the two sisters—all this potentially bears upon the sustained development of Elinor and Marianne as interlocked and comparatively realized character-spaces.

For the same reason, every thing seems to count within the story as well. If each co-protagonist's insecure—and always subtly shifting—place lends a charged significance to the unfolding narrative discourse (which, like Mrs. Dashwood, "knew not on which child to bestow principle attention" [353]), each turn of the plot is as consequentially fraught in the referenced world itself. We've already seen how that potential for overcrowdedness which is registered through Austen's ostensibly delimited formalism is dramatically literalized in the rented cottage that becomes a key space within the novel as a whole. More generally, the co-protagonists' lack of secure formal space is both motivated by, and intertwined with, the anxious economic situation that establishes and governs the plot. The opening of the novel enacts what we might call a fable of disinheritance, hinging on the juxtaposition of two versions of the relationship between person and property.

> The family of Dashwood had been long settled in Sussex. Their estate was large, and their residence at Norland Park, in the center of their property, where, for many generations, they had lived in so respectable a manner as to engage the general good opinion of their surrounding acquaintance. . . . [T]heir fortune, independent of what might arise to them from their father's inheriting that property, could be but small. Their mother had nothing, and their father only seven thousand pounds in his own disposal, for the remaining moiety of his first wife's fortune was also secured to her child, and he had only a life interest in it. (3–4)

The first sentences of the novel dramatically comprehend the consequences of landed wealth for individual identity, with the house at the "center" of the "large" estate hauntingly literalizing the security of the landed subject, surrounded by and confirmed through that "acquaintance" which both shelters and reflects back on this property. (Right away we might recast such centrality—here coded as a *social* condition within the world of the story itself—in relation to the discursive structure that will govern the narrative.) The second passage, following on the heels of this opening, depicts individuals emerging only in the painful disjunction between their property and their subjectivity—between who they are and what they have. "Their mother had nothing": and the limited wealth available to Mr. Dashwood is also distinctly tied to an uncertain temporal framework, a nontransmissible "life interest" that contrasts with the stable flow of property across "many generations." Remarkably, these two different conditions apply to the very same people. Both descriptions announce the inheritance—the tangled economic identity—of Marianne and Elinor. It is the disjunction between these two passages that shapes the world in which the two sisters reside. "King'd" and "unking'd,"[11] Marianne and Elinor seem to have everything and have nothing, just as they are both valued *and* imperiled by the narrative structure. Each of their particular temperaments or worldviews stems from this condition and, simultaneously, as I've been suggesting, the dynamic and pervasive contrasting *of* these worldviews stems from it as well.

If the structure of comparison that marks both story and discourse in *Sense and Sensibility* is the underlying *given* of the novel, the plot begins, properly, at this moment—when a fixed and direct relationship between person and property (or between interior consciousness and social circumstance) breaks down. Before this sociohistorical moment, like the identities of Marianne and Elinor *before* they interacted as sisters, or the formal strategy of this novel *before* it had co-protagonists, is only the nonnarratable. Comparison arises out of displacement: the disinheritance and eviction that opens the novel doesn't merely set the plot in motion but also motivates, and is motivated by, its narrative structure. The Dashwood sisters are deprived of any internally grounded identity; instead they need to define themselves through a constant and shifting sequence of comparisons. Like these sisters, the "middle class," a category taking on much more active political meaning at the moment Austen writes, does not have an intrinsic social, or circumstantial, identity, but emerges only contingently, in negative relation to both the landed aristocracy and the unpropertied working class.[12] By placing its co-protagonists between the stability and centeredness of landed wealth and the "nothingness" that lurks on the other side of disinheritance, Austen's novel suggestively formulates the material and categorical insecurity that underlies this emergent class. In their struggle to gain a social footing, both Marianne and Elinor are only negatively situated: each one of them is locked between two rivals who delimit what the Dashwood sisters are *not*. Not coincidentally, Edward and Willoughby both consider two different marital choices—on the one hand, the unpropertied Lucy Steele and Eliza, and on the other hand, the aristocratic Miss Morton and Miss Grey. With all four of these characters personality slides into wealth: whether the fifty-thousand and thirty-thousand-pound fortunes of Miss Grey and Miss Morton or the social nothingness of Lucy ("Lucy has next to nothing herself" [260]) and Eliza ("he had left the girl . . . with no creditable home, no help, no friends" [209]).

This double set of double oppositions is the most immediate and consequential echoing, or reduplication, of the psychosocial (and narrative) doubling between Marianne and Elinor themselves. It is only in contrast with these rivals that the uncertain social space which these two sisters occupy comes into relief—as *neither* the emphatic nothingness of Eliza and Lucy nor the absolutized financial security of Miss Morton and Miss Grey.[13] Each of the co-protagonists emerges somewhere between these two opposed, and juxtaposed, states of identity—and emerges, simultaneously, into a world where social identity is constituted through juxtaposition. As Mrs. Jennings bluntly lays out Edward's choice: "Nobody in their senses could expect Mr. Ferrars to give up a woman like Miss Morton, with thirty thousand pounds to her fortune, for Lucy Steele that had nothing at all" (272). This nothingness—that horizon which haunts the Dashwoods' disinheritance from the opening page—

is repeated by Lucy herself, who says "I shall have no fortune" (132) and by Mrs. Jennings, who says that Lucy "has next to nothing herself" (260). In relation to Miss Morton, Elinor also has next to nothing, but she still insists that she is distinct from Lucy Steele, who is "undoubtedly inferior in connections, and probably inferior in fortune to herself" (140). In fact, Elinor's own status in relation to Edward emerges strictly in comparison with Lucy; both Mrs. Ferrars and Edward himself can only think of Elinor in relation to the abject Miss Steele. Comparing Elinor with her prospective daughter-in-law, Mrs. Ferrars concludes that "It would have been beyond comparison . . . the least evil of the two, and she would be glad to compound *now* for nothing worse" (297; Austen's emphasis). Edward's very attraction *to* Elinor is legible only in this same relational context: "'till I began to make comparisons between yourself and Lucy, I did not know how far I was got'" (368), just as Colonel Brandon later uses the same term to express how Marianne can comprehend her own identity only vis-à-vis the impoverished Eliza: "'[S]he may now, and hereafter doubtless will, turn with gratitude towards her own condition, when she compares it with that of my poor Eliza, when she considers the wretched and hopeless situation of this poor girl. . . . Surely this comparison must have its use with her'" (210).

I want to conclude this essay by engaging in a slightly more specific "comparison" of the two Dashwood sisters. But to be precise, I don't want to compare their characters so much as their modes of response to this world *of* comparison—of insecurity, displacement, and competition. In this sense, each of the distinct personalities that we can discover or argue for within the oppositional structure that organizes Austen's novel is expressive of—even as it emerges through—opposition itself. (As J. M. Findley describes Hegel's *Phenomenology*: "The logical 'movement' which the *Phenomenology* . . . exhibits, is throughout the logic of the 'side' or 'aspect' or 'moment' of that which, while it can be legitimately distinguished in some unity, and must in fact be so distinguished, nevertheless represents something basically incapable of self-sufficiency and independence, properties which can only be attributed to the whole . . . a reference to which is accordingly 'built into' each such side."[14] I would note here that Findley's *formal* terms to describe the Hegelian dialectic—"self-sufficiency," "independence"—can also be starkly social terms, as my reading of *Sense and Sensibility* is suggesting.) Elinor and Marianne are inflected into the narrative *as* co-protagonists, encounter their disinheritance, and get thrust into marriage plots at precisely the same moment. At the outset, the novel deliberately conflates two separate conditions: the Dashwoods' economic displacement (a fundamentally social problem) and the (biographical) transition by Marianne and Elinor from unnarrated childhood to unmarried adulthood. Within the deliberately defined parameters of *Sense and Sensibility*, of course, these two conditions seem indissociable. As Mrs. Dashwood comments early on: "'In a few months, my dear Marianne,' said she, 'Elinor will in all probability be settled for life. We shall miss her; but *she* will be happy'" (17). For Elinor (or Marianne) to "settle"—that crucial word in this novel—means both to move beyond the interim period between childhood and marriage and to leave the insecure social position between wealth and nothingness.

One of the most remarkable aspects of Austen's novels is the continual replaying, and distension, of this same temporal framework—the short period between childhood and marriage—through different characters, settings, and narrative structures. This is of course a temporal, rather than characterological, middle. Austen's novels relentlessly foreground the one period during which female identity is unhinged from fixed social demarcations; and, in almost every case, this unhinging of identity is related to the separation of "income" and "rent," or of the character's interior desires for herself and her ability to actualize herself on these terms. To make this condition symbolically coherent, Austen firmly differentiates it from the psychosocial reality of what precedes and what follows. The narratives thus all insist on the fiction of a "before" and "after": a nonnarratable childhood implicitly defined by the lack of separation between consciousness and world and the "happy" endings in which the protagonist who has, in the course of the narrative, become radically disjoined from the world is reintegrated. (While Austen's endings have been well scrutinized, it's worth pointing out how much they rely on an equally de-realized opening. If the marrying protagonist can never be shown as a married protagonist, Austen's novels waver between lack of interest in and outright hostility toward children—and none more so than *Sense and Sensibility*. As the narrator memorably encapsulates this orientation in the opening pages of *Sense and Sensibility*: "the whole was tied up for the benefit of this child, who . . . had so far gained on the affections of his uncle, by such attractions as are by no means unusual in children of two or three years old; an imperfect articulation, an earnest desire of having his own way, many cunning tricks, and a great deal of noise" [4].)[15] Perhaps it is only in setting her marriage plots against this fantastically stable background that Austen is able to render the glaring period of insecurity on which all the novels come to focus. And, like a nightmare, the fundamental economic uncertainty returns in the next novel, each narrative "settlement" erased by the recurrence of another unmarried protagonist and another grid of social circumstances—and narrative strategies—surrounding this uncertainty.[16]

Sense and Sensibility unfolds within this particularly "unsettled" social and temporal situation: where objects can't be precisely grasped, identities are not securely formulated, and no person has an intrinsically grounded or stable value. A social anxiety—extending far beyond any individual's psychology—is pervasive in this novel, where "every thing [is] in such suspense and uncertainty" (133). This suspense is shared: As John Dashwood comments to Elinor: "'your friends are all truly anxious to see you well settled'" (224), or, as Mrs. Jennings comments of Willoughby and Marianne, "'I hope, from the bottom of my heart, he won't keep her waiting much longer'" (181). This most essential form of "waiting"—between engagement and marriage—structures many briefer instances of impatience in the novel. Waiting is so difficult both because everything is unsettled and because the consequences are so steep. Implication can quickly become transformed into a new, and permanent, condition, as in John Dashwood's speculation about Marianne: "'You would not think it perhaps, but Marianne was remarkably handsome a few months ago; quite as handsome as Elinor.—Now you see it is all gone'" (237).

Barton cottage becomes the key site in which the insecure financial, social, and temporal position of the Dashwoods is explored. When John Dashwood blithely asserts to Elinor that "'you are most comfortably settled in your little cottage and want for nothing'" (222), he picks precisely the two keywords—"comfortable" and "settled"—that are inadequate to their situation. And his confidence that Elinor "want[s] for nothing" reminds us that Mrs. John Dashwood has insisted that the disinherited family should want nothing: "'They will live so cheap! Their housekeeping will be nothing at all. They will have no carriage, no horses, and hardly any servants; they will keep no company, and can have no expenses of any kind'" (12). The proliferation of "nos" in this passage (like that "all gone" of John Dashwood's comment about Marianne) itself seems to emerge from the blunt economic summary we have already noted: "Their mother had nothing."

Situated in this precarious home, the sisters are continually aroused by surprise visits, by the shock of misrecognition, anticipation, disappointment, and unexpected experience. It is in the flow of these events—which constitute the protracted and incrementally unfolding plot of *Sense and Sensibility*—that the uncertain middle of the character-system is given temporal form. In *Don Quixote*, Cervantes protracts the individual's empirical encounter with an outside world, distending the simple act of perception with complicated sequences of desire, projection, apprehension, retrospection, regret. This temporality suffuses *Sense and Sensibility*, in local scenes and in the overarching plot, but the sister's empirical adventures are shaped through the constraints of the unmarried and economically insecure. While Don Quixote rides his horse into the windmills—in a mobile projection of consciousness onto world—Marianne, in a subtle inversion of this paradigmatic scene, is thrown off by observing *another* person riding a horse, toward the cottage.

> Amongst the objects in the scene, they soon discovered an animated one; it was a man on horseback riding toward them. In a few minutes they could distinguish him to be a gentleman; and in a moment afterwards Marianne rapturously exclaimed,
>
> "It is he; it is indeed;—I know it is!"—And was hastening to meet him, when Elinor cried out,
>
> "Indeed, Marianne, I think you are mistaken. It is not Willoughby. The person is not tall enough for him, and has not his air."
>
> "He has, he has," cried Marianne, "I am sure he has. His air, his coat, his horse. I knew how soon he would come." (86)

Waiting for the horse to get closer—or for the man on the horse to make himself known—Marianne's social vulnerability (embodied here in the potential relationship with Willoughby) and epistemological uncertainty converge. In this scene and many others, Marianne furiously seeks to close the gap between expectation and circumstance; she uses the energy of her mind to intentionally seal these rifts, trying to force condition into harmony with cognition. Elinor, on the other hand, seeks to protect herself from such rifts between expectation and circumstance by establishing a consciousness that is almost systematically detached from, rather than fulfilled in, the exterior world that it apprehends. We might simply say that Elinor is elaborately careful, continually seeking to recognize the objective force of circumstances before they encroach on Elinor herself, Marianne, or her mother. But in this alertness Elinor elevates her consciousness in a way just as aggressive as Marianne. Elinor privileges reflection or introspection rather than projection; the mind becomes separated from a world that hems it in precisely through its continual response to—and analysis of—this world. Elinor's coping strategy, we might say, is not to transcend the gap between mind and circumstance but to widen it, exploiting it as an occasion for increased thoughtfulness. Consider this early assessment of Edward Ferrars:

> "I have seen a great deal of him, have studied his sentiments . . . and, upon the whole, I venture to pronounce that his mind is well informed, his enjoyment of books exceedingly great, his imagination lively, his observation just and correct, and his taste delicate and pure. His abilities in every respect improve as much upon acquaintance as his manners and person. At first sight, his address is certainly not striking; and his person can hardly be called

handsome, till the expression of his eyes, which are uncommonly good, and the general sweetness of his countenance, is perceived. At present, I know him so well, that I think him really handsome; or, at least, almost so. What say you, Marianne?" (20)

Here again we get at least as profound a sense of the agent of judgment as of the object that she judges. While Elinor comments on Edward's "observation" and "the expression of his eyes" she simultaneously conveys the depth of *her* observation, as exemplified in this very judgment: "I have seen . . . at first sight . . . [I] perceived." The passage enacts a double construction: his eyes and her eyes, as it were. There is something unsettling in this strange meeting of the lovers' eyes, as Austen manipulates an exemplary trope of direct or passionate communication. The glance falls askew; Elinor seems to transform perception into thought, and thus distances herself—as the thinking agent—from the object she perceives. "At present, I know him so well, that I think him really handsome; or, at least, almost so." The fall off from a "passionate" encounter is not so much determined because Elinor only finds Edmund "almost" handsome, but rather because Elinor's relationship to an external world, more generally, is so indirect. She must impose a distance between her observation and his face, the distance of reflection itself. In this way the "almost" that seems to gratuitously modify Elinor's attraction is already built into the "think[ing]" that frames this attraction in the first place.

To think, for Elinor, is always, simultaneously, to formulate herself *as* a thinker, and as someone distinguished from the objects that she thinks about. While Marianne (as well as Mrs. Dashwood) tries to actualize her interiority by continually projecting it onto nature (or circumstance), Elinor shrewdly finds an opportunity for interiority within the very rupture of thought and world. Thus Elinor aggressively tries to absorb each shock *into* cognition and to build thought out of disappointment: "She was not immediately able to say anything, and even when her spirits were recovered, *she debated for a short time,* on the answer it would be most proper to give" (173; emphasis added). Elinor continually cultivates these precarious moments of internal response. Such psychological portraiture can be extremely subtle, as in the bare hint of an "idea" that grows up within Elinor between the moment when Mrs. Jennings comes rushing in and when she begins to speak:

Mrs. Jennings . . . entered the drawing-room, where Elinor was sitting by herself, with an air of such hurrying importance as prepared her to hear something wonderful; *and giving her time only to form that idea,* began directly to justify it by saying,

"Lord! my dear Miss Dashwood! Have you heard the news!" (257; emphasis added)

It is just enough for Austen to frame Elinor's *processing* of the conversation over the conversation itself to demonstrate this co-protagonist's basic strategy. Facing something unexpected (and, as usual, sitting at home and having it come rushing into her), she immediately begins to convert her surprise into reflection. Thought itself—the act of thinking—functions as a strategic response to the shock that it registers.

In this sense Austen dramatizes the process of focalization, as the way in which Elinor processes the events of the novel is itself a crucial event in the novel.[17] And, as we know, the novel as a whole begins to center itself around Elinor's consciousness, while Marianne gets shifted to a disturbingly externalized position—an object for Elinor's consciousness. In fact, thinking is the tool that Elinor uses to assert an independence from events; she seeks to *leave* events in thinking about them, just as Marianne might refuse them by rushing out of a room. Similarly, for Mrs. Dashwood and Marianne, speech is a necessary consequence of thought: they can't honor their interiority except by vocalizing it. For Elinor, on the other hand, speech is the enemy of thought, since reflection grows only in the breach between understanding and circumstance. "But break my heart, for I must hold my tongue," says Hamlet, for whom, like Elinor, the activity of reflection is the triumphant and residual consequence of silence or, at least, of broken communication. "Elinor conjectured that she might as well have held her tongue" (157).

There is more to say about the dynamics of this response, as well as the far-from-simple cognitive processes illustrated by Marianne. But rather than simply offering the reader two abstracted examples of human personality, Marianne and Elinor demonstrate two modes of coping with a specific and historically grounded social condition. The insecure economic position of the two sisters motivates, I have been arguing, the very presence *of* two sisters, as a character-pair in which each individual emerges only in relation to the other. Crowded together into a delimited amount of narrative space, Elinor and Marianne illustrate the way that people must jostle for social space, or a satisfactory alignment of circumstance with intention. Locked together in continual juxtaposition, Marianne and Elinor embody the essentially contingent identity of those many individuals—then or now—who are unable to define themselves through a fixed or stable economic ground. Both their responses to and the condition of socioeconomic insecurity emerge only in relation to the narrative form. To put this differently, the novel never lets its form get *outside* of, and merely serve to objectify, the condition it is representing. In this way, *Sense and Sensibility* avoids the risk that inheres in so many subsequent traditions of social realism: externalizing or reifying the conditions of social vulnerability and deprivation that are confronted. Instead, the novel resolves those conditions of "heat and inconvenience" (ultimately legible as overcrowdedness and inadequate shelter) into the resolutely interior, but still comparative, terms of the title. Insecurity is not, after all, a strictly objective condition, but is produced only in the dialectical intersection *of* an interiority that insists upon its distinct and integral value and external circumstances which continually threaten to disable, denigrate, or damage it. If Austen's mixture of sympathy and irony, or her development of the technique of free indirect discourse, demonstrates this "middle" ground between the exterior and the interior, the underlying organization of this novel's character-system (simultaneously substantializing and displacing intentional agency) does too. In Marianne's energetic projections and Elinor's equally embattled reflection, Austen sketches out two different responses to a shared social condition. Both Marianne and Elinor are trying to preserve the integrity of their interior life, to defend their intrinsic value as human beings, in a system that cannot adequately accommodate the interior or comprehend the intrinsic. If the reader is left to choose between the two sisters, this choice is finally not between two sets of characteristics, but between these two compelling modes of response. Beneath any static opposition of "reason" and "emotion" is this dynamic world of comparison, displacement, and insecurity, which all of Austen's novels chart and through which all of her characters emerge.

Notes

1. Jane Austen, *The Novels of Jane Austen*, ed. R. W. Chapman, 3rd ed., 5 vols. (Oxford: Oxford University Press, 1932–34), 57. All subsequent quotations refer to this edition.

2. A number of other Bruegel paintings also explore (and arguably hinge on) the relationship between the event of falling and the compositional arrangement of multiple persons within a single structure. Canonically exemplified in *The Fall of Icarus* (an iconic image for the dialectical play of central and peripheral figures), this relationship is also crucial to the disturbing *Parable of the Blind* and to *The Procession to Calvary* (which features numerous forms of falling while ingeniously positioning the protagonist at the hidden center of its intricate composition). I discuss this and other Bruegel paintings at further length in the essay, "Partial Representation," in *The Work of Genre: Selected Essays from the English Institute*, ed. Robyn Warhol (Cambridge, MA: English Institute in collaboration with the American Council of Learned Societies, 2011).

3. Marilyn Butler, *Jane Austen and the War of Ideas* (Oxford: Clarendon Press, 1975), 184.

4. On the contrary, many critics have argued that the merit of the novel lies outside of its overtly comparative organization. Susan Morgan, for example, claims that the novel is "flawed

by a structure too visibly formal" ("Polite Lies: The Veiled Heroine of *Sense and Sensibility*," *Nineteenth-Century Fiction* 31, no. 2 [1976]: 188–205; 188), and Marilyn Butler likewise dismisses the "cumbrous" (195) and "didactic" (182) structure of this novel. Butler insists, in fact, that Austen herself "was impatient with the rigidity of her framework" (195), and that the subsequent novels "are more sophisticated in conception, and . . . capable of more interesting treatment of the central character" (182). Butler's essay is important for establishing a kind of double reading of *Sense and Sensibility* that sees the *structure* of the novel as fundamentally unoriginal—merely "typical of the feminine variant of the anti-Jacobin novel" (188)—while locating Austen's still latent originality in the "soften[ing]" (195) of this structure. It is peculiar that much criticism of *Sense and Sensibility* hinges on detaching the novel from its own structural premise.

5. James Joyce, *Ulysses*, ed. Hans Walter Gabler (1922; New York: Vintage Books, 1986), 173.

6. Margaret is introduced by name in the final sentence of chapter one, which is both foregrounded and isolated as a single paragraph: "Margaret, the other sister, was a good-humoured well-disposed girl; but as she had already imbibed a good deal of Marianne's romance, without having much of her sense, she did not, at thirteen, bid fair to equal her sisters at a more advanced period of life" (7). The marginalization of this third sister at the edge of the character-system is connected here, explicitly, to her position at the threshold of childhood.

7. For a more extensive discussion of "character-space" and "character-system" in Austen, see Alex Woloch, *The One vs the Many: Minor Characters and the Space of the Protagonist in the Novel* (Princeton: Princeton University Press, 2003), 43–124. This discussion of *Sense and Sensibility* develops a reading that I briefly touch on in *The One vs the Many* (62, 349).

8. Jane Austen, *Letters*, ed. Deirdre Le Faye, 3rd ed. (Oxford: Oxford University Press, 1995), 275.

9. Austen, *Letters*, 323.

10. "Mrs Palmer was several years younger than Lady Middleton, and totally unlike her in every respect. . . . Her manners were by no means so elegant as her sister's but they were much more prepossessing. . . . Her husband was a grave looking young man of five or six and twenty, with an air of more fashion and sense than his wife, but of less willingness to please or be pleased" (106). In this passage comparison operates on multiple, spiraling levels: a simple difference in age flows into Elinor's nuanced distinction between two kinds of manners, and this more qualitative discrimination informs the implicit, strictly internal contrast between "fashion" and "sense."

11. I take these resonant phrases from the Act V prison soliloquy in *Richard II*, "[. . .] Sometimes am I king, / Then treasons make me wish myself a beggar, / And so I am. Then crushing penury / Persuades me I was better when a king; / Then am I king'd again; and by and by / Think that I am unking'd by Bolingbroke, / And straight am nothing" (*Richard II*, 5.5.33–39).

12. Historians such as Dror Wahrman and John Raynor have persuasively shown that early-nineteenth-century England is saturated with cultural and political representations of the middle class as precariously situated in that excluded middle between "a patrician elite on the one hand and the plebs on the other" (Dror Wahrman, *Imagining the Middle Class: The Political Representation of Class in Britain, 1780–1840* [Cambridge: Cambridge University Press, 1995], 4) and "conscious of their differences both from the gentry and from the main mass of the people below their economic level" (John Raynor, *The Middle Class* [London: Longmans, Green and Co., 1969], 16). Wahrman argues more particularly that even *as a* newly constructed cultural category—rather than a sociological entity—the "middle class" has

a particularly contingent meaning: "[T]he category of 'middle class' does have an inherent vagueness in relation to social structures and social relations, which renders it perhaps more dependent upon linguistic choices and rhetorical constructions than the categories of 'working class' or 'nobility'" (8).

13. *Sense and Sensibility*, in fact, enacts continual forms of doubling, from the ghostly repetition of the two Elizas (both buried in a subplot that, itself, emerges as an explicit duplication of Marianne's condition and persona) to the mechanical confusion of Edward and Robert Ferrars in the novel's most ostentatious plot device. (The Ferrars brothers' antagonism in the story is so marked that they never appear simultaneously in the discourse.) It's remarkable how many selves seem stuck with a sibling, down to Mrs. Jennings's fleeting mention of her servant's unnamed sister (appropriately in terms of dislocation): "'I believe I could help them to a housemaid, for my Betty has a sister out of place, that would fit them exactly'" (260).

14. J. M. Findley, "Foreword" to G. W. F. Hegel, *The Phenomenology of Mind*, trans. A. V. Miller (Oxford: Oxford University Press, 1977), v–xxx; at ix.

15. Such a coding of childhood—essentially as the absence of a reflective self—is intimately connected to the problems of character-space we're examining. We've already seen how Margaret's (inscribed) disappearance is connected to her "unadvanced" age of thirteen. In a similar way, the (precarious) emergence of the co-protagonists within the novel is connected to their emergence out of childhood. But while we get absolutely no information about their past, the novel makes clear that each sister's sense of self has developed through a process of differentiation that extends far back into the sisters' shared youth. Unrecorded, their childhood has already produced the distinct temperaments of the two sisters and produced them in relation to one another—just as the governing *narrative* premise of the novel, the comparative juxtaposition that's anchored in the division between the two co-protagonists, seems to precede the story that is told.

16. The last sentence and paragraph of *Sense and Sensibility* certainly works in this way, offering a resolution so conventional in design but skeptical in tone that it can only send us back toward the insecurity it putatively eases. Most famously, these lines insist on a sequence of double negatives that, for our purposes, demonstrate a final connection between the novel's own syntax and the troubling structure of comparison that has organized the narrative—and which is maintained right up to the conclusion: "[A]mong the merits and happiness of Elinor and Marianne, let it not be ranked as the least considerable, that though sisters, and living almost within sight of each other, they could live without disagreement between themselves, or producing coolness between their husbands" (380). The narrative's negative substitution of "without disagreement" for "agreement" and "not . . . least considerable" for "most considerable" thus echoes the final positioning of Elinor and Marianne as, appropriately, "almost within sight of each other." It would be surprising if *Sense and Sensibility* didn't end with attention to *both* sisters, and this version takes advantage, one last time, of a fixity that can only be elaborated on the level of the narrative discourse. In other words, however close—or distant—the referenced proximity of the two sisters' homes, it cannot equal the effective conjoining of the two sisters within the form that conveys this ending. This fixity is crucially precarious, of course: the characters are permanently left, as it were, at the unstable threshold between independence and juxtaposition (or, in Hegelian terms, at the very hinge of a dialectical reversal). Why can't the sisters see each other? Why do they remain, all the same, "almost" within sight of each other? They cannot *quite* see each other, perhaps, because they are too close: the perceiving self that would organize such vision of the other already depends *upon* her relationship to the other. They cannot quite see each other, perhaps, because they are too much at odds: the self that *would* see is formed only in recoil from—and thus through

negation of—the other. In either case, the final state of subjectivity that is secured in this last sentence is one that locks the sisters together, "Elinor and Marianne," simultaneously turned upon and canceling out the other.

17. On focalization see Meike Bal, *Narratology: Introduction to the Theory of Narrative*, trans. Christine van Boheemen (Toronto: University of Toronto Press, 1985). Elinor continually equates cognition with freedom: she has "leisure enough to think" (104); "leisure enough for thinking over the past" (178); she finds herself "at liberty to think" (82) or, as the end of volume one amplifies this, "at liberty to think and be wretched" (135). This ironic close suggests that Elinor profits from unease itself, that thought is cultivated particularly well out of the kind of disappointments that Marianne's own energetic projections continually produce.

TWO

The Make-Believe of a Middle

On (Not) Knowing Where You Are in *Daniel Deronda*

HILARY M. SCHOR

> . . . *and by Mr. Vandernoodt, whose acquaintance Sir Hugo had found pleasant enough at Leubronn to be adopted in England.*[1]

Pity Mr. Vandernoodt! This knowledgeable man of the world appears only twice in George Eliot's *Daniel Deronda*, and when he is absent, is recollected by nobody.[2] The first time he appears, in chapter one, Gwendolen Harleth asks him to introduce her to Daniel Deronda, who has been observing her at the gambling table and has (she thinks) jinxed her play; the second time, in chapter thirty-five, when he reappears at Topping Abbey, he offers Daniel information we already have, about Gwendolen's husband Henleigh Grandcourt and his liaison with a married woman, Lydia Glasher, with whom Grandcourt has had several children, now seemingly disinherited by his marriage to Gwendolen. Not much narrative time has passed between these two meetings (three months), but hundreds of pages have gone by. We are, in fact, exactly halfway through the book, and the reader is now in a position to feel superior to the worldly gentleman, busy with his scandal and guesses—and yet, certainly on rereading, we cannot help but ask, what if Mr. Vandernoodt had managed to carry out his assignment in chapter one and thereby introduce our two protagonists, bring the two plots together? Is his failure, in fact, the reason there is any plot at all, let alone so very much of it? Is he the key to this complicated two-plot novel, with its crazy time scheme and relentless games of narratorial knowledge? Truly, if there ever were such a novelistic thing, Mr. Vandernoodt is a man in the middle.

What does it mean for a novel to have a middle? Readers and in particular teachers of long novels have some working ideas on the topic (the middle, most simply, is where you, and more often your students, tend to bog down), and one might be tempted to turn to narrative theory for a sharpening of our terms. And narrative theory would oblige: middles don't only come between the beginning and the end, the first and the last chapter. "If in the beginning stands desire," says Peter Brooks authoritatively, "and this shows itself ultimately to be desire for the end, between beginning and end stands a middle that we feel to be necessary."[3] But for Brooks, middles, like everything else in narrative, can only be found retrospectively—although, curiously, he never makes this point explicitly. The middle is something we find at the end, when we have rearranged the plot into story, when we know what the characters desired and how they achieved, or did not, fulfillment. It is, further, a point that characters themselves reach, when "the 'dilatory space' of postponement and error" is over, when the many choices which characters have faced again and again, "taking us back again over the same ground," have been resolved finally into the "choice of ends," and the proper end has at last been reached.[4] Then, and only then, do we (readers and characters alike) know where the middle (now well and safely behind us) lies. Clear enough. But even this minimal clarity may be illusory, and no novelist makes this more evident than George Eliot, and no novel more aggressively than *Daniel Deronda*.

Daniel Deronda has two plots, and it begins in the middle of both of them. It is more famous for the former quality than for the latter, and subsequent generations of readers have tried mightily to resolve the relationship between the two plots, all agreeing with early critics that this is no ordinary multiplot novel.[5] Most readers have adopted the expedient answer of imagining it as two novels and simply preferring one to the other—invariably choosing the story of the charming and erring Gwendolen Harleth over that of the more stolid, and certainly more fortunate, Daniel Deronda, the one falling prey to a disastrous marriage and developing a somewhat inconvenient conscience; the other, learning the secret of his parentage, choosing a vocation, and marrying the woman he loves. But these finicky readers have failed to learn the lessons of the novel's opening, which teaches us that plots are not so easily unmixed.

It teaches us this precisely by beginning so resolutely in the middle, pushing us to separate and then recombine the two characters it presents together, initially such equivalent terms of mystery. The first sentence of the novel is usually taken to be its opening sentence, "Was she beautiful or not beautiful?"

and on this interrogatory note has rested the novel's claim to epistemological interest. But its first sentence actually occurs in its authorial chapter epigraph:[6] "Men can do nothing without the make-believe of a beginning." Even Science, the narrator goes on, "is obliged to start with a make-believe unit . . . when his sidereal clock shall pretend that time is at Nought." "Poetry has always been understood to start in the middle," but "Science, too, reckons backwards as well as forwards, . . . and with his clock-finger at Nought really sets off *in medias res*." "No retrospect," she opines, "will take us to the true beginning."

But such opining raises an interesting question for narrative theorists: will even "retrospect" (on which, as the novelist noted long before narratology, narrative knowledge depends) ever take us to the true middle? Are we already there, already in the middle, when the book begins, but in ways we can only understand later? What form does this middle take, as we stand with our characters at a roulette table (fitting emblem of the accidents of plot) in the opening chapter? The novel gives us little guidance, looping us instead into confusion. The epigraph, as we have seen, sends us towards questions of novelistic form, to the (pseudo)science of middles, "in medias res." The book title ("The Spoiled Child") and the opening description of the heroine, Gwendolen Harleth, send us to questions of character, more familiar questions for novel readers. Yet even here, problems of form again intrude on our meditations: "Was she beautiful or not beautiful? And what was the secret of form or expression which gave the dynamic quality to her glance?" We are told that these were "the questions raised in Daniel Deronda's mind" as he watched a young woman gambling in Leubronn, but more basic readerly questions must hang, unanswered. Four pages go by before we learn the young woman's first name, her last name comes a full page later, and still another page turns before Gwendolen learns Daniel's name. Daniel himself must have learned her name by chapter two, when he returns some property to her, but we do not see him learn it—only in chapter fifteen do we confirm that he did learn it, having (of course) asked the ubiquitous, all-knowing Mr. Vandernoodt. By the time we come to that knowledge (that is, by the time we learn how the hero learned the heroine's identity) we have spent twelve chapters of flashback learning what brought Gwendolen to Leubronn and another five chapters learning what brought Daniel there. It will be a full twenty-six chapters (from her departure from Leubronn in chapter two until their meeting at Diplow in chapter twenty-nine) before Daniel and Gwendolen meet again—or rather, meet for the first time. Only well into the middle of the novel, that is, are we in a position to understand the book's beginning, and its pivotal opening act, the "beginning" of the plot, when Daniel redeems the necklace Gwendolen pawned for travel money, and sends it to her with an anonymous note, wrapped in a torn handkerchief, saying "a stranger . . . has found Miss Harleth's necklace" (12).

No wonder we are confused, everywhere tangled in the middle of things. What makes *Daniel Deronda* such a good test case for "middles" is more, however, than the trappings of mystery (strangers, torn handkerchiefs, and redeemed jewels), though these will all return in my analysis. Nor is it the fact that this novel reveals multiple strands of plot whose connection is long delayed, for it is equally many chapters in *Bleak House* before we are sure how Lady Dedlock and Esther are related, and we are far into *Felix Holt* before Felix Holt and Harold Transome finally meet. "What connexion can there be?" asked the narrator in *Bleak House*;[7] "'Relationships must branch out,'" asserts a character late in *Daniel Deronda* (558). "'It is like a Chinese puzzle that one has to fit together,'" says another; "'I feel sure something wonderful may be made of it, but I can't tell what'" (558). The novel everywhere abounds in metaphors of connection and confusion, yet this novel offers something more (and more puzzling) than "finding out relationships" or "fitting [things] together . . . ." More than any novel in the tradition, when we say of *Daniel Deronda*, "this novel begins in the middle," the novel answers, "the middle of what?" This is a novel, precisely, that does not ever want us truly to know where we are, for in this novel, wherever we are, we can only be sure that we cannot easily get "there" from "here."

Not that we do not try mightily. And so I have done: I have begun with a character in the middle, with Mr. Vandernoodt, who is (as Barbara Hardy once noted) a "functional character," one we recognize from narrative theory, there to make connections, offer background information, move plot along.[8] But he fails: here, as elsewhere in the novel, connections do not work in the expected ways, and narrative knowledge similarly does not move smoothly through the middle of this novel. This is in part because of what Claudia Johnson, paraphrasing F. R. Leavis, calls the "confused asymmetry" of the novel.[9] *Daniel Deronda* begins over and over, withholds knowledge of a major plot twist (the secret of the hero's identity) from the hero himself until near the final chapter, and in a thousand subtle ways keeps its protagonists from ever occupying a shared plotline. But beyond its doubleness, this is a novel that trades in ambiguity and confusions of knowledge, keeping readers and characters alike uncertain of what is happening. And without such knowledge, how can we find the beginning, the end, or (most particularly) the middle of the novel?

My argument here is, in part, that it's not immediately clear just how you find the middle of any novel. Readers could, for instance, identify the middle of a novel by marking a point halfway through its pages. Drop a book ten times and judge where it opens—is that not the middle? Or we could be more scientific. We could identify a point of greatest interest, or greatest confusion, or even greatest coincidence, the moment when everything seems to be happening at once. We could work thematically, and mean the middle to be the moment of greatest mixture, when things have come together, or we can mean the middle to be, like poor Mr. Vandernoodt or (more consistently) our nominal hero, Daniel Deronda, a person in the middle, the one around whom these plots swirl and gather or, as Daniel himself will put it, the person who enters the greatest number of plots, the person who "meddles" the most. We can mean simply the moment when things have clearly begun and not yet ended—the moment of greatest narrative (and hence social) possibility, when questions of "what if?" still radiate around our heroes. In *Middlemarch*, Eliot's previous experiment with the fiction of limits, the middle suggests not just the moment of finding the average, accepting the ordinary, being (as Gwendolen Harleth will put it in this novel) "middling," but of finding the proper ending—of finding a secure (if ungainly) exit from the "narratable," as D. A. Miller memorably diagnosed the problem in his reading of *Middlemarch*, into the un-happening ordinariness of everyone else.[10] But notice how in our analysis of "middles" we have already slid from the merely pragmatic—the middle is halfway through whatever we are reading—to the thematic, where most of the key words are in motions, to the normative: the middle is the point of consensus, where all novels long to be. My argument is both more epistemologically and more politically concerned. It is that questions of the middle depend largely upon whom (and about whom) we are asking. While I am interested in these questions of where the middle is, and how we know when we are in it, I am considerably more interested in the question of how we come to be in the middle, and who we are when we get there. For both readers and characters, I will argue, these questions resolve into one even more challenging to answer: whose middle is it? The middle is a kind of warfare, and in *Daniel Deronda*, I will argue, largely because of our vexed identification with Gwendolen, we become deeply aware of the struggle between the characters not only "in" but "over" the middle. But this struggle has a bias to it, for if recognizing the middle is largely (as I will argue) a problem of knowledge, of knowing where you are in the novel, then the knowledge of women, in the middle of their plots, is by definition very different from the knowledge of men. For George Eliot, the middle is the place in the plot where women characters, in particular, must not only learn new things, but must learn the limits of what they think they already know. Middles are not only confusing, arbitrary, and seemingly up for grabs—they are also particularly and pointedly gendered.

No wonder, then, that they are also so alluring, and here we must return to narrative theory, to suggest a way that a feminist reading of this novel might shift the meaning of the middle considerably. To quote again from Peter Brooks, "we are condemned to the reading of erroneous plots, granted insight only insofar as we can gain disillusion from them," yet "the process remains necessary if we are not to be caught perpetually in . . . the illusory middle" (142). Brooks, of course, means "illusory" in the sense of "we are deluded," rather than "the middle doesn't exist," but in his reading, dominated as it as by the power of closure, he might almost mean the latter. I am tempted to assert that, at least for the purposes of *Daniel Deronda*, we might question whether endings exist at all. To hint briefly at the way these themes might play out in this novel, what is so great about an ending? And what exactly is so terrible about being lost in the middle, lost in error? The novel is certainly squeamish about wandering: the Princess Halm-Eberstein, Daniel's mother, formerly the great singer Alcharisi, is described as "a forcible nature whose errors lay along high pathways," and the narrator offers one of her rare rebukes of Daniel for not appreciating or (to use her stronger word) feeling "admiration" at both the height and the error. And error is certainly linked to the central note of the novel, sounded in its epigraph and repeatedly by Daniel Deronda: "let thy chief terror be of thine own soul," announces the author before we begin. "'Turn your fear into a safeguard. Keep your dread fixed on the idea of increasing your remorse,'" as Daniel instructs Gwendolen (386). Like any novel, *Deronda* leads us to fear that most awful of things, making a mistake; not getting to a proper end. But I want to ask, throughout this essay, if error and wandering, if mistakes, if middles, can't instead be far more productive, a far more illuminating as well as disillusioning, place to reside?

To do this, I will rest in the middle of the novel for as much of this essay as I can, resisting the lure of closure, trying to keep in motion the several definitions of "middling" I have laid out here, but moving always towards my central points: who are we in the middle of novels, and how do we (and the characters with whom we are so powerfully identified) know what we know? My argument here will be that the question of middles is shaped by Deronda's central formal innovations: the temporal displacements with which the novel (and I) began; the complicated double-plot structure; the problem of unequal readerly, characterological, and narratorial knowledge. I hesitate to call the latter a formal problem—we are not accustomed to thinking of knowledge as synonymous with form—but I want here to focus on its formal implications: that until the end of the novel, Gwendolen Harleth is mistaken. She is making a generic error, thinking herself the heroine of her own life, central to the story (a romance, of course) in which she appears. This is a lesson we are slowly schooled in, a punishment we see growing for her throughout the second half of the novel—but it is one that suggests that Gwendolen, and we, are at worst entirely lost in a by-way, something trivial, reading a novel that is not moving towards an ending but only nearing its middle as the book nears its ends. *Daniel Deronda,* I am arguing, may be made up of nothing but middles—and we may never get our just readerly rewards, any more than Gwendolen gets hers. But this serious displacement of our readerly expectations is foreshadowed by the temporal confusions with which the novel opens, and there I will begin.

i. in the meantime . . .

> [< MEAN a.2 + TIME n., prob. after Anglo-Norman en meyne temps (1327)
> [< Anglo-Norman mene, men, meen intermediate, middle, middle-sized (cf. Old French< classical Latin medinus (see MEDIAN a.2).
>
> **The time intervening between one particular period or event and another**
>
> *"Gwendolen, as we had seen, passed her time abroad in the new excitement of gambling." (130)*

Many novels give us the sense that things are happening in the meantime ("when we last saw our heroine," they say, or "the reader will remember . . . "), but *Daniel Deronda* imparts a quality less of movement than of holding us still, of returning us in time and beginning again—"as we had seen . . . ." Some of that is the convention of the multiplot novel, which commits itself to the bifurcation of our attention, but that doubled vision is intensified here by the extensive delays between the plots, and by the temporal disruptions within them, disruptions that Eliot refined consciously to impress a sense of distance upon her readers. For this reason we, no less than the central characters, spend much of the middle of the novel lost in time, between the two plots and the (at least) two timelines. This feeling of repetition, of constantly trying to move forward only to rejoin our earlier place supplied with slightly different knowledge, further contributes to our identification with the characters, particularly with Gwendolen Harleth, who faces the most difficult choices-in-time while she is, like the reader, lost somewhere in the middle.

These disruptions are perhaps most noticeable at the beginning of the novel, where we begin with Daniel's observation of Gwendolen at the roulette wheel at Leubronn, and their delayed introduction, and wait till chapter twenty-nine for both characters to be together in time. When Gwendolen departs for her family's home at Offendene at the end of chapter two, we are moved backwards one year to her family's arrival at the house, and follow Gwendolen through her introduction to the neighborhood, the arrival of the wealthy Mr. Grandcourt, and their odd little courtship, until, as she is preparing herself to accept his offer, she meets his mistress, Lydia Glasher, and their illegitimate children. At this point Gwendolen is still active: she proudly asserts that "'I will not interfere with your wishes,'" and flees the country, traveling that same night (at the end of chapter fourteen) to Leubronn, which we saw her leaving at the end of chapter two. We then return to Leubronn in the "present" (the time in which Gwendolen has already left), only to encounter Daniel, his guardian, Sir Hugo Mallinger, and Sir Hugo's nephew, who is none other than Grandcourt—or, as the novel puts it, "While she was going back to England, Grandcourt was coming to find her . . . " (130). It is Daniel who tags the connection for us:

> "She's gone home," said Deronda coldly, as if he wished to say no more. But then, from a fresh impulse, he turned to look markedly at Grandcourt, and added,
> "But it is possible you know her. Her home is not far from Diplow: Offendene, near Wancester . . . "
> But [Grandcourt] answered, with his usual drawl, "Yes, I know her . . . " (135)

We, knowing more than Daniel, know the extent of their acquaintance, which Daniel will learn only later from Grandcourt's gentleman, Lush; in the meantime, we are left with only this sense of missed connection and overlapping acquaintance.

The narratorial trick, particularly the hint of Daniel's "fresh interest," is that the scene also seems to prepare us for the romance between the eponymous hero and Gwendolen, which other characters seem to expect as well. But those carefully laid expectations are disrupted by another regression in the time scheme. Sir Hugo, speaking our readerly desires, asks Daniel, "'You won't run after the pretty gambler, then?'" Daniel answers, "'Decidedly not'"—but the narrator displays more unexpected knowledge, this time closed to everyone except Daniel and us:

> This answer was perfectly truthful; nevertheless it had passed through Deronda's mind that under other circumstances he should have given way to the interest this girl had raised in him, and tried to know more of her. But his history had given him a stronger bias in another direction. He felt himself in no sense free. (136)

With this, we are off for five chapters of retrospection, largely expository, bringing us Daniel's history—his mysterious origins, his childhood as the ward of Sir Hugo (a guardianship Daniel reads as his own bastardy), his desultory education and wandering vocational yearnings, culminating in his discovery of a young woman about to drown herself in the Thames. He has rescued her and brought her to the home of his friends, only to receive her story in turn, ending "'I am a stranger; I am a Jew.'" This extensive digression ends, "This was the history of Deronda, *so far as he knew it*, up to the time of that visit to Leubronn, in which he saw Gwendolen Harleth at the gambling table" (191; emphasis added); the remainder of that disclosure ("as he knew it") is of course held from us till the end of the middle section, when Daniel learns that he, too, is a stranger and a Jew.

In the meantime, we are poised between two separate plots and several different time frames. Only after we have been brought to Leubronn again can we finally depart from it, turning back to the diegetic present, beginning with Gwendolen's much-delayed arrival at Offendene, where she had been "deposited as a feme sole with her large trunks" (192) and carrying her through her engagement to Grandcourt, in the midst of which, finally, she is introduced to Daniel Deronda, when Grandcourt announces that "my cousins are at Diplow," where they meet in chapter twenty-nine. The delay increases our sense of hesitation, as well as our sense of Gwendolen's increasing powerlessness, as knowledge is withheld from both of us. Only at the moment of their much-delayed meeting do we fully realize the extent to which we already know what Gwendolen cannot—that these "cousins" include the man who has already shaped her fate, and will continue to mix his "history" with hers. But we also know that Daniel is "in no sense free," and we know what Daniel cannot, that Gwendolen has been tortured by her decision to marry Grandcourt. The narrative, in short, has already mixed that "history" for us, but only by playing repeatedly with our sense of time, predetermination, and destiny.

The central temporal disruption within the novel clearly takes place in these opening chapters, and I will return to them at the end of this section, but I want first to note how far such disruption travels into the middle of the novel, and how much it challenges our sense of straightforward motion through the center of the plot. Before Gwendolen agrees to marry Grandcourt, she meets with the eccentric musician Klesmer. Her letter summoning him reaches him "pat between too early and too late" as he is leaving Quetcham, and he must stay the night at Wancester to meet with her, but this meeting is delayed while readers learn of his engagement to Catherine Arrowpoint and his unexpected departure from Quetcham. And this delay is deliberate: after completing these chapters, Eliot rearranged their order so that the information about Klesmer's engagement comes to us after Gwendolen's note, rather than before, shaping our sense that Gwendolen lacks the necessary knowledge to understand those around her. At a moment when we sympathize deeply with Gwendolen, it also lessens our identification with her—and our sense that her view of the world is, to say the least, shuttered by her lack of experience. At this, as at other turns of her own plot, Gwendolen does not realize just how incomplete her awareness of the world is.

We might feel comforted by our greater awareness, for this disruption, like the digression in book one that informs us of Daniel's past history, convinces us that we understand what Gwendolen does not, but there are other disruptions in the novel that do the opposite. Rather, they ally our confusion with Gwendolen's and keep us from feeling confident of the little that we do know. When Daniel returns to London and goes to visit Mirah, after his return from Leubronn, we hear of a visit he made to Frankfurt and his encounter with a stranger in the synagogue there. But this visit, which occurs chronologically between chapters twenty and twenty-one, and hence before Daniel's visit to Diplow and his meeting with Gwendolen, is not narrated until he returns to London from Diplow (chapter thirty-two); suggesting its relation not to the "Gwendolen" plot but to the "Mordecai" plot—Mirah's brother, in whose history Daniel is now somehow to entangle himself. These scenes primarily impress a reader with the sense that time is not entirely reliable—that the interweaving of plot has some unexpected effect on the order of things. At least initially, both seem to link our confusion with Gwendolen's, secure in her romantic daydreams. But notice how both of these disruptions produce knowledge that we have that Gwendolen does not share—in both cases, with Klesmer and Daniel, she is speaking with men who have vast "histories" closed to her, and these histories (the stories of Jewish men and the singing women they love) will shape her plot far more than she imagines.

The sharpest example of this temporal confusion, and one that suggests powerfully the relationship of time to problems both of plot and knowledge, comes at what we might consider the end of the middle of the novel, when Daniel and Gwendolen meet unexpectedly in Genoa, when finally all the cards in the deck will be laid out for us. Gwendolen has traveled to Genoa on a yacht with her husband, and Daniel has traveled there to meet his hitherto mysterious mother, the singing Jewess whose revelations truly upend Gwendolen's romance. At first this meeting seems securely placed in the love plot: Daniel and Gwendolen had last seen each other in London, in a series of meetings that leave several other characters convinced they are on the edge of an affair. Daniel has visited Gwendolen at her London home, at her request, in Grandcourt's absence; when her husband returns and finds Daniel there, he decides to take Gwendolen yachting in the Mediterranean, and after a painful scene between the two of them, we leave the couple and return to Daniel, caught in the misery of Gwendolen's longing for succor. But again, the narrator plays with our sense of what we have just read. The next chapter begins with the revelation that "Deronda had abstained from saying 'I shall not see you again. . . .'" Only here do we learn that before meeting Gwendolen he has had a visit with Sir Hugo and been given a note from the long-absent mother, who "desires to see you": he is off to Genoa to await a rendezvous with her (521–22). The next four chapters focus on Daniel's time waiting in Genoa (time in which he thinks of Gwendolen and the intertwining of "their two lots") and his encounters with his mother. Gwendolen in fact crosses his mind only briefly when, in a letter from his friend Hans, he hears that "'your Vandyke duchess,'" as Hans calls Gwendolen, "'is gone with her husband yachting to the Mediterranean. Shall you by chance have an opportunity of continuing your theological discussion with the fair Supralapsarian?'" (551). But Daniel resists seeing any future (any chance or opportunity, certainly no "continuity") in another meeting with Gwendolen, for we are told immediately that "The nonsense about Gwendolen, conveying the fact that she was gone yachting with her husband, only suggested a disturbing sequel to his own strange parting with her." Daniel is wrong, and their parting is only temporary, but the novel seems to support his sense of their disconnection. After describing Daniel's second meeting with his mother (increasing our sense that those vivid and painful scenes, and not his with Gwendolen, are the heart of this section of the novel, called, significantly, "The Mother and the Son") the narrator returns us to Gwendolen and Grandcourt yachting on the Mediterranean—only to have them meet, abruptly and unexpectedly, with Daniel on the steps of the hotel in Genoa.

Eliot has placed us, again, vividly, in the middle, and she has placed the disruption in Gwendolen's consciousness. Gwendolen has been dreaming of meeting Daniel in the cold, in the snow, over Mount Censis; instead, she sees him in Genoa, where she is "warm in her light woollen dress and straw hat" (577). Eliot has briefly made Daniel an interruption in Gwendolen's plot, coming across her path again like fate, but she abandons Gwendolen floating out to sea with her husband, estranged and half-mad, desperate for salvation. Instead of remaining in the boat with Gwendolen, we return to Daniel, studying his strange reluctance to leave Genoa that evening without seeing Gwendolen, his going to a synagogue (of course the last place Gwendolen would imagine him—does she know there are such places?) and wandering back onto the Strand, where he sees a drenched Gwendolen return, alone, after the drowning of her husband. While we weren't looking, Grandcourt died; with no warning, jarringly, the two plots are intertwined again.

These are all deliberate authorial choices—as we might quip, at this moment, middles are not born, they are made, and in this case, remade. Eliot had to choose: where should she place Daniel's second confrontation with his mother? It appears chronologically after his meeting with Gwendolen on the stairs, and initially, that is where Eliot placed the chapter. But she changed her mind, and moved the chapter so that it appears in the novel before that meeting with Gwendolen and Grandcourt. This does not shift the characters' knowledge in any significant way, but it radically changes ours, giving us a very different perspective in particular on Gwendolen, in part throwing our attention more fully on her and her struggles, but also reminding us of the failures of her knowledge. Gwendolen (who has no sense that Daniel is in any other plot, except that, when she saw him in London, he "looks different") is aware of his presence but not of his story, and in that way, as well as in the presentation of the chapter, her progress to her fatal voyage with Grandcourt is uninterrupted. This makes sense certainly in terms of building readerly suspense: no doubt Eliot wanted Daniel through with his portion of the plot before we rejoined Gwendolen—she wanted our suspense about Gwendolen out at sea undisturbed by wondering what Daniel's mother could want in her second meeting. But she also wanted us to know (again, what Gwendolen cannot) that Daniel is now free to marry Mirah, and will therefore never marry Gwendolen. She wanted us, in short, to appreciate that while Gwendolen was at sea physically she is "at sea" mentally as well, utterly unaware of what awaits her even once she is back safely on dry land. She is freeing us to worry about Gwendolen, toying with us as we watch Gwendolen struggle in the boat, and then aligning our sympathies with Daniel as he watches Gwendolen return to the shore, wondering (as we do, along with him) if she has actually murdered her husband. Our readerly knowledge, if not entirely our sympathies, is being shifted away from Gwendolen and towards her observer; this prepares us (if anything could—and I think Eliot is very aware that nothing will) for the end of the novel, when all focalization moves to Daniel, and Gwendolen becomes a minor character in his plot, rather than a major character in her own. But this is done by moving us around in time—putting us in the middle and then shifting that middle repeatedly to render us ever more uncertain of our bearings, ever more uncertain that we know all this is going on around us.

With these smaller disruptions in mind, I want to return to the central narratorial trick of the first part of the novel, the one that shapes the progress in particular of Gwendolen's narrative: the repetition of Grandcourt's marriage proposal interrupted (not ended) by the gambling episode at Leubronn. This is the central action of the book, the "error" that the plot most needs to correct, Gwendolen's mistake in marrying Grandcourt. But it is also the central plot element that needs temporal rearrangement by the careful reader, the one that needs to be seen as a beginning and not a middle, although that is where it appears to us. If the book were reordered properly, Gwendolen would arrive at Offendene, meet Grandcourt, meet Lydia Glasher in the glade, promise not to marry him, go to Leubronn, hear of her loss of fortune, and then return to Offendene, where she will, after this minor delay, accept his offer of marriage. In this version of the plot, Daniel will not even be a blip on a screen; he will be a minor glance in the major plot, which brings Gwendolen into marriage. The most obvious effect of moving the visit to Leubronn forward in the novel is to introduce the relationship between Daniel and Gwendolen; it is also, of course, to give a name to her moral scruples, the conscience that already led her to leave Grandcourt the first time. But the central effect of this movement-through-time is, I would argue, to highlight the impossibility of Gwendolen's choice, the feeling that she is already mired in plot by the time she hears Grandcourt's proposal. Gwendolen herself notices the uncanny nature of the repetition, one that the other temporal derangements of the novel train us to see as well. "What was the good of choice coming again" (245), she asks, a question the novel will rephrase repeatedly in its repetitions without difference. When she faces the second proposal (the first never having quite taken place, evaded by her act of flight), Gwendolen is given an image of shuffling through a book, much as we do:

> Again she seemed to get a sort of empire over her own life. But how to use it? Here came the terror. Quick, quick, like pictures in a book beaten open with a sense of hurry, came back vividly, yet in fragments, all that she had gone through in relation to Grandcourt . . . her own pledge (was it a pledge not to marry him?) (245)

Gwendolen tries to do what we do, look backwards and gauge exactly the extent of her promise to Lydia—which was, simply, "I will not interfere with your wishes." The words she dreads, "I will not marry him," are never said, but they are what she means, and she knows it. We know it as well, and this is the broken promise that haunts the remainder of the book.

Lest we be tempted to forget Gwendolen's failed promise, the same image and the same words come back at a later moment of confusion, when Gwendolen imagines murdering Grandcourt. To Gwendolen, "the strife within her seemed like her own effort to escape herself," and she "clung to the thought of Deronda." "And yet," says the narrator, "quick, quick, came images, plans of evil that would come again and seize her in the night, like furies preparing the deed that they would straightway avenge" (581). The "quick, quick" is the sign of the disjointed time, for the word quick in this book suggests always its opposite: that we are frozen in time.

For Gwendolen, this is also a sign of her powerful desire to escape knowledge, to act unthinkingly: "'I wish I had never known it,'" she says to herself of Lydia's secret (246), and she has a sense of being pulled backwards into other people's stories, of the world of (sexual) knowledge being "full of backwards secrets" (251). We see this world in considerably more complexity—for we see both Gwendolen's desire to escape Grandcourt and the financial traps, the loss of freedom, that lead her precisely to choose the one thing she knows enough not to choose. Our sense of how she is mired in these choices, the way time conspires against her and the way her own movements only trap her further, can only be increased by two powerful images that come at the moment when she makes her (hopeless) choice: the first, when "Yes came as gravely from Gwendolen's lips as if she had been answering to her name in a court of law" (255); the second, after her acceptance, when Grandcourt stands near Gwendolen "not unlike a gentleman who has a felicitous introduction at an evening party." Here, at last, is the introduction long delayed from chapter one, but it is not the introduction we had hoped for—and, unlike that first scene in which we saw Gwendolen still free to choose, "She could not go backward now . . . " (260).

ii. mixing it up

> mixed: [Orig. < Anglo-Norman mixt, mixte mixed, spec. of mixed blood (early 12th cent. in a legal context), of the nature of both a real and a personal action (c1290: see sense 2a) and Middle French miste, mixte mixed, consisting of different elements or qualities (12th cent. in Old French) and their etymon classical Latin mixtus partaking of two or more kinds, composite, mixed, varied, mixed with water.
>
> **Consisting of different or dissimilar elements or qualities; not of one kind, not pure or simple; composite.**
>
> *"Of course, it makes a difference if the objects of interest are human beings; but generally in all deep affections the objects are a mixture—half persons and half ideas. . . . " (355)*

In chapter twenty-nine, after many a missed opportunity and narratorial aside, Daniel Deronda and Gwendolen Harleth finally meet. From that point until chapter sixty-five, when Gwendolen effectively disappears from the novel, they are brought together often, and readers become accustomed to their meetings. Indeed, such comings-together are the custom of all novels, even multiplot novels, and they might be the chief way that we can recognize that we are in the middle: the different plots have made each other's acquaintance, come into the same room, taken a chair, and begun conversing. As characters from one plot cross into another, and all the plots jostle together in the mix, we feel a sense not just of curiosity (how will all this be sorted out?) but of control—we, and only we (or so we believe) know what is happening to everyone; we may not know how all the differences will be resolved, but we know that they shall be resolved in time. What happens in the middle, as the plots announce themselves, mingle, fall apart, and come back together, is what we think of as the plot of the book, in which we (and only we) are at home. But such readerly ease is not to be trusted, and it is what Eliot challenges, if she does not absolutely throw it over. For that reason, it is worth our asking, what is it that brings Gwendolen and Daniel together—what is the connection, the secret mixture, of their two stories?

Surprisingly, the plot element that brings them together is a particularly odd form of consanguinity: it is Sir Hugo Mallinger's desire to purchase the lease of one of his own properties, Diplow, from his nephew Henleigh Grandcourt (the heir to the estate) for the protection of Sir Hugo's wife and daughters. The expenses of his marriage have left Grandcourt more open to Sir Hugo's offer (he would have been less eager had he successfully married the heiress Catherine Arrowpoint), and Sir Hugo charges a reluctant Daniel Deronda to meet with Grandcourt and persuade him to consider the offer. This is doubly painful to Daniel, who does not like Grandcourt and, beyond that, believes (as do most characters in the novel) that he himself, Sir Hugo's illegitimate son, should be the heir. Into this remarkably byzantine (and quite deceptive, we might add) inheritance plot comes the young Gwendolen, another object (we initially believe) that should "belong" to Daniel, and instead belongs to Grandcourt.

None of this is true—but in defense of Eliot's elaborate plot-spinning, we must concede that she does not need it to be true; it is not, in fact, what brings these plots together. Instead, they are held together by what both Gwendolen and Daniel believe to be an apt metaphor, the imagined resemblance of his unknown mother to Lydia Glasher—a connection they both make when they meet. The "mixture" of these plots similarly works by analogy, not just of one erotic relationship to another, or one property plot to another, but to a series of erotically charged objects that move throughout the novel, repeatedly linking characters who may never meet to one another, and binding Gwendolen, Daniel, and a host of others together. It is these "objects" of interest, both human and material, that form the connections of the novel, that make up its middle—and these objects form, as the novel itself says, a chain of make-believe, a succession of "makeshift links."

Two statements, one from each of them, separated by some hundred pages, suggest that what they see instead is a kind of emotional symmetry, or, put more loosely and yet more accurately, a kind of analogy: the first is Gwendolen's, when she first learns of Daniel's purported bastardy, after her meeting with Lydia Glasher:

> An image which had immediately arisen in Gwendolen's mind was that of the unknown mother—no doubt a dark eyed woman—probably sad . . .
>
> What she had now heard about Deronda seemed to her imagination to throw him into one group with Mrs Glasher and her children. . . . Perhaps Deronda himself was thinking of these things. Could he know of Mrs Glasher? If he knew that she knew, he could despise her; but he could have no such knowledge. Would he, without that, despise her for marrying Grandcourt? (281)

That she draws this connection is not so surprising—Gwendolen is obsessed with the wrong she has done Lydia, the fear that she has married Grandcourt simply for money, and the anxiety that everyone knows it; for this reason, she sees everywhere reminders of her own shame. What is more remarkable is that for Daniel as well thoughts of his mother and his confused birth interweave themselves with his thoughts about Gwendolen and her painful marriage, and both stories propose themselves as problems not just of sexual secrets but secret knowledge. After Mr. Vandernoodt tells Daniel the story of Grandcourt's relationship with Lydia Glasher, Daniel draws exactly the right conclusion, and makes an unexpected connection:

> Since the early days when he had tried to construct the hidden story of his own birth, his mind had perhaps never been so active in weaving probabilities about any personal affair as it now had begun to be about Gwendolen's marriage. This unavowed relation of Grandcourt—could she have gained some knowledge of it, which caused her to shrink from the match—a shrinking finally overcome by the urgency of poverty? (370)

In terms of the plot, this is an uncanny moment: Daniel has in fact exactly guessed not only Grandcourt's secret relations but Gwendolen's knowledge of it; and like Gwendolen, he makes an essential connection between the secrecy of his own upbringing and the trauma of her marriage. But Daniel has unexpectedly answered (and in the negative) Gwendolen's silent question: would he despise her if "he knew that she knew" of Lydia before the marriage?

What links the plots of the two principal characters is not just a story of bastardy and deceit, but an obsession (characterological and narratorial) with knowledge and guilt. Gwendolen cannot rest until she tells Daniel the story of how she came to marry Grandcourt, just as (at the book's end) she cannot rest until she tells him the story of how she longed to kill him. But there is a similar unrest about all sorts of secrets in the middle of this novel, which suggests the problem with which I began: how can we know (anything, anyone) in the middle; how do characters know themselves while others gain and share knowledge of what seems to be secret to them? This confusion is acted out most strongly by Gwendolen Harleth, as she gradually learns that what she thought was most secret is known; that (as we knew from the beginning, and as the narrator tells us starkly) "her husband *all the while* knew it" (emphasis added). It is not that she has otherwise spared herself: throughout, Gwendolen treats herself fiercely in her scorn of her own marriage. As the narrator explains in free indirect discourse, "She had not consented in ignorance, and all she could say now would be a confession that she had not been ignorant. . . . Her right to explanation was gone" (275). But her one comfort has been that Grandcourt does not know her secret—that her shame is merely her own. When she learns that that is a lie, she is forced again to go backwards through her own story, to live through it again: Lush tells her that "'Mr Grandcourt was aware that you were acquainted with the unfortunate affair beforehand'" (509), and "she lived back in the scenes of her courtship, with the new bitter consciousness of what had been in Grandcourt's mind" (513). Just as the temporal disruptions of the novel cast us back relentlessly in time, so here the games of knowledge force characters, and in turn force us, to return to the beginning of everything.

This suggests something different about the combinatory power of the two-plot structure: that it works by playing games with the characters and with the readers, while we watch both knowledge travel across time and space. But of course, you cannot watch knowledge; you can, however, watch objects, the infinitely moveable signs of the people who own them. That is the business of the middle of any novel. The middle of *Daniel Deronda* (that "mixture," as the novel calls it, made up of "half persons and half ideas") carries this to an extreme, as the work of the novel is staged less through persons than through a series of objects highly linked to the people who wear, carry, or barter them, who make the relationships between people thinglike by giving us external objects to track. This is truly odd, but it also offers us a useful guidebook to finding the middle: the middle of the book is simply the place where all "things" are in motion. People move about fretfully; inheritances go from testators to heirs, often missing their intended (or our desired) inheritors along the way; objects float along and carry the plot with them. In this way, *Deronda* is no more uncanny than any other realist novel, bent on imbuing objects with life, memory, meaning, making them at once agents and symbols of plot, but here, it seems to give the objects more agency than it does the characters, making them, like our beloved Mr. Vandernoodt, a different kind of narrative middlemen.

Eliot works this out carefully through a group of linked objects that travel backwards and forwards through the novel. The plot proper began, remember, in Leubronn, in chapter two, when Gwendolen pawned and Daniel redeemed for her (anonymously) a necklace of turquoise stones made, as Gwendolen's mother says later, "out of your dear father's chain" (231). The necklace is the sign not only of Gwendolen's failed plot of independence (she attempted to pawn it to have travel money) but her unpayable debt to Daniel: "she had returned home—carrying with her, against her inclination, a necklace which she had pawned and someone else had redeemed" (130). The necklace resurfaces chapters later, when Gwendolen once more goes to sell her jewelry to help her impoverished family, but this time it is the one object she holds back from the intended sale, for (as she says later, when she wears it in front of Daniel and her husband) "I lost it once, and some one found it for me" (379). Once the necklace appears on Gwendolen as a married woman, it becomes a sign of some secret between Daniel and Gwendolen, a sign of a shared plot (what the narrator calls "the little affair of the necklace" [278]), and a sign of further resentment for Grandcourt. "'Oblige me by not showing whims like a madwoman in a play,'" he orders his wife: "'Don't carry on telegraphing'" (381).

But the redeemed necklace links itself up to a number of other bijoux in the course of the novel, suggesting again the complicated mixture that makes up the middle of any novel. The jewels Grandcourt has ordered Gwendolen to wear rather than her turquoise or emeralds are diamonds that once belonged to his mother; he had given them, when an impressionable young man, to Lydia Glasher, and has demanded them back on the occasion of his wedding to Gwendolen. Lydia, bad fairy that she is, has told Grandcourt she will send them to Gwendolen on the day of her marriage, but before that she, too, has raised the specter of madness. When she reminds Grandcourt that she could appear at the wedding herself, he says, "'Of course, if you like, you can play the mad woman'" (293), but the diamonds themselves carry with them some contagion of madness. When Lydia is first asked to relinquish them, she "burst(s) into hysterical crying and [speaks], again almost with a scream" (294); when the diamonds are given to Gwendolen, with a note from Lydia, Gwendolen "scream(s) again and again with hysterical violence" (301). Grandcourt watches Lydia's passion with "a baffling sense that he had to deal with something like madness" (295); later, when Gwendolen's screams shatter his wedding night, he can only repeat himself: "Was it a fit of madness?" As Grandcourt notes of this transference of mania with jewelry, "In some form or other the furies had crossed his threshold . . . " (301).

We might take the point further, for the "middle" consists largely of a series of such threshold-crossings. Following the jewels in *Daniel Deronda* not only connects Grandcourt, Gwendolen, and Lydia in their passionate triangle, but connects Daniel, Mirah, and his mother. Daniel wears a ring that belonged (like Gwendolen's necklace) to a "dear father" long dead. That ring is the only object he bears to visit his mother, who writes "Bring with you the diamond ring that Sir Hugo gave you. I shall like to see it again"—saying, that is, not I would like to see you, but I would like to see it (527). He pawns that ring to the Cohen family, when he goes in search of Mirah's brother, Ezra; he redeems it after he finds Mordecai; he leaves it off when he studies Hebrew with Mordecai, only to have it stolen by Mirah and Mordecai's father, Lapidoth, for "among the sensibilities still left strong in [him] was the sensibility to his own claims, and he appeared to himself to have a claim on any property his children might possess" (660). Lapidoth takes the ring and abandons his family, and it is the discovery of this theft that reduces Mirah to shame in front of Daniel, and leads him to propose marriage to her. Like Lapidoth, who assumes that "any property of Daniel's (available without his formal consent) was all one with his children's property" (675), Daniel assumes that property and relationship travel together, for his proposal to Mirah is that "we have no sorrow, no disgrace, no joy apart" (677). "Say you will take me to share all things with you," says Daniel (677); the willingness to share his things (and their inevitable loss) with her is what makes the marriage bond real.

The only surprise to this chain of consanguinity and ownership is that the novel doesn't last long enough for the diamond ring to be recovered yet again—the past, like everything else in *Daniel Deronda,* repeats infinitely, and, like the ghosts Daniel's mother sees, the ghosts that have led her to write to him and return to him his true inheritance (not the diamond ring of his father but the casket-bound letters of his grandfather), there seems little escape from these recurrences. "What was the good of choice coming again?" Gwendolen Harleth asked; "Quick, quick," the novel answered twice. The power of the links forged in *Daniel Deronda* is that they offer not different second choices, but the same choices, the same jewels, the same ghosts, come back again. The ghosts travel eerily backwards and forwards in time, as the jewels seem to do.

When Daniel first intuits Gwendolen's moral dilemma, "It was as if he saw her drowning while his limbs were bound" (387); he will see her saved from drowning before the book's end, but he will not be able to rescue her. When Gwendolen watches her husband drown, in the Mediterranean, she will see his dead face rise up again and again, but it is a face she has already seen, in a spectral moment in the first volume of the book, when a face appears from a locked cabinet in her mother's house at Diplow, helped by some "medium" to appear. The Princess Halm-Eberstein, when she meets her son at last, offers one final metaphor for this relentless connection of past, present, and future—this novel of "backwards secrets." To her father, the Princess says to Daniel, she was only a "makeshift link," a connection between himself and her son who would carry on his heritage. The princess mattered only because the true son and heir would pass through her; Daniel is her father's belief become real, the ultimate "object" of a fiction. But for Gwendolen, screaming at the sight of the diamonds that mark her barter-price, weaving her father's chain around her as she moves between Deronda and Grandcourt, we might argue that these links (however makeshift, however make-believe; however, to use Peter Brooks's term, "illusory") are all too terribly real. They have left her chained to a plot that makes coincidence fate and objects punishments; a plot that she can never entirely understand.

iii. meddling, marrying, and middling

> [< Anglo-Norman medler (c1165), variant of Anglo-Norman and Old French mesler, meller (c1000 in Old French as mescler; French mêler (1740)) < post-classical Latin misculare (9th cent.) < classical Latin miscere to mix (see MIXED a.2)
>
> To concern oneself or interfere (with).
>
> *"I can think of no medium so good as Mr Deronda." (268)*

There is another (proper) name for "link" in *Daniel Deronda*, and that is Daniel himself. It may take some eight hundred pages to unfurl, but by the end of the novel we know why the book bears his name like a defiant banner: he is the character who, through sympathy, curiosity, and relentless coincidence, has brought together all these characters into a chain of reaction. We might remember Mab Meyrick's joyful declaration on learning that the Vandyke duchess is the cousin of Rex and Anna Gascoigne: "'It is like a Chinese puzzle that one has to fit together'" (558). Mab is sure something wonderful may be made of it, but what? We might guess that when the pieces are fit together they form a portrait of Daniel Deronda.

The novel, in a metaphor we well remember from *Middlemarch,* refers to Daniel as a "medium," a middle path between extremes, a kind of spiritual aether (an effective description of his paucity of characterization as well) floating between plot elements, fulfilling a messianic promise while also, unlike poor Gwendolen, successfully completing the marriage plot that is the exit exam for any novel. Daniel not only *is* a "middle," he successfully *traverses* the novel's "middle," in part (here the book becomes vicious in its rebuking of Gwendolen) by accepting his own role as simply middling. "'I make it a virtue to be content with my middlingness,'" Daniel smugly announces to Gwendolen. "'I cannot imitate you,'" she replies. "'To be middling with me is another phrase for being dull'" (350). And many a reader, confronted with Daniel's comfortable ordinariness, might level a similar accusation at him—the long succession of scenes painting his somewhat tepid moral crises doubtless accounts for the remarkable numbers of readerly drop-offs in the middle of *Daniel Deronda.*

Daniel, however, offers a more pungent account of his own life in the middle: "'I seldom find I do any good by my preaching. I might as well have kept from meddling,' said Deronda, thinking rather sadly that his interference about the unfortunate necklace might end in nothing but an added pain to him" (479). Without pausing too long over his remarkable narcissism, we might agree with him in every other way: he "might as well have kept from meddling." But he didn't. Daniel has named accurately (as deliberately as Eliot did, with her movement of a middling chapter to chapter one) the "true beginning" of the plot. But it is interesting to note that Gwendolen also marks that beginning as the most significant moment: "'You began it when you rebuked me . . . '" (387), she says.

What exactly, we might still be wondering, very late in the novel, did begin when Daniel meddled? Certainly, to return to the note of the previous section, he "crossed over," entering Gwendolen's life, becoming part of her story. And this action in itself is enough to create anxiety. The novel's nervousness about "togetherness with separation," particularly when made flesh in Daniel's determination to marry a Jewish woman, and his separation from British society at the book's end, ought otherwise to have alerted us to a real queasiness about "meddling," mixing, mixing-in, but this form of middling, unlike intermarriage or religious assimilation, meets more with ambivalence than absolute disapprobation. Daniel is accused of worse forms of admixture, essentially of pandering and adulterating, when Grandcourt accuses him of keeping Mirah as a mistress; but he is more likely to "mix" by entering into the sympathies of others, by joining too eagerly with their fantasies, their schemes, their plots. And this too eager sympathy is at once where one plot comes from (the sympathy for Gwendolen with which he "began it") and the death of other forms of plot.

It is certainly the death of at least one version of Gwendolen Harleth's plot. *Deronda* differs from others of Eliot's late novels in that the plot of education, the plot where the heroine's moral enlightenment comes at the hero's hand and in turn goes hand in hand with her marriage, does not here reach erotic fulfillment. This plot was most successful in *Felix Holt, the Radical* (where Esther Lyon, a less dangerous if also less alluring Gwendolen Harleth, proves her redemption when she renounces an inheritance, choosing instead to marry her pontificating mentor, the eponymous Felix), but the erotics of instruction carries over into *Middlemarch* as well. Will Ladislaw is, quite obviously and probably blessedly, no Daniel Deronda, but the progress in which "Miss Brooke" is swallowed up in *Middlemarch* and Dorothea Casaubon, having "learn[ed] what everything costs," leaves Freshitt Hall and Tipton Grange for the streets of London, still promises that marital rewards and moral certainty will travel together. No such unity in *Daniel Deronda*—at least not for Gwendolen Harleth.

Yet our expectations have clearly been aroused. The beginning of the middle, the moment when Gwendolen and Daniel come together and do not (yet) meet, promises us that their fates will be (permanently, which is to say closurally) bound together; we could not have predicted the subsumption of her plot into his, or her curious silencing at the book's end, or the grief that she brings to her youthful failures of moral imagination. But more than that, we could not have predicted that they would not have married. Indeed, we are not alone in our imaginings. Other characters are quick to explain to us why this should have happened: even Lady Mallinger, no ingenious plotter, confesses "it had passed through her mind that after a proper time Daniel might marry Mrs Grandcourt—because it seemed so remarkable that he should be at Genoa just at that time—and although she herself was not fond of widows she could not help thinking that such a marriage would have been better than his going altogether with the Jews" (679). Sir Hugo, Rex, Hans, characters trained like us to read coincidence as destiny, follow this "remarkable" path to an unremarkable ending, hoping to find the lead characters successfully tucked into the marriage bed. The redoubtable Kate Meyrick, seeking a fictionally appropriate partner for Daniel, explains that "'When I drew a wedding for a frontispiece to "Hearts and Diamonds," I made a sort of likeness of him for the bridegroom, and I went about looking for a grand woman who would do for his countess, but I saw none that would not be poor creatures by the side of him'" (560). "'You should have seen Mrs Grandcourt then,'" replies the equally firm Mrs. Meyrick, but perhaps the title itself, conjuring the fatal diamonds of Gwendolen's wedding night, ought to remind us that a silver-fork novel of courtship is no place for either Gwendolen or Daniel.

The person most surprised by the ending of *Daniel Deronda* is, of course, Gwendolen herself, who seems to be as disastrous a spinner of love plots as any popular romancer. But this we might say is because she is no necromancer: she cannot conjure the portions of the novel she does not appear in. As Barbara Hardy describes it, "For her, he is a character in her private drama, a support, a mentor, and, at the end, a pillar of strength. For the reader, she is visibly only a small part of his life, and the part he plays in her story is far removed from his relationship with Mirah, Mordecai, his mother, and the destiny of the Jewish people" (28). This is made clear as Gwendolen's portion of the novel diminishes as the book nears its end—in the final volume, only one chapter is focalized through her; all the rest is Daniel and his (Jewish, messianic, nuptial) world. But as Eliot makes painfully clear, Gwendolen could not at all see that other world, for it is removed from her not only by her selfishness but by the structure of the world she does live in—how could she ever cross that threshold? Daniel, not surprisingly, has a far keener sense of this than Gwendolen herself does. Reflecting on her fate before he meets her in Genoa,

> Strangely her figure entered into the pictures of his present and future; strangely (and now it seemed sadly) their two lots had come in contact, hers narrowly personal, his charged with far-reaching sensibilities, perhaps with durable purposes, which were hardly more present to her than the reasons why men migrate are present to the birds that come as usual for the crumbs and find them no more. (531)

It is true that Gwendolen has somewhat birdlike interests—she observes only once that Daniel seems different from usual, and she takes no notice of his comings and goings, never asks about his profession or his interests, and fails to rise to the bait even when she finds he is studying Hebrew. Indeed, it would seem that she isn't even sure that Jews can marry, from her strained response when he tells her of his newly discovered heritage. Yet the narrator seems curiously intent on punishing Gwendolen for not being in a position to read the remainder of the novel in which she appears.[11]

The point of *Daniel Deronda*, as Henry James noticed long ago, is for Daniel to announce to Gwendolen that he is a Jew;[12] there is no comparable announcement that Gwendolen can make. As Leslie Stephen remarked, "As we cannot all discover that we belong to the chosen people, and some of us might, even then, doubt the wisdom of the enterprise, one feels that Deronda's mode of solving his problem is not generally applicable" (189); F. R. Leavis noted somewhat more acerbically that "there is no equivalent of Zionism for Gwendolen."[13] Her closural promise (that "'it will be better for me to have known you'") is not really an ending at all—it is, like most of Gwendolen's brighter moments, an acknowledgment of new knowledge, not a program for action.

But our interest in Gwendolen's end, an interest that began when we saw her making the first of many bad (if inevitable, if forced) choices, and decided, like Daniel, that we wanted to meddle, ought not to blind us to the difference that the lack of a clear ending makes when we go to find the middle of her plot. For Daniel, we need no such rearranging: his plot began before he met Gwendolen, when he rescued Mirah from the river: that was the "history" that made him feel, when he met Gwendolen, that he was no longer free. In the course of the novel's middle, he moved uneasily between three pivotal figures (Gwendolen, his mother, and Mordecai, all of them variously mixing him up) until he saw where fate had placed his plot. But once his identity was fixed and his romantic desire and vocational ambitions were like so many ducks in a row, he could shoot straight through to his ending. No such progress for Gwendolen, and therefore, we must conclude, no such self-evident alignment—or rather, only a continuing middle, one that has hardly allowed her such a clean exit from the shooting gallery of plot. And yet we might ask, are middles so clearly to be dreaded?

> "I was telling [Grandcourt] a capital story last night, and he got up and walked away in the middle. I felt inclined to kick him." (369)

Let us give the last word to Mr. Vandernoodt, who chides Grandcourt not for being a sexual predator or a sadist, but for having no interest in his story. Grandcourt will not stay till the end—though we might remember that a man who is most looking-about when least looking-at might be forgiven for thinking that he already knows the end of every story. But he does not—least of all of his own, for although he is warned (both by sailors on the docks and by his own wife) of the dangers of his last sail, Grandcourt's "soul was garrisoned against presentiments and fears" (580). Grandcourt can walk away in the middle because he believes stories are all middle—he never looks back to beginnings, because he has no fears of the end.

What is the dread that this novel evokes so constantly? As I have hinted, I suspect it is precisely a fear of middles. Middles keep us humble—or they ought to, in a George Eliot novel. It is always too early to know if you are the heroine of your own life, or (as Henry James memorably put it of Gwendolen Harleth), "Gwendolen's history is admirably typical—as most things are with George Eliot: it is the very stuff that human life is made of. What is it made of but the discovery by each of us that we are at the best but a rather ridiculous fifth wheel to the coach, after we have sat cracking our whip and believe that we are at least the coachman in person?"[14] When James rewrote this novel as *The Portrait of a Lady*, he made no such mistake—but then, he took no chances on anyone displacing Isabel Archer. The heroine remained front and center; no messianic history marred her despair, telling her to buck up in spite of it. Of course, James also seems to have left his heroine stuck with Gilbert Osmond, or with a portly bunch of disappointing suitors. We might all prefer to return to Offendene with Mrs. Davilow, if those are our choices.[15]

"Maidens choosing." "What was the good of choice coming again?" "I wish I had never known it." "'I know everything,'" Gwendolen finally says at the book's end. "'It is all perfectly right, and I wish never to have it mentioned'" (648). What is the plot that comes after knowledge? Brooks, Miller, et al. would tell us that it is not plot at all—that, once the illusions have faded, after we have learned our lesson, we enter a kind of stasis, an end to narration, an end to possibility. And yet the ending of *Daniel Deronda* is more truly read not as coming "after," indeed, not as an ending at all, but for Gwendolen Harleth at least, as a middle—and a rather promising one at that. "Is it absolutely necessary that Mrs Grandcourt should marry again?" (683). So modern readers have queried after many a novel—and so Daniel Deronda asks at the end of this one. His own jealousy speaking, perhaps, but a certain rebellion against marriage and death, nonetheless. At the least, he offers such a rebellion (however hypothetically) for the heroine, and for once, the narrator does not interrupt: his opening-up of her ending, his invitation to other, more disruptive plots, is allowed to stand.

The final chapter of *Daniel Deronda* can similarly be seen as replaying the elements of "middling" I have identified in this essay: for all its certainty, it finesses the problem of temporal continuity, the first thing Eliot questioned in her novel, by placing Daniel not in novelistic but in messianic time, as he sails out of vocation and into history. It has eliminated the two-plot problem, the relentless interweaving of one character's destiny with another's, by simply asserting (as Daniel does, when he takes his "virtual farewell" from Gwendolen) that "If we had been much together before, we should have felt our differences more, and seemed to get farther apart. Now we can perhaps never see each other again. But our minds may get nearer" (689). No need, in this theory of plot, to be anywhere near any other character;[16] characters (and their stories) can continue to grow together simply by the fact of being apart, something the rest of this novel challenges fiercely, but is the novel's final answer to the multiplot problematic.

But middles, I have been arguing, turn out less to be problems of time and space, than simply a trick of *authorial* knowledge—we are in the middle because we do not (yet) know enough. Or rather, we are in the middle because we think we are at the center, but we are wrong; we are not even the coachman, but are straggling behind, trying to catch up to the main plot. And I have been arguing that women's knowledge, at least in the Victorian novel, is necessarily going to lag behind men's. Gwendolen's ignorance is the fate of a maiden "choosing," as the third book's title claims, when she as yet knows nothing of the world. Hence the bitter irony of the next book's title: "Gwendolen gets her Choice." Her choice of what, exactly? She knows no more of Daniel's messianic vocation than she did of Grandcourt's illicit relationship, so well known in the county that not only our Mr. Vandernoodt (who "likes to know the manners of my time") has it at his crafty fingertips, but the reverend Mr. Gascoigne, mild country clergymen, has heard the rumors of what Vandernoodt calls Grandcourt's "anecdotic history," his going "rather deep into pleasure." She knows no more of the contemporary lives of Jews than she knew of Grandcourt's viciousness, which she learns only when she realizes that he has known all along that she knew of Lydia's existence before their marriage, and that as Daniel later says, "Grandcourt can bite" (369). As Gwendolen says to Klesmer of her desires to be an actress, "'Of course I cannot know what goes on about theatres'" (219); no more can she know that men have mistresses and illegitimate children, or that (as even Mr. Vandernoodt could not conceive) they have Jewish mothers, undying grandfathers, and tiny-footed girlfriends with Talmud-reading brothers. She will know all of this, at last, by the book's end; what she is to do with such knowledge is not yet clear; why should this close off all possibilities of all other kinds of knowledge still to come, knowledge available to you only when you know some of what you don't know?

If middles are a kind of narratorial lag time, in which various forms of knowledge catch up to each other, middles may be both the heroine's natural enemy and her best friend—or at least they hold the potential to be that, if she is not forced into an ending when the pages of the book come to an end. George Eliot closed *Middlemarch* with the seemingly wise statement that "every limit is a beginning as well as an ending," but she went on to make clear what she meant: "marriage, which has been the bourne of so many narratives, is still a great beginning." Gwendolen Harleth is spared both such an ending and such a beginning; instead, she is offered something far more radical, a chance to continue as she is. There may be nothing more interesting, after all, for a heroine (or for that matter, a novel) to do than to choose to live in the necessary, illusory, make-believe middle.

Notes

1. George Eliot, *Daniel Deronda*, ed. Graham Handley (Oxford: World's Classics, 1984), 345. All quotations from the novel are from this edition.

2. For readers who will otherwise fret through the entire essay, Mr. Vandernoodt is "a man of the best Dutch blood imported at the revolution . . . one of those commodious persons in society who are nothing particular themselves," and "as good a foil as could be found" (345). "'Mr Vandernoodt,'" says Gwendolen when she first wonders who Deronda is, "'you know everybody . . . .'" He will reappear in various forms of "reader's friends" in the novels of Henry James, and he has clearly traveled to Leubronn from one of Thackeray's watering places, doubtless a later incarnation of "Tom Eaves," the gossiping narratorial presence of *Vanity Fair.* He appears, or rather is quoted, once more in the course of this novel, when the narrator comments that Gwendolen "found her only safety in a chill haughtiness which made Mr Vandernoodt remark that Mrs Grandcourt was becoming a perfect match for her husband" (517). His endlessly digressive narratives, I must concede, are an irritation to Deronda, for he has "the mania of always describing one thing while you were looking at another," and continually insists on "Lord Blough's kitchen" while touring the kitchen at Topping Abbey (356). Mr. Vandernoodt, we might note, raises the possibility that there might be a wrong middle after all.

3. Peter Brooks, *Reading for the Plot: Design and Intention in Narrative* (Cambridge, MA, and London: Harvard University Press, 1984), 96.

4. In Brooks's summary, "the metonymies of the middle produced, gave birth to, the final metaphor" (29). My interest, as will be clear in the middle of my essay, is much more clearly in the metonymies, as it is in "error," one of the most interesting words in *Daniel Deronda*, as it is in every novel since *Paradise Lost.*

5. The clearest exposition of these issues remains Barbara Hardy's, in *The Novels of George Eliot: A Study in Form* (London: The Athlone Press, 1963). Her reading of the novel in the introduction to her Penguin edition is a model of formal clarity, and I will return to her analysis at several points in my text. But these questions go back to the novel's earliest readers: R. H. Hutton commented on the novel's publication that "no book of hers before this, unless, perhaps, we except *Adam Bede,* ever contained so fine a plot, so admirably worked out" (David Carroll, ed., *George Eliot: The Critical Heritage* [London and New York: Routledge and Kegan Paul, 1971], 366; or *The Spectator,* September 9, 1876). Other critics, it must be noted, such as an anonymous reviewer in *The Saturday Review* (September 16, 1876), concluded that "we are at sea throughout." But the most interesting responses are the attempts to reconcile the two plots, not merely the most famous and most draconian, F. R. Leavis's re-editing of the novel into "Gwendolen Harleth," or Sir Leslie Stephen's comment that "The story is really two stories put side by side and intersecting at intervals. Each gives a life embodying a principle, and each illustrates its opposite by the contrast" (Leslie Stephen, *George Eliot* [London: Macmillan, 1903], 185). Hardy notes a similar concern in the reviews of *Felix Holt,* where a

writer in *The Edinburgh Review,* for October 1866, complained that "'the story has the defect of running in two parallel lines with only an occasional and arbitrary connexion'" (*George Eliot: The Critical Heritage,* 283), but *Daniel Deronda*'s division of our attention, although far more intricately worked out, has called up far more hostility than that earlier novel.

6. Its first sentence is, most properly, "let thy chief terror be of thine own soul," the opening line of the novel's motto. The opening sentences then move, in interesting order, from imperative to declaratory to interrogative, a progress that anticipates the structure of my own argument here.

7. Charles Dickens, *Bleak House,* ed. Stephen Gill (Oxford: World's Classics, 1996), 235.

8. Tzvetan Todorov, "Narrative-Men," in *Poetics of Prose* (Ithaca: Cornell University Press, 1977), 67–79.

9. Claudia L. Johnson, "F. R. Leavis: The 'Great Tradition' of the English Novel and the Jewish Part," *Nineteenth-Century Literature* 56 (September 2001): 198–227.

10. D. A. Miller, *Narrative and Its Discontents: Problems of Closure in the Traditional Novel* (Princeton: Princeton University Press, 1981).

11. The more interesting parallel is with Mirah, who similarly has no idea what Daniel's life is like apart from his visits to her. At the end of the novel, she convinces herself that Gwendolen is simply another woman on whom Daniel took pity, and she manages to forget that she was ever jealous at all. Of course, the plot has proved her right, and proved Gwendolen wrong, but structurally their roles are exactly the same: each is left in ignorance of what Daniel Deronda is doing when he is not with them. And it is interesting that neither of them knows of Daniel's visit to his mother, the visit that will play so major a role in both their stories.

12. "It makes one wonder whether the whole heavy structure of the Jewish question in the story was not built up by the author for the express purpose of giving its proper force to [the blow to Gwendolen's ego]." Henry James, *Partial Portraits* (London and New York: Macmillan, 1888), 90.

13. F. R. Leavis, *The Great Tradition* (New York: George Stewart, 1950), 83.

14. James, *Partial Portraits,* 89.

15. See Carolyn Dever, *Death and the Mother from Dickens to Freud* (Cambridge: Cambridge University Press, 1998), for a similar reading of the optimism of leaving the heroine alone with her mother at the book's end. Dever, however, reads the novel as having an ending; I do not.

16. See John Picker, *Victorian Soundscapes* (Oxford: Oxford University Press, 2003), for a similar reading about necessary distance in the novel.

THREE

Before and Afterwardsness in Henry James

KENT PUCKETT

> *"'ere today, somewhere else tomorrow," that's 'is motto.*
> —Henry James, notebook entry, August 22, 1885

> *But, as we all know, the absence of evidence is not evidence of absence.*
> —Donald Rumsfeld, news briefing, August 5, 2003

Getting the middle right was hard for Henry James. If, as he suggests in the preface to *The Tragic Muse* (1890), it was his delight in "deep-breathing economy and [. . .] organic form" that kept his novels from reproducing the excesses of what he famously called "large loose baggy monsters," that sought-after structural tautness seemed most likely to give way in the middle. He writes that

> . . . the centre of my structure would insist on placing itself *not,* so to speak, in the middle. It mattered little that the reader with the idea or the suspicion of a structural centre is the rarest of friends and of critics—a bird, it would seem, as merely fabled as the phoenix: the terminational terror was not the less to break in and my work threaten to masquerade for me as an active figure condemned to the disgrace of legs too short, ever so much too short, for its body. I urge myself to the candid confession that in very few of my productions, to my eye, *has* the organic centre succeeded in getting into proper position.[1]

A novel's middle is tricky: the structural balance, the produced and proportional difference between a middle or center and everything else is, given James's interest in "organic form," simply difficult to achieve; too much or too little here or there results in shapes awkward enough to pose a threat to form, in figures fragmented, stunted, or foreshortened that seem the inevitable consequence of wishing too hard for a perfect body. In the developmental story that James tells again and again in the prefaces, the story of how this little germ grew up into that kind of novel, the "just right" stroke that would at last land the middle in the middle seems maddeningly elusive: the world, running over with relations, has only too much to give, and the impossibility of knowing what would be enough gets right in the way of seeing where one's middle should go.

The middle is hard to handle even within the context of James's brief discussion of it in the preface to *The Tragic Muse*. On the one hand, it names a pervasive attribute of a novel structured around one or another point of view: to look for the middle in these terms would be to look for a "center of consciousness" around and through which the stuff of a novel could be organized. The middle, in this case, would refer to a mostly theoretical point posited in order to allow for the hermeneutic motion between different parts understood as bound together into an internally coherent whole. On the other hand, James seems also to refer to the modest Aristotelian idea of the middle as that which "follows something else and is followed by something else": "The first half of a fiction insists ever on figuring to me as the stage for the second half . . ." (6).² Constructing a fiction is about proportions, and getting the proportions right means having a first half and a second half that make sense in terms of each other and that help each other to make sense. The novel in that case comes to look like a folding screen; its wholeness hangs, as it were, from the hinge of a mundanely material middle. The presence of both senses of the middle—as luminous hermeneutic center and merely material point—produces a situation just as monstrous as any of the prefaces' other organic forms gone bad. Their simultaneous resemblance and difference threaten to make a lot of nonsense out of James's discussion of the middle.

Eve Kosofsky Sedgwick has seen in this slip a moment when what seems simply muddled in James's novel talk instead figures a sensuousness with which the prefaces might otherwise seem to have little to do: "But, confusingly, these spatial metaphors refer to the interrelation among characters' points of view [. . .] but also (and quite incommensurably) to the relation between the first half and the latter (or, anthropomorphically, the lower and/or back) half of each novel."³ The middle is for Sedgwick polymorphous, a place within the novel too excessively *there;* it thus becomes an idea resistant enough to systematization to stand in for a pleasure that would similarly exceed our efforts at simple description. The middle, so hard to do, can only be *done* (in the vague and suggestive Jamesian sense of that word), and bringing into proximity the first and the second versions of the middle produces a situation in which a novel's brains cannot be kept safely separate from other, less reputable parts of its body. The middle, hard to hold on to, is delightful precisely because it marks a point at which the terms of James's nascent novel theory resist abstraction in order to cultivate a writing that is pleasurable because it is particular. There is also another kind of excess at work here. If the middle sometimes seems a place where the body of a novel is—according to an idea about novels that the prefaces both support and lament—too wide, weird, or short, so can it come off as poorly timed, falling somewhere before or after what would seem its proper place. James's middles can thus seem to resemble his characters insofar as those characters are, according to Kaja Silverman, often "conspicuously either too early or too late," too early or too late, that is, in relation to one or another primal scene that would take the position of center within a whole narrative of development.[4] Characters in James tend, in other words, to have more than a little trouble knowing what they need to know when they need to know it. In this, they are like a novel form that was itself both early and late: James writes in "The Future of the Novel" that the novel "is a form that has had a fortune so little to have been foretold at its cradle. . . . It arrived, in truth, the novel, late at self-consciousness, but it has done its utmost ever since to make up for lost opportunities."[5]

It is thus appropriate that James's discussion of the middle is itself oddly timed, appearing as it does in the preface to *The Tragic Muse,* a novel for which the middle isn't that much of a problem. James's troubled take on the middle applies, he says, to almost all of his novels; if, in that case, the middle is *everywhere* a problem, why mention it in one preface instead of another? Why mention it here instead of there?[6] James accounts for his discussion with a reference to his "mortal horror of two stories, two pictures, in one," a horror brought on by the difficulty that came with working to resolve the story of Nick Dormer's agonized decision to "chuck" politics for art and the story of Peter Sherringham's efforts to get Miriam Rooth, the tragic muse of the novel's title, to "chuck" the dramatic art that kindled his desire so that she might respectably marry him. Though this awkward division of labor does, as James sees, pose problems, they are not exactly the problems about which he writes in the preface to *The Tragic Muse*. While the presence of several seemingly central characters does indeed complicate the novel's ability to focus attention, the economic problem posed by the jostling presence of two interwoven tales is not especially about the successful articulation of a middle point coming appropriately after the beginning and before the end.⁷ So, while the middle (as opposed to the center, about which, if we're talking about Jamesian centers of consciousness, there is already no shortage of writing) is as important to *The Tragic Muse* as it is to any novel, it seems no *more* important to it than it is to any novel, a fact that would mean little if it weren't for the fact that the middle is so absolutely important to the novel that James had written just before: *The Princess Casamassima*. As we will soon see, that earlier novel's most spectacular event is not-so-spectacularly situated at the novel's most middle point; as a result, where *The Tragic Muse* is just another novel whose prickly middle causes problems, *The Princess Casamassima* is a novel that not only *has* a middle, but also is importantly and centrally *about* the middle.

The Princess Casamassima (1886) was very much on James's mind as he began to write *The Tragic Muse;* he was in 1887 still smarting from the relative silence with which *The Princess* had been greeted and welcomed his new next novel as a chance for change: he writes to Grace Norton in the summer of that year, "I am just beginning a novel about half as long (thank God!) as the *Princess*. . . . "⁸ Of course, *The Tragic Muse* was in the end every bit as long as *The Princess,* a fact that gives it the feel of an unexpected and unwelcome repetition. It was meant to be half as long as its precursor, and in expanding to twice its intended length, ends up looking like the latter half of a much larger figure made up of two equally long novels. The recognition that the middle might be a problem thus appears as both belated (in James's late-blooming reference to it in the prefaces) and precocious (in its unannounced early performance in *The Princess*).⁹ Just as the middle tends to encourage excess, so too in this case does the developmental quirk visible in the relation between these novels from James's "middle years" and their prefaces produce at the level of theory and practice a surplus registered in the fact of so very many words and the oddly timed preface to *The Tragic Muse. The Princess Casamassima,* both because it falls where it does in relation to James's other novels and because of what it does with its own middle, can be taken as a long meditation on middleness: Why is the middle a problem? What does the middle do? Why, when the middle is otherwise elusive in James, is it given such particular pride of place in *The Princess Casamassima*?

The Princess Casamassima is about a "little cockney bookbinder" named Hyacinth Robinson. Hyacinth, who is the product of a brief and fatal liaison between a French seamstress and an English aristocrat (she kills him after he jilts her), bears a social order that will not recognize him a grudge. He is raised in something like squalor by Amanda Pynsent, a kind-hearted seamstress, and suffers an early and defining trauma when "Pinnie," as he calls her, takes him to visit his disgraced dying mother in the Millbank Prison infirmary. As a result of his hurts, his shame, and his sympathy for "the People," Hyacinth works for the first half of the novel to insinuate himself into a shadowy anarchist underground dedicated, however vaguely, to society's overthrow. Towards the middle of the novel—make that *at* its middle—he succeeds and offers his life to the anarchist Diedrich Hoffendahl: he later tells the Princess, a jaded and beautiful aristocrat who initially takes Hyacinth up because she is interested in "the great cause," that "I took a vow—a tremendous, terrible vow" (327). He has promised to execute, when called upon, one or another terrorist plot that will almost certainly result in the loss of his life. After making that promise, he sees something of the world (Paris and Venice), experiences a change of heart, finds that he loves a lot of what an otherwise barbarous culture has produced, and commits suicide in order to escape the terms of his vow and what looks like an insoluble and familiarly Jamesian tension between art and life.

Hyacinth's vow is as much the middle of the novel as his cleverly reflective "vessel of consciousness" is its center:[10] not only does it take place at the novel's very middle, falling physically between the two volumes of its New York Edition, but it also stands as the culmination of Hyacinth's political career, the crisis of his life, and the point that bisects that life in terms of its significance. Things happened before he made his promise and things happened after he made his promise; insofar as Hyacinth's brief life is in the end a whole and narratable thing, his vow is that point against which all other aspects of that life can be read: the promise, we are told, "altered his life altogether—had, indeed, as he might say, changed the terms on which he held it" (326). Beforeness and afterwardsness are, as Deborah Esch points out, built into the very structure of the promise as a speech act defined by the inevitable and unpredictable difference between before and after: "What James calls Hyacinth's 'deep dilemma,' his 'impossible stand,' is a function of the intervention of time into the configuration of promise and redemption in the narrative. An interval opens up between the promise and the demand that it be kept...."[11] The constitutive difference between what a promise means today and what it will mean tomorrow is only an especially concentrated form of a structure that reappears locally in Hyacinth's divided self—"there were times when he said to himself that it might very well be his fate to be divided, to the point of torture" (165)—and more generally in the many ways in which the difference between past and future, present and future, or past and present drive the characters and the plot of *The Princess*.

If "the noncoincidence of the utterance and its fulfillment" in time constitutes a key dilemma within *The Princess Casamassima,* so is it the very engine of a psychic economy defined by the pressure that the past exerts on the present.[12] Using the language of psychoanalysis, we might think of Hyacinth in terms of his "afterwardsness" (Jean Laplanche's term for Freudian *Nachträglichkeit* or "deferred action"). *Nachträglichkeit* names the process according to which old memories take on new kinds of significance in relation to new experiences and new stages of psychic development. The phenomenon of *Nachträglichkeit* raises a number of important and importantly novelistic questions: In what ways are past and present related? Are old traumas really responsible for new actions? What, if anything, separates past from present from future? Because these are, as we have begun to see, also *The Princess Casamassima*'s questions, a turn to Freudian *Nachträglichkeit* will be—or, rather, will have been—useful.

Laplanche and Pontalis point out that "Freud uses the term '*nachträglich*' repeatedly and constantly" to refer to the relation between experiences that seemed the first time around to lack significance and later experiences that make their early, missed significance felt.[13] At first glance, the logic of deferred action would seem to provide fodder for critics who would see psychoanalysis as a determinist reduction of psychic life to a more or less elaborate effect of infantile trauma; some primal scene or primal repression, some early trauma or forgotten seduction will inevitably emerge as the truth of analysis and analysand. Indeed, Laplanche points out that Freud worked, if with difficulty, to solidify exactly this sense of the past's relation to the present: "Freud . . . never wavered in his conviction that what comes before determines what happens after."[14] At the level of theory if not practice—in *The Interpretation of Dreams,* "Little Hans," and the "Wolf Man"—Freud maintains what Laplanche calls the *determinist* sense of *Nachträglichkeit*'s temporal mechanism—the past really determines what happens in the future. To focus exclusively on that direction of *Nachträglichkeit,* however, would be to miss an important aspect of its operation both in and after Freud: while common sense would reduce its effect to a linear, forward motion (the past *causes* the future), *Nachträglichkeit* also seems to work in reverse. As much as Freud worked to limit his concept to one direction, it seemed nonetheless to resist that limitation; where it was to go forward, it seemed sometimes also to go back. That, for instance, the Wolf Man comes later to "understand" the significance of his parents' sexual act seems more *retroactive:* "He received the impressions when he was one and a half; his understanding of them was deferred, but became possible at the time of the dream owing to his development, his sexual excitations, and his sexual researches."[15] In this instance, present knowledge *produces* the past as differently significant—as different—from what it had been. The future, in this instance, *makes* the past. It is this other direction of *Nachträglichkeit* that Lacan emphasizes: "The past and the future correspond precisely to one another. And not any old how—not in the sense that you might believe that analysis indicates, namely from past to the future. On the contrary, precisely in analysis, because its technique works, it happens in the right order—from the future to the past."[16] For Lacan, this is the "right order" because the truth of psychoanalysis as talking cure depends upon it: "he simply presupposes all the resubjectivizations of the event that seem necessary to him to explain its effects at each turning point at which he restructures himself—that is, as many restructurings of the event as take place, as he puts it, *nachträglich*, after the fact."[17] Or, again to use Laplanche's terms, "it is the *later* which is perhaps more important, and alone allows us to understand and to interpret what we persist in calling *the prior*."[18]

The point is that Freud's thinking and writing about psychic causality consistently pose the difference between the forward and backward motion of *Nachträglichkeit* as a problem. At the level of the text, deferred action doesn't always go only forward or only backward; and neither does it go back and forth both at once. Rather, Freud's writing regularly forces the reader to decide between one of two available but incommensurate positions: forward or back. It is for this reason that Laplanche takes "afterwardsness" as a translation more appropriate than deferred action or retrospective fantasizing for this phenomenon: "So either one decides to split up and divide the term in translation, or one chooses a term that will allow the readers to stay with Freud's term and reinterpret it for themselves. That's why I propose a translation that is not interpretive: I suggest the term *après coup*, and 'afterwards' in English. In all cases in Freud it's possible to use either 'afterwards' or 'afterwardsness.'"[19]

In order to get the double and contradictory movement of afterwardsness across, Laplanche rehearses a moment from *The Interpretation of Dreams*:

> A young man who was a great admirer of feminine beauty was talking once—so the story went—of the good-looking wet nurse who had suckled him when he was a baby: "I'm sorry," he remarked, "that I didn't make a better use of my opportunity." I was in the habit of quoting this anecdote to explain the factor of afterwardsness in the mechanism of the psychoneuroses.[20]

Freud's use of the story (the protagonist of which sounds appropriately like James's idea of the novel as a form that "has done its utmost ever since to make up for lost opportunities"[21]) is significant for Laplanche precisely because it isn't clear from the telling in which direction the erotic charge of the young man's story moves: either *retrogressively* from the adult's mischievous sense of what he would have done if he knew then what he knows now or *progressively* from an infant sexuality the force of which continues to be both felt and expressed in the psychic and erotic life of adults.

And if afterwardsness is a problem in Freud, the middle is an important part of its structure; the middle is the point that allows the analyst and the reader to enter into the work of interpretation. What, in other words, makes afterwardsness *work,* what in both directions makes events legible is a moment that comes in between and that allows the difference between before and after to become meaningful: the analyzable psychic life is made up, says Laplanche, of "two scenes linked by associative chains, but also clearly separated from each other by a *temporal barrier which inscribes them in two different spheres of meaning*" (Laplanche's emphasis). The simple fact of relating beginning to end (a relation both dependent on and constitutive of some kind of middle) puts us in a position where if we would read for significance we would need to decide but cannot finally decide between reading forward or backward, from trauma to symptom or from symptom to trauma.[22] This is why Laplanche prefers "afterwardsness": it holds us suspended between these two available but partial interpretations.[23]

The Princess Casamassima is, I would argue, characterized at every level by its afterwardsness. Afterwardsness is central to the temporality of the vow; the vow is necessarily the sometimes messy structural meeting of a before—when the promise is made—and an after—when the promise is kept. Hyacinth's relation to his origin is also structured in terms of its afterwardsness: although Hyacinth meets his poor, incarcerated mother early in life (he meets her briefly, as I have said, in one of the novel's celebrated opening scenes), the life-defining significance of the visit emerges only afterwards: "The strangeness of the matter to himself was that the germ of his curiosity should have developed so slowly; that the haunting wonder, which now, as he looked back, appeared to fill his whole childhood, should only after so long an interval have crept up to the air" (166). The muddled naturalistic logic of the novel remains interesting and, I would argue, *Jamesian* because it fails ever really to announce its proper order: Hyacinth is a great reader and seems as much a product of novels and plays as of his social context or of any real genetic imperative. Are Hyacinth's adult feelings, sensitivities, and actions the inevitable result of his genetic inheritance, or is that inheritance rendered significant and legible as a plot only because of the novel-reading that James tells us the adult Hyacinth has done? And, again, as I have already suggested, that the middle is *afterwards* announced as a problem in the preface to *The Tragic Muse* but worked out *before* in the body of *The Princess Casamassima* seems not only to underscore the significance of this problem, but also to reproduce it as theory. As was the case with Hyacinth, what we see in James becomes significant only afterwards. *The Princess* thus becomes both a meditation on and an instantiation of problems that seem the inevitable result of James's particular investment in the middle. Importantly, these different aspects of the same problem with the middle come together—where else—at the middle of *The Princess Casamassima*.

Although *The Princess Casamassima* is divided into six books, the novel's middle in fact falls between books two and three; in fact, the first volume of the two-volume New York Edition of the novel ends with the end of book two and the second volume begins with the beginning of book three.[24] At the end of book two, Hyacinth is on his way to meet the terrorist mastermind, Diedrich Hoffendahl, in front of whom he will make a solemn promise to commit a violent and probably suicidal terrorist act; book three, as we will see, begins well after Hyacinth has had his midnight meeting with Hoffendahl. What falls in between those two volumes is arguably the novel's most important event: Hyacinth's vow. Book two, more specifically, ends in this way: Hyacinth makes a spontaneous speech against the system at the "Sun and Moon," a pub where erstwhile revolutionists gather; it impresses Paul Muniment, the most serious and impressive of the London radicals ("Hyacinth was sure he had extraordinary things in his head; that he was thinking them out to the logical end, wherever it might land him; and that the night be should produce them, with the door of the club-room guarded and the company bound by a tremendous oath, the others would look at each other and turn pale" [206]). After the speech, Paul invites Hyacinth to meet the great Hoffendahl, who has come to London to recruit participants for one or another plot:

> They all walked away from the "Sun and Moon," and it was not for some five minutes that they encountered the four-wheeled cab which deepened so the solemnity of their expedition. After they were seated in it, Hyacinth learned that Hoffendahl was in London but for three days, was liable to hurry away on the morrow, and was accustomed to receive visits at all kinds of queer hours. It was getting to be midnight; the drive seemed interminable, to Hyacinth's impatience and curiosity. He sat next to Paul Muniment, who passed his arm around him, as if by way of a tacit expression of indebtedness. They all ended by sitting silent, as the cab jogged along murky miles, and by the time it stopped Hyacinth had wholly lost, in the drizzling gloom, a sense of their whereabouts. (296)

The passage's final dissolve only amplifies an ambiguity that has defined the whole of the scene. The errand on which the four men have entered should be among the most motivated of the novel; no one, however, seems to have much of an idea of what it is all about. This is, of course, disturbing in part because it is finally about violence, about hatching a plot to plant a bomb, to shoot a man, to do damage for reasons that will remain, like details of the scene, unclear. The tone of the thing—the hour, the weather, the mode of transportation—seems to take over, putting the atmospheric cart before the narrative horse. And if the weather is murky, so is the affective field in which these characters move; expressions are tacit, significant, excessive, maybe meaningless, maybe not. We lose, like Hyacinth, all sense of our whereabouts as chapter, book, and volume fade to black.

The beginning of the next book, book three, exacerbates or at least sustains this confusion:

> Hyacinth got up early—an operation attended with very little effort, as he had scarcely closed his eyes all night. What he saw from his window made him dress as rapidly as a young man could do who desired more than ever that his appearance should not give strange ideas about him. . . . (299)

It is not for another page or so that we realize that *three months* have passed since the previous scene and that Hyacinth now finds himself waking up in a spare room at Medley, a country house rented by the Princess Casamassima. Until that's clear—and the text seems to delight in withholding that information—we can have no idea where Hyacinth is in fact waking up; that he exhibits an anxious concern about fitting in with his surroundings tells us nothing—it is, after all, the truth of Hyacinth's character that, as nice as he always looks, he never fits in. That book two ends in the late evening and book three begins early in the morning produces a narrative ellipsis that goes unnoticed long enough to suture the scenes together; learning, as we will, that much time has passed between night and day will require us to tug at those stitches, giving the middle an affective significance that it didn't necessarily need to have. As if to add to this effect, the ellipsis is made into even more of a fetish by the fact that it falls in between chapters; indeed, in between the two discrete physical volumes of the New York Edition of the novel. The three lost months and the all-important promise that stand between his evening with Paul and his morning with the Princess are left somehow to hang in the air, dislocated and lost.[25]

What falls between the pages is arguably the novel's most important scene, the moment when Hyacinth makes his promise. The scene is, because of its absence, the novel's middle in a way that something coming at the end of the first part or the beginning of the second never could be. In this way, the excluded middle of *The Princess Casamassima* seems like a performed solution to problems that will be afterwards announced in the preface to *The Tragic Muse:* carving out a precise absence at the novel's midpoint is, it seems clear, an ingenious way to keep still a middle that might otherwise swell all out of proportion or simply float away. If, however, digging a hole where the middle should go works to pin down what will in the preface to *The Tragic Muse* seem all too elusive, we might wonder why this scene of all scenes, a scene the presence of which would have pinned down the notoriously vague politics of *The Princess Casamassima*, should be sacrificed to structural convenience. As happy, in that case, as this move might make the formalist worried only about securing the tenuous relation between beginning, middle, and end, the absenting of the meeting with Hoffendahl offers only anxiety to the reader worried more about politics and political violence. Why, with so much at stake, would James withhold Hyacinth's promise and thus the promise of the political real from *The Princess Casamassima*?

Thought of in these terms, *The Princess*'s absent middle might be taken as the index of a more general political ambivalence that has given critics much about which to write. Is the novel, considering the quality of its treatment of terrorism in the 1880s, a heavy-handed joke, or is it rather a canny kind of political analysis? There are, on the one hand, those who would see James's novel as pure political fantasy: Rebecca West famously called *The Princess* "a mad dream," and James's anarchists have been said to belong "decidedly in the realm of comic opera."[26] John Lucas writes that "at the very point where we need precision we meet a baffling vagueness. The ignorance of the characters too often suggests the ignorance of their creator."[27] There are, on the other hand, those who have tried to salvage a properly political James. Lionel Trilling, for instance, writes: "For the truth is that there is not a political event of *The Princess Casamassima*, not a detail of oath or mystery or danger, which is not confirmed by multitudinous records."[28]

James, in fact, plays in his preface with the idea that he might not have known enough about his subject: "There was always of course the chance that the propriety might be challenged—challenged by readers of a knowledge greater than mine" (48). Knowing little, however, does little to undermine James's carefully guarded position. On the one hand, James converts his "not knowing" into a virtue: "Shouldn't I find it in the happy contention that the value I wished most to render and the effect I wished most to produce were precisely those of our not knowing, but only guessing and suspecting and trying to ignore, what 'goes on' irreconcileably, subversively, beneath the vast smug surface?" (48). On the other hand, James was, as Trilling notes, "nourished like any other on conversation and the daily newspaper,"[29] and shared in a general anxiety that characterized the period in which the novel was written. If he didn't know a lot, that meant simply that he knew as much as the next guy. In January 1885 James writes to Grace Norton: "There is very little 'going on'—the country is gloomy, anxious, and London reflects its gloom. Westminster Hall and the Tower were blown up two days ago by Irish Dynamiters." James is, in this regard, a man very much of his time, a man of a time Mike Davis describes as that "half-century during which the bourgeois imaginary was haunted by the infamous figure of the bomb-throwing nihilist or anarchist."[30] It was exactly the "haunting" quality of that threat that James wanted to capture; rather than write an article about terrorism, he wrote a long novel and in so doing sought, as he writes in his preface, to represent "the sketchiness and vagueness and dimness" of a violence that seemed omnipresent to what elsewhere he called his "imagination of disaster."[31] If, though, all this "sketchiness" does much to reproduce an anxiety effect that would have been all too familiar to readers of his novel, what does James gain by so pointedly dropping Hoffendahl's only appearance and, most importantly, Hyacinth's "sacred" vow into the lost middle of his novel? In what follows I want to pursue the question of why James arranges his novel in this way in terms of that vow. How are we, stuck as we are with a novel hovering awkwardly between farce and fact, to assess the political decisions it represents? What does Hyacinth want from his terrorist act? And why, at last, does he refuse to carry it out? These questions will in the end return us to the middle.

In answer to the first question—why does Hyacinth make his vow—we might say that, according to the logic of James's novel, he can't do much else. *The Princess Casamassima* is, among other things, James's odd and oddly strained effort to produce a naturalist novel, one written self-consciously under the influence of Zola.[32] Read in this way, the novel is a working-out of the consequences of Hyacinth's genetic inheritance, the consequences of a self divided between the English blood of his father, the dissipated duke, Frederick Purvis, and the French blood of his mother, the "wild" seamstress, Florentine Vivier.[33] This problematic provenance could be taken as that which drives all else along; it puts Hyacinth in a place where he might most poignantly feel and diagnose the injustices of a corrupt social order, it gives him an inborn revolutionary credibility that James makes much of (his is, at different moments in the novel, the gloriously spilt blood of 1789, 1848, and 1871), and it sets the stage for the crisis of conscience that leads to Hyacinth's suicide. It is also what convinces Paul Muniment, who introduces Hyacinth to Hoffendahl, that he is the right man for the job. Not only is Hyacinth sure that his friend Poupin "had taken upon himself to disseminate the anecdote of his origin, of his mother's disaster" (282), but that origin also seems to be the cause of Hyacinth's spontaneous speech to the men of the Sun and Moon, a speech which stands as the clear precursor to his awful vow. After one disgruntled radical, a certain Delancey, taunts the others, calling them "afraid, afraid, afraid," Hyacinth responds:

> The next moment Hyacinth found that he had sprung up on a chair, opposite to [Delancey], and that at the sight of so rare a phenomenon the commotion had suddenly checked itself. It was the first time he had asked the ear of the company, and it was given on the spot. He was sure he looked very white, and it was even possible they could see him tremble. He could only hope that this didn't make him ridiculous when he said, "I don't think it's right of him to say that. There are others, besides him. At all events, I want to speak for myself: it may do some good; I can't help it. I'm not afraid; I'm very sure I'm not. I'm ready to do anything that will do any good; anything, anything—I don't care a rap. In such a cause I should like the idea of danger. I don't consider my bones precious in the least, compared with some other things. If one is sure one isn't afraid, and one is accused, why shouldn't one say so?" (294)

The terms and the spontaneity of his speech suggest something like pure reflex: Delancey's attack feels "like a quick blow in the face"; Hyacinth finds himself on the stump without knowing how he ended up there; he speaks, he says, because he "can't help it." The speech is accompanied by familiar physical symptoms: he trembles, he blanches, he stammers (the rapid and close repetition of "I"—"I don't," "I want," "I can't," "I'm not," etc.—in his short speech produces the effect of a stammer that is at other moments named directly: "he seemed to himself to stammer and emit common sounds" [198], he "blushed and stammered" [286]). We might, of course, read Hyacinth's performance as a simple and appropriate response to the severity of the commitment he feels himself making; joining up with the anarchists is, as he awkwardly suggests, maybe to choose death. There is, however, something excessive in the style of Hyacinth's speech that we should consider. The act seems all the more reflexive because it is almost purely phatic: Hyacinth says little else in his speech than "I am now speaking politically." His tortured syntax, the abstraction of his speech, his tendency to shift course mid-sentence: these are signs that the speaker, though he can speak, has nothing much to say. What's more, the play between Hyacinth's speech and James's narration, a play indexed by the sudden odd shift from the jerkily repeated "I" to the stiff impersonality of the "one" in his last line, suggests that stammering might go all the way down in *The Princess Casamassima*. Why, in other words, does the strained person-ness of the passage, frenetically secured at some expense to the speaker (I-I-I-I-I-I-I-I-I), give way at last to this curious anonymity? Why after so many "I"s (ten in only eight lines) does he ask "why shouldn't *one* say so"? In an essay called "He Stuttered," Gilles Deleuze writes that there are moments in novels when an otherwise absolute difference between a character's speech and a narrator's language collapses: "It is no longer the character who stutters in speech; it is the writer who becomes a *stutterer in language.*"[34] That, according at least to one familiar reading of the novel, James knew no more about politics than Hyacinth makes moments like these vibrate between the related registers of a character's speech and a narrator's language. Where, in other words, we might want to see Hyacinth's inability to say anything as an effect of what he doesn't know, we might in this case see it as equally an effect of what *narration* (rather than James) doesn't know. Not knowing, an absolute condition positively rendered here as a kind of stammering, cuts sharply across the distance between narration and character in a way that both reverses and exceeds the force of free indirect style. *Exactly the same* absence of knowledge drives style for both Hyacinth and narration, making identical the quality of their respective stammers. In all these ways, Hyacinth's sudden stump speech comes across as a brilliantly nervous and nearly automatic formal performance that is more about a relation to politics than about politics as such.

That an imperative more formal than genetic drives Hyacinth's speech makes sense here: if the literary naturalism with which James explicitly associates *The Princess* is "often characterized, implicitly or explicitly, as instancing the hard facts of racial determination and the contest between individual will and genetic fate," in Hyacinth it is, as the novel again and again tells us, neither Englishness nor Frenchness that drives him; it is, rather, the relation between the two that gives his character its meaning and force.[35] "He didn't really know whether he were French or English, or which of the two he should prefer to be" (127). His paradoxical inheritance is that which stands in the middle of those two competing terms: a relation, the formal quality of which reappears in the form of his curiously abstract but still fluid speech (one Channel, it seems, is as fluid as another).[36] James's naturalism thus seems an expression of Walter Benn Michaels's "logic of naturalism," which he identifies as a "a set of interests and activities that might be said to have as their common denominator a concern with the double identities that seem [. . .] to be required if there are to be any identities at all."[37] What drives Hyacinth to speak at this moment is neither any particular fact about his past nor some kind of cleanly constitutive absence; rather, James exploits the conventions of literary naturalism in order to posit as the center of Hyacinth's character something messier than pure presence or absence, something more like a fold or what Michaels would call a "working-out" of conflicts that would result from the fact of those conflicts being forced into such close, overlapping, awkward proximity.[38]

With this, we simply name Hyacinth's kinship with other Jamesian folk who act without the felt pressure of what Leo Bersani calls "vertical" motives. That we find a fold between one thing and another where we might have expected a birthmark or juicy secret come lately to light makes *The Princess Casamassima* another "narrative surface . . . never richly menaced by meanings it can't wholly contain." To continue with Bersani: "Complexity consists not in mutually subversive motives but rather in the expanding surface itself which, when most successful, finds a place in its intricate design for all the motives imaginable."[39] The expressive middle of Hyacinth Robinson, because it is a fold instead of a fixed point, spreads out to do whatever the novel needs it to; if there is, in other words, a force to neither-Frenchness-nor-Englishness, it is a force that might be recruited for any kind of work. That is, in itself and after Bersani, not much to notice; that it is mobilized as such within the frame of the naturalist novel—or, at least, James's version of the naturalist novel—is something else. We should take this first as a bit of Jamesian ingenuity; how, the novel seems to ask, might one retain the possibly saleable form of the naturalist novel without reducing one's characters to automatons driven along by a single biological imperative? If James's characters are not deep, neither are they stupid; indeed, if Hyacinth is any example, they are more at risk, as James says in his preface, of coming off as "too divinely, too priggishly clever" (37). Second, and more importantly, this arrangement creates a contradiction within *The Princess,* one the novel spends most of its energies trying to resolve. If Hyacinth is, like *The Princess Casamassima,* structured around, driven on by a sort of fold, he is also at last forced to choose between the two terms that come awkwardly together to produce that fold: Englishness and Frenchness, culture and anarchy, aesthetics and politics, nonviolence and violence, etc. In other words, Hyacinth seems organized according to two incompatible models: one defined by its demand that one choose and another defined by its structural resistance to the very idea of choice. Hyacinth is a choice asked to choose: "It made him even rather faint to think that he must choose" (165).

Hyacinth Robinson makes a promise at the middle of *The Princess Casamassima:*

> The only thing settled was that it was to be done instantly and absolutely, without a question, a hesitation or a scruple, in the manner that should be prescribed, at the moment, from headquarters. Very likely it would be to kill some one—some humbug in a high place; but whether the individual should deserve it or should not deserve it was not Hyacinth's affair. (333)

This promise, as I have already suggested, structures the whole of *The Princess Casamassima;* it divides the novel into two, stands as a figure for an afterwardsness that characterizes the novel at several levels, and is the most concentrated source of narrative desire in the novel (will it happen? when will it happen? who will it be?). It is both what retroactively makes sense of Hyacinth's life (he becomes *that* boy who grew up to be a terrorist) and leads with an almost plodding inevitability to the novel's bloody conclusion. The promise, in as many ways as we can describe, makes the middle of *The Princess Casamassima*. It is in that case all the more odd that Hyacinth at last fails to keep his promise. Towards the end of the novel the long-awaited order arrives in the form of an enigmatic letter, the contents of which are never directly revealed to the reader: "The letter," as Peter Brooks puts it, "is a blank."[40] Although Hyacinth receives the letter, seems at first to accept that he will assassinate one or another duke, and takes the pistol with which this assassination will be carried out, he does not finally act; Hyacinth Robinson breaks his promise and shoots himself. In breaking the terms of his vow, the figure that seemed, both thematically and structurally to hold the novel together, Hyacinth threatens to break up *The Princess,* to pull from under it a rug that had been counted on to tie James's cluttered room together. We must, in that case, ask: what keeps Hyacinth Robinson from keeping the promise that makes the middle of *The Princess Casamassima?* The novel raises, only to dismiss, a number of possibilities.

Is it because Hyacinth renounces the political use of violence? Although, as we have seen, James had an active "imagination of disaster" and thought society corrupt, he was no radical. In *A Little Tour of France* (1885) James offers this in response to terrorist activity in Lyons:

> Of course there had been arrests and incarcerations, and the *Intransigeant* and the *Rappel* [left-wing newspapers] were filled with the echoes of the explosion. The tone of these organs is rarely edifying, and it had never seemed less so than on this occasion. I wondered, as I looked through them, whether I was losing all my radicalism; and then I wondered whether, after all, I had any to lose. Even in so long a wait as that tiresome day at Lyons I failed to settle the question, any more than I made up my mind as to the possible future of

the militant democracy, or the ultimate form of a civilization which should have blown up everything else.[41]

Although James's reluctance to endorse the political use of violence seems more a matter of mild good taste than real moral outrage, we can nevertheless see that he has little time for a certain kind of radical. In his review of Turgenev's *Virgin Soil,* a novel on which he drew heavily for the plot of *The Princess,* James describes that novel's protagonist, Nezdanov, as "the 'aesthetic' young man [who], venturing to play with revolution, finds it a coarse, ugly, vulgar and moreover very cruel thing; the reality makes him deadly sick . . . " (29). Insofar as parallels between these novels have been thoroughly worked out elsewhere, we might simply take Hyacinth's reaction as a repetition of Nezdanov's visceral reaction to the violence of revolution.[42] Hyacinth, however, never really repudiates the political use of violence. In fact, the novel tends even at its most serious moments to take a peculiarly light tone when it comes to the possibility of political assassination. About Hyacinth's mission, we are told that "Very likely it would be to kill some one—some humbug in a high place; but whether the individual should deserve it or not deserve it was not Hyacinth's affair" (333). Hyacinth's response is not only surprisingly low-key, but also sort of comic; the metrical lilt of "humbug in a high place" gives the phrase a familiar if inappropriate shave-and-a-haircut feel. So, if Henry James would have found the shooting of a duke "coarse, ugly, and vulgar," the same, it seems, can't be said of Hyacinth Robinson.

We might, instead, think of Hyacinth's final refusal to act in terms of the opposition that has most often been taken to structure *The Princess:* the opposition between aesthetics and politics. In a long letter to the Princess, written towards the end of his modest tour of Italy and France, Hyacinth both owns and makes clear his rejection of Hoffendahl's general position: "The monuments and treasures of art, the great palaces and properties, the conquests of learning and taste, the general fabric of civilization as we know it, based, if you will, upon all the despotisms, the cruelties, the exclusions, the monopolies and the rapacities of the past, but thanks to which, all the same, the world is less impracticable and life more tolerable" (396). Hyacinth finds himself, as he looks over the triumphs of a long and continuous European culture, favoring its Arnoldian "sweetness and light" over the possibility of revolution: "What was supreme in his mind today was not the idea of how the society that surrounded him should be destroyed; it was, much more, the sense of the wonderful, precious things it had produced, of the brilliant, impressive fabric it had raised" (382–83). *The Princess Casamassima* is dotted with references to Arnold, and Hyacinth's late discovered allegiance to culture follows a familiar

Arnoldian pattern; insofar as Hyacinth's good taste puts him at odds with his socioeconomic context, he ends up looking distinctly "alien" in Arnold's sense of the term. If it has been Hyacinth's problem that he feels all too divided, the structure of Arnoldian disinterestedness gives him an out; adopting and emulating culture allows Hyacinth to sublate the two terms of what had hitherto stood as a painful contradiction in his character. Trilling saw long ago that Hyacinth was after something *between* the terms of the proliferating pairs that fill *The Princess Casamassima:* "He is a hero of civilization because he dares do more than civilization does: embodying two ideals at once, he takes upon himself, in full consciousness, the guilt of each."[43] In order to negotiate the negation of the negation of his divided self, Hyacinth opts to trade terrorist cell for culturalist clerisy.

If, though, the novel repeatedly opens itself up to a reading based on Hyacinth's eventual choice of culture over its destruction, that choice is not for Hyacinth equivalent to the choice of shooting or not shooting a duke. Hyacinth writes in the same letter that, though his sympathies have shifted, "You can't call me a traitor, for you know the obligation that I recognize" (396). He remains committed to the terms of his vow well after he understands that he is all for sweetness and light; not only does choosing the aesthetic not mean *not* choosing violence, but it also seems even to support his respect for the vow as vow, for the vow as an end unto itself. If the practical man of politics (a Paul Muniment) could turn his back on a vow or comrade, Hyacinth, increasingly sensitive to an ideal ethical disinterestedness, finds himself at this late point in the novel unwilling to break his promise.

Indeed, as the letter continues, Hyacinth turns his attention to what appears to be the anarchist's simple bad taste:

> You know how extraordinary I think our Hoffendahl (to speak only of him); but if there is one thing that is more clear about him than another it is that he wouldn't have the least feeling for this incomparable, abominable old Venice. He would cut up the ceilings of the Veronese into strips, so that every one might have a little piece. I don't want every one to have a little piece of anything, and I have a great horror of that kind of invidious jealousy which is at the bottom of the idea of a redistribution. (397)

The problem with Hoffendahl is that he doesn't know enough or can't feel enough to like Venice. It is not clear from Hyacinth's letter which comes first: ideology or vulgarity. What is clear is that Hyacinth finds himself in a position at this later point in the novel to *name* Hoffendahl. Where earlier descriptions treat him as something like a god (quietly omniscient and omnipresent in his effects), Hoffendahl is here reduced to the diminutive "our Hoffendahl," and Hyacinth writes (in conspicuously smooth Jamesian prose) as if he is in possession of ideas that would supersede the terms of Hoffendahl's "jealous" little mind. In this, Hyacinth strikes a distinctly Nietzschean pose, spotting in his anarchist friend a bad case of *ressentiment:* "To the psychologists first of all, presuming they would like to study *ressentiment* close up for once, I would say: this plant blooms best today among anarchists. . . . "[44] Where sweetness and light have allowed Hyacinth to cultivate a sovereign forgetfulness, the ragtag revolutionists of *The Princess Casamassima*, men of *ressentiment*, remain trapped in and motivated by a pathological internalization, fixed in a state that feels like a physical hurt: "Everywhere, everywhere, [Hyacinth] saw the ulcer of envy—the passion of a party which hung together for the purpose of despoiling another to its advantage" (405). As a result, the world—at both its worst and its best—becomes an insult: "Beauty and goodness are, for [the figure of *ressentiment*], necessarily as outrageous as any pain or misfortune that he experiences."[45] Such is the nature of the "invidious jealousy" that Hyacinth finally sees in Hoffendahl; giving everyone a "little piece" is not to satisfy every possible want "a little," but to reduce life to a state in which there would be no way to want anything more. To Hyacinth's expanded sense of things, "redistribution" names a violent, unwanted, and general impoverishment: "I don't want every one to have a *little* piece of anything." He wants, we take it, everyone to have rather a little *more:* "'I think there can't be too many pictures and statues and works of art,' Hyacinth broke out. 'The more the better . . . '" (413).[46]

While we will want to listen to this proto-Nietzschean strain in *The Princess*, it, too, cannot account for Hyacinth's final, suicidal refusal to act; Hyacinth continues to respect the terms of his vow long after he comes to this conclusion. Because Hyacinth's commitment to his vow has seemed oddly impervious to evidence and to ideas that might make him rethink the sacredness of his vow to Hoffendahl, his decision at last *not* to act seems all the more arbitrary:

> This loathing of the idea of a *repetition* had not been sharp, strangely enough, till his summons came; in all his previous meditations the growth of his reluctance to act for the "party of action" had not been the fear of a personal stain, but the simple extension of his observation. Yet now the idea of the personal stain made him horribly sick; it seemed by itself to make service impossible. (582)

Although the thought of his mother as a bad example clearly disturbs Hyacinth, it is not her crime that the passage emphasizes; the crime is indeed mentioned only in passing. It is rather *repetition* as such that seems to bother Hyacinth, that produces in him a revulsion strong enough to get between him and his vow. This compulsion *not* to repeat has been seen to lead not only to the breaking of his promise but also in different ways to his suicide. On the one hand, Sheila Teahan writes: "Thematically or conceptually, his failure to carry out the assassination is a betrayal of the revolutionary cause. But in textual or performative terms, Hyacinth's bid for a radical break with patterns of repetition (by avoiding a repetition of his mother's crime, by dissociating himself from a political movement perceived as duplicating the mystifications of the ruling class) renders his suicide revolutionary."[47] And, on the other hand, critics have pointed out that, insofar as Hyacinth is the bastard son of a duke, he is himself a kind of duke. His suicide is, in that case, a more successful assassination than it at first looks and ends the novel with the purest and most final form of repetition, a last return to the quiescence of death. Thought of in these terms, because Hyacinth's suicide is a way absolutely to own *both* his father's aristocratic title *and* his mother's crime (like Hyacinth, she killed a duke), it is the most perfect and most capacious of repetitions and is thus one well suited to usher in the necessary silence of a novel's end. Still, whether we view Hyacinth's suicide as a move that paradoxically masters the drive towards death or as a paradigmatic case of an organism living only so that it might at last "die in its own fashion," we are no closer to understanding the relation between his ostensible refusal to repeat and his turn away from a particular political act.[48]

All of which returns us to the afterwardsness of *The Princess Casamassima*. Afterwardsness, we remember, is Laplanche's term for Freudian *Nachträglichkeit;* where other terms place emphasis on either the progressive or the retrogressive aspects of Freud's concept, "afterwardsness" allows the ambiguity of his thinking on the matter to stand. *The Princess Casamassima* is a novel of afterwardsness because it interrogates the concept through its formal preoccupation with the middle and its thematic interest in the temporality of the vow; the novel also appears as an instantiation of afterwardsness in the related forms of the promise, the prefaces, and Hyacinth's variously divided self. I want to go on now to suggest that afterwardsness provides us not only with an interpretive scheme with which to unpack the novel but also a way to understand the value and varieties of political action and inaction in it. Afterwardsness is, among other things, that aspect of psychic life that makes the interpretive work of psychoanalysis possible. To say that psychic events are meaningful is to say that they are meaningful as past traumas and present symptoms that are, in turn, meaningful in terms of each other. What makes this double movement between the past and present possible isn't any necessary causal relation, but rather the fact that past and present are understood as parts of a greater analyzable whole: in analysis experiences are, says Lacan, "placed within a parenthesis of time, within a form of time."⁴⁹ What, in turn, makes that "form of time" a form (in a sense related to James's sense of "organic form") is the articulation of one or another point around which it might be organized. Although that point is often thought of in terms of an end, in terms "of a final settling of accounts [. . .] when every event will receive retroactively its definitive meaning, its final place in the total narration,"⁵⁰ in *The Princess Casamassima* that structuring work falls, as we have seen, to *the middle*, to the site of Hyacinth's vow, to that "temporal barrier which inscribes [before and after] in two different spheres of meaning." It is, in other words, the middle that makes sense of things; it is the middle that makes meaningful the temporal and structural difference between a before and an after. How, with so much at stake, would one go about locating or producing the point that would do all this work?

Hyacinth, as I have already said, turns his back on the party of action not because he renounces the use of violence, and not because he chooses art over politics, and not because he resists the *ressentiment* that he comes to associate with Hoffendahl. Although he is affected by these ideas, Hyacinth maintains that he will nevertheless respect the terms of his vow. He chooses, as I have already said, *not* to act because of his "loathing of the idea of a *repetition*." We might read this loathing as Hyacinth's wish as the protagonist of a naturalist novel to transcend the terms of his genetic inheritance and to do what his mother could not: to become something else. Hyacinth, however, is in this passage disturbed not by a particular repetition (the repetition of his mother's criminal act) but by the idea of a repetition, an idea that is bound up with a temporal logic that he has begun to associate with Hoffendahl's politics. The novel is filled with an abstract and self-consciously hackneyed rhetoric that accentuates the "eventness" of revolutionary activity: when it comes, it will be a sudden "scare," a "general rectification," or "a new era." Each of these terms offers the revolutionary act and, implicitly, revolution itself as the willed production of "a temporal barrier [between] two different spheres of meaning," into, in other words, a *before the revolution comes* and an *after the revolution comes*. If narration seems from the start to feel that these terms lack seriousness, it is the index of Hyacinth's development within the terms of *The Princess* that he comes more and more to resemble narration. We need not, however, see this turn towards narration as an absolute turn away from revolution; indeed, what Hyacinth performs might be taken less as a rejection of revolution as such than as the recognition of a theoretical difference within thinking about revolution. Hyacinth is, to take things a little too literally for a moment, less a follower of Bakunin than of Kropotkin.[51] Where Bakunin was all for "a spontaneous, formidable, passionate, energetic, anarchic, destructive, and savage uprising of the popular masses," Kropotkin warns enthusiastic revolutionists that "'The Year I of Liberty,' has never lasted more than a day, for after proclaiming it men put themselves the very next morning under the yoke of law and authority."[52] The difficulty here is not that men want liberty or that they use violence to get it; it is rather the logic of "the Year I" that seems to Kropotkin to lead to bad political repetition: "How many fiery innovators are mere copyists of bygone revolutions?"[53] What Kropotkin warns against is the idea that one could simply make a middle, that one could simply put in place a point that would once and for all divide human time into night and day; formal faith in that kind of a break seems to Kropotkin to lead to exactly the kind of repetition that at last produces loathing in Hyacinth. Hoffendahl's revolution, a revolution by committee, begins to look more and more to Hyacinth like a return of that which it would replace.[54]

If, however, Hyacinth outgrows his early sense of what a revolutionary action might mean—"Isn't it a new era?" (130)—he never does turn fully away from an idea of revolution as a possible and, indeed, historically inevitable good; well after he writes his letter to the Princess, the letter that announces both his allegiance to culture and his disdain for the anarchist as man of *ressentiment*, he has this thought about the days to come:

> What was most in Hyacinth's mind was the idea, of which every pulsation of the general life of his time was a syllable, that the flood of democracy was rising over the world; that it would sweep all the traditions of the past before it; that, whatever it might fail to bring, it would at least carry in its bosom a magnificent energy; and that it might be trusted to look after its own. (478)

Why so watery a revolution? Revolution, it seems, is an "oceanic feeling" for Hyacinth; it is a "flood," a "floating," a "pulsation" quite at odds with the feel of Hoffendahl's more arid anarchist program; Hoffendahl is compared to "a great musician," under whose knowing fingers all the different parts of the revolution will come to life. His, however, is a *dry* sound: "The day would come when Hyacinth, far down in the treble, would feel himself touched by the little finger of the composer, would become audible (with a small, sharp crack) for a second" (334). The short, sharp shock of Hoffendahl's style resembles the sound of chopping blocks and gunfire; it is also altogether different from the liquid feel of Hyacinth's thinking about revolution and the flowing Jamesian prose in which that thought is rendered (this is another moment at which it is hard to tell two voices pulsing and stammering together apart). Where Hoffendahl hears in revolution the staccato sound of so many hard "cracks," Hyacinth responds more to the pedal point of a revolutionary "pulsation," a notion running against the Bakuninist violence with which Hyacinth and the novel had flirted. We might, in fact, hear in Hyacinth's music something at once radical and conservative. In a different but related context, Neil Hertz has seen "pulsation" as a figure that straddles the difference between dumb repetition and radical change, between habit and desire in George Eliot: "As we have seen, this region is gestured towards by Eliot's repeated allusions to rudiments, her fondness, as we have seen, for words like *pulse* and *pulsation*, which figure at once an elementary sameness, the repetition of a beat, and an equally elementary difference, the opening up of a temporal gap."[55]

If "pulse" carries with it these overlapping senses of return and renewal, what are we to make of Hyacinth's revolutionary pulsation? On the one hand, we might read his as a fantasy of return to what Freud, writing about another case of "oceanic feeling," "dismisses [. . .] as a delusionary cure for human suffering traceable to the 'limitless narcissism' of infancy."[56] Just as the child, flush with precarious infant omnipotence, knows not what it is to want, so will the subject of revolution somehow be above or beyond it all: " . . . there was joy, exultation, in the thought of surrendering one's self to the wave of revolt, of floating in the tremendous tide, of feeling one's self lifted and tossed, carried higher on the sun-touched crests of billows than one could be by a dry, lonely effort of one's own" (478). The happiness of this revolution is the happiness of a life of total, floating "surrender"; it is a life that lacks nothing. The trouble, as Jonathan Lear points out in a different context, is that a life that lacks nothing is a life that lacks lack:

> . . . to characterize such a condition as a life lacking in nothing hints at the idea that the truly happy life is somehow beyond lacks—that is, beyond desire. The hint is of a life which is beyond the exigencies and pressures of life itself. The fantasy of a happy life becomes tinged with the suggestion of a life beyond life—a certain kind of living death.[57]

The twin fantasies of an achieved return to a state beyond want that would reduce the pang of desire to the need always already met and a total revolution that would make desire historically residual meet for Hyacinth at a point of "happy" annihilation. Here we might take Hyacinth's fantasy as a subtle performance of the anxiety (James's anxiety) that accompanies all utopian revolutions: when the revolution comes, we will be bored to death.

We might, however, see this moment as a more particular and less annihilating return: a return to his early and formative visit to his mother in the Millbank Prison infirmary. The visit has all the characteristics of a "seduction" in Laplanche's sense of the term; because it is affectively charged and because Pinnie does not tell Hyacinth that the woman, wild and "starved" for his infant kiss, is his mother, this meeting is like many significant encounters between adults and children: "These are experienced as messages but they are necessarily enigmatic. Precisely because these messages escape our understanding, they captivate us. . . . "[58] The mother's enigmatic message takes a number of forms: she shouts in French; she reaches out to him from her prison bed; she, still a stranger to Hyacinth, demands a mother's embrace. These are supplemented with another form of message: her speaking, weakening pulse: " . . . she had but the thinnest pulse of energy left . . . " (85). The presence of the mother's pulse at so early and important a moment forces us to reconsider not only the terms of Hyacinth's oceanic feeling but also the character of this particular return. The pulsation and "magnificent energy" of revolution reads, that is, like an *amplification* of the mother's barely remembered pulse, a figural return less about the violence with which Florentine Vivier was so spectacularly associated and more about an effort to repeat with a difference profound enough to be something *more* than a repetition. Thought of as the result of a kind of feedback (a pulse fed back to itself until it becomes a roar), Hyacinth's oceanic revolution would function neither as repetition nor as break, but as a figural amplification that would own without fixing in place what had been, rendering it in the process so much more itself as to become something new.[59] That is, after all, what Hyacinth wanted: the only revolution that would be good enough would be the revolution at the end of which everyone would have *more* than "a little piece of anything" (397). The good-enough revolution would have more than enough to give.

Where it might have seemed that—in absenting the middle of his novel, in placing a hole where Hyacinth's vow should have gone—James had carved out of his novel the most perfect of middles, *The Princess* at last turns its back on that model: Hyacinth, acting only in the name of a loathing for the logic of repetition, breaks his vow, undermining not only its content but also its pride of structural place in *The Princess Casamassima*. Instead of acting for the party of action, Hyacinth turns his pistol on himself. As was the case with his vow, the suicide is not directly represented in the novel. Instead, we see with the Princess, who has arrived only too late to save Hyacinth, what has happened.

She and Schinkel show up to find that Hyacinth has locked himself in his room and isn't responding to knocks; Schinkel puts his shoulder to the door:

> The door collapsed: they were in the light; they were in a small room, which looked full of things. The light was that of a single candle on the mantle; it was so poor that for a moment she made out nothing definite. Before that moment was over, however, her eyes had attached themselves to the small bed. There was something on it—something black, something ambiguous, something outstretched. Schinkel held her back, but only for an instant; she saw everything, and with the very act she flung herself beside the bed, upon her knees. Hyacinth lay there as if he were asleep, but there was a horrible thing, a mess of blood, on the bed, in his side, in his heart. (590)

It is a beautiful death. The single candle that illuminates the room seems out of necessity to have taken the place of the "cleverly reflective" consciousness that has only just been snuffed out. It, as a dim and yet central source of light, lends the scene palpable atmospheric effects: that the room is filled with "things" off of which the light plays offers, without any need of further description, a vivid sense that the room is all at once confused, crowded, delicate, and arranged. Hyacinth, of course, is finally just another thing in the room, and the fact that the candle offers him nothing more than it offers his stuff gives us an initial sense that the novel is without him oddly belated, just another roomful of junk lacking anything to hold it all together. There is, however, order here. Though James suggests that there is a "mess of blood" in the room, it is a mess most carefully arranged within this final frame, with the wound itself—it is "in the heart"—functioning as a center around which the rest of the composition is concentrically arranged: if James's description goes from out to in (from room to bed to shirt to heart), the scene encourages us to go from in to out: from heart to shirt to bed to room to house and so on. And though we can see that this is "what he would have wanted," we must nevertheless wonder at the significance of this last beautiful thing in a novel filled with them. Why at this last moment risk the bad taste of a beautiful death? What is gained arranging a room around Hyacinth's broken heart?

The problem with both the form and the ideal result of Hyacinth's vow is that they support the notion that a single event—a violent act, the assertion of authority, the just-right middle of a novel—might make violent totalizing sense of what comes both before and after. Hyacinth's suicide, driven by the rejection not of any particular position but of a way of thinking about the significance of events in time, replaces the end of the novel with a much different middle.[60] Just as Hyacinth reproduces at the level of fantasy his mother's weakening pulse as the torrent of revolution, so does his suicide rewrite the middle: "Hyacinth lay there as if he were asleep, but there was a horrible thing, a mess of blood, on the bed, in his side, in his heart." At the novel's end we see the emergence of a shape, a set of rings emanating concentrically out from a wound in Hyacinth's heart; where the vow was a middle that ordered because it divided, Hyacinth's heart, broken and spilling over from heart to side to bed to room, makes visible a different kind of order, a fluid order the surface of which is agitated but not broken by the light splash of his suicide. The novel uses Hyacinth's body, puts its material, hemorrhaging shape in competition with a middle in which it seems to have lost faith and to lay claim to the problem of the middle as one that should rightly remain a problem. The middle, a figure that both occupied and exceeded the prefaces, is in that case at its best when it is left to overflow its bounds; it is when it is fixed too firmly in place that it becomes a matter for the "imagination of disaster."[61] If it has become all too clear in recent years that the worst kinds of violence might be authorized by the belief that everything changed on this or that day, Hyacinth, in wrenching the novel's middle away from its place in between the beginning and the end, casts doubt on the notion that an end invented as the necessary effect of a merely asserted middle can justify any and all means.

Notes

1. Henry James, *The Tragic Muse* (London: Penguin Books, 1995), 5. Subsequent references to *The Tragic Muse* appear in the body of the essay.

2. Aristotle, *Aristotle on Poetry and Style,* trans. G. M. A. Grube (Indianapolis: Hackett, 1989), 16.

3. Eve Kosofsky Sedgwick, *Touching Feeling: Affect, Pedagogy, Performativity* (Durham: Duke University Press, 2003), 53. See the rest of Sedgwick's brief but excessively suggestive discussion of the "misplaced middle" in the prefaces: 52–53.

4. Kaja Silverman, "Too Early/Too Late: Subjectivity and the Primal Scene in Henry James," in *Novel: A Forum on Fiction* 21, no. 2/3 (Winter 1988): 162.

5. Henry James, "The Future of the Novel," in *The Critical Muse: Selected Literary Criticism,* ed. Roger Gard (London: Penguin Books, 1987), 335.

6. James returns self-consciously and, it seems, belatedly to this discussion in the preface to *The Wings of the Dove,* which, he says, "happens to offer perhaps the most striking example I may cite (though with public penance for it already performed) of my regular failure to keep the appointed halves of my whole equal." Henry James, *The Wings of the Dove* (Oxford: Oxford University Press, 1984), xliv.

7. About the center, James asks, "What has become in that imperfect order, accordingly, of the famous centre of one's subject?" (8). For more on what *is* exceptional about the structure of *The Tragic Muse,* a structure organized around a central character who is not a clear "center of consciousness," but who is rather oddly "dense or opaque," see Joseph Litvak, *Caught in*

the Act (Berkeley: University of California Press, 1992), 242–47. Because Miriam Rooth is *not* a center in the sense we tend to associate with James (we never, as James says, "go behind" Miriam), she is a center "that wanders from its assigned post, pervading and disfiguring the text that tries to master it" (245). I will, in what follows, be interested in a much different kind of middle.

8. Henry James, *Selected Letters*, ed. Leon Edel (Cambridge, MA: Harvard University Press, 1974), 217.

9. The prefaces were, of course, all written after the individual novels they accompany as "a kind of epitaph or series of inscriptions," writes R. P. Blackmur, "for the major monument of his life, the sumptuous, plum-coloured, expensive New York Edition of his works" (15). It is more than this essay can do to navigate to proliferating temporal relations of preface to novel, of preface to preface, and of the prefaces to the whole New York Edition. On the timing of the New York Edition, see R. P. Blackmur, "Introduction" to Henry James, *The Art of the Novel: Critical Prefaces* (New York: Charles Scribner's Sons, 1934); Philip Horne, *Henry James and Revision: The New York Edition* (Oxford: Clarendon Press, 1990); and Sedgwick, *Touching Feeling: Affect, Pedagogy, Performativity*, 35–67.

10. James's discussion of Hyacinth in the preface leads to one of his more thorough discussions of this aspect of his narrative technique: "I should even like to give myself the pleasure of retracing from one of my own productions to another the play of a like instinctive disposition, of catching in the fact, at one point after another, from *Roderick Hudson* to *The Golden Bowl*, that provision for interest which consists in placing advantageously, placing right in the middle of the light, the most polished of possible mirrors of the subject" (42).

11. Deborah Esch, "Promissory Notes: The Prescription of the Future in *The Princess Casamassima*," *American Literary History* 1, no. 2 (Summer 1989): 323.

12. Esch, 323.

13. Jean Laplanche and J.-B. Pontalis, *The Language of Psychoanalysis*, trans. Donald Nicholson-Smith (New York: W. W. Norton & Co., 1973), 111.

14. Much of what Freud says about deferred action takes place in the context of his rejection of Jung's idea of a retrospective fantasy that simply "gives priority to the present over the past." Laplanche, "Notes on Afterwardsness," in *Essays on Otherness* (London: Routledge, 1998), 262; and John Fletcher's "Introduction" to that same volume, 15.

15. Sigmund Freud, "From the History of an Infantile Neurosis," in *The Standard Edition of the Complete Psychological Works of Sigmund Freud*, vol. 17, trans. James Strachey (London: The Hogarth Press, 1962), 37–38.

16. Jacques Lacan, *The Seminar of Jacques Lacan, Book I: Freud's Papers on Techniqe, 1953–1954*, ed. Jacques-Alain Miller (New York: Norton, 1988), 157.

17. Jacques Lacan, "The Function and Field of Speech and Language in Psychoanalysis," in *Écrits*, trans. Bruce Fink (New York: W. W. Norton & Company, 2002), 48. For the Lacan of the Rome Report, the logic of *Nachträglichkeit* works because in analysis temporality is itself the effect of a "full speech": "Let's be categorical: in psychoanalytic anamnesis, what is at stake is not reality, but truth, because the effect of full speech is to reorder past contingencies by conferring on them the sense of necessities to come, such as they are constituted by the scant freedom through which the subject makes them present" (48).

18. Jean Laplanche, *Life and Death in Psychoanalysis* (Baltimore: Johns Hopkins University Press, 1985), 25.

19. Laplanche, "Notes on Afterwardsness," 263.

20. Quoted in Laplanche, "Notes on Afterwardsness," 264.

21. James, "The Future of the Novel," 335.

22. Properly speaking, the trauma resides somewhere in the middle: "On this model, neither of the two experiences is traumatic in and of itself. The earlier experience need not have been traumatic when it occurred, because it was registered but not understood. The later experience, for its part, can be innocent in itself—as, for instance, the experience of mild sexual arousal in a situation that triggers a reminiscence of the earlier occasion. What becomes explosive is the cocktail of both those experiences." Jonathan Lear, *Happiness, Death, and the Remainder of Life* (Cambridge, MA: Harvard University Press, 2001), 45.

23. Afterwardsness looks like a contradiction because psychoanalysis—in and after Freud—is pulled artificially in two directions: it works both as a *determinist* system that looks for real past traumas that would account for present psychic life and as a *hermeneutic* system that sees the past as a construction creatively produced to make sense of the present. Laplanche suggests that this split (seen locally in Freud and more generally in the constitution of the psychoanalytic community as a whole) is the result of psychoanalysis's early abandonment of the seduction theory, which Laplanche returns to and updates: for Laplanche the individual is in part constituted by the "implantation of enigmatic signifiers from the other." In other words, the child is first formed as a self in relation to an external world—which, of course, both includes and is exemplified by the mother—from which it receives real messages that it can perceive but not understand, in part because it lacks the developmental know-how to interpret them, and in part because they are also obscure products of the other's unconscious. These necessarily enigmatic messages, which constitute what we might call an "ordinary seduction," not only continue to exert a pressure on the individual after they have been internalized but also contribute to the very consolidation of the psychic apparatus insofar as these "processes mark the boundaries between inside and outside as sites of exchange and targets of parental care," a fact that constitutes an important part of Laplanche's contribution to Freud's "unfinished Copernican revolution" (31). That these messages are both historically real and essentially enigmatic means that their significance must be understood both in terms of the determining effect of the past on the present and in terms of their availability to a necessary hermeneutic restructuring. We will return to the presence of the enigmatic message in *The Princess Casamassima* shortly. See John Fletcher's "Introduction," "Interpretation between Determinism and Hermeneutics," and "Time and the Other" in Laplanche, *Essays on Otherness*, 1–52, 138–65, 234–59.

24. *The Princess Casamassima* took a number of different physical forms before finding its way into the New York Edition: it was first published serially in *The Atlantic Monthly* from September 1885 to October 1886. Though it was meant to appear in twelve issues, it appeared finally in fourteen. It was then published in three volumes in 1886 and as a single volume later that year. The two-volume edition of *The Princess* appeared in 1908 as volumes five and six of the New York Edition of the novels and tales of Henry James. The publication history of *The Princess* thus comes to perform the search for the middle that James describes in the prefaces and enacts, as we will see, in *The Princess Casamassima*.

25. John Carlos Rowe sees this ellipsis as a means of exposing social contradiction in James's novel: "The formal structure of the novel is the representation of such contradiction; the melodramatic and suspenseful discontinuity in the narrative, which we have sketched above, is merely a synecdoche for a pervasive feature of James's structural organization." John Carlos Rowe, *The Theoretical Dimensions of Henry James* (Madison: University of Wisconsin Press, 1984), 186. Here, I draw on and develop an argument I began in *Bad Form: Social Mistakes and the Nineteenth-Century Novel* (New York: Oxford University Press, 2008).

26. A. H. Quinn, quoted in Oscar Cargill, "*The Princess Casamassima:* A Critical Reappraisal," *PMLA* 71, no. 1 (March 1956): 102.

27. Quoted in Christine DeVine, "Revolution and Democracy in the London *Times* and *The Princess Casamassima*," *The Henry James Review* 23, no. 1 (2002): 56.

28. Lionel Trilling, *The Liberal Imagination* (New York: The Viking Press, 1950), 68.

29. Trilling, *The Liberal Imagination*, 68.

30. Mike Davis, in Jon Weiner, "Mike Davis Talks about the 'Heroes of Hell,'" *Radical History Review* 85 (2003): 227–37; 227. Davis locates the beginning of that "half-century" in 1878. To associate that fear with the bourgeois imaginary is not, however, to say that there was no reason to be afraid. The first half of the 1880s was marked by a steady and often successful stream of assassinations and bombings in London and beyond; between 1883 and 1885 successful and unsuccessful attacks were made on the Local Government Board Offices in London, the offices of *The Times*, two underground railways, Victoria Station, Scotland Yard, St. James's Square, Nelson's Column, London Bridge, the House of Commons, Westminster Hall, and the Tower of London (most of these attacks were connected to Irish nationalists). These local attacks were vaguely associated with attacks and assassinations occurring at the same time in Russia, France, Italy, Germany, and Spain. See DeVine, Trilling, and Derek Brewer's introduction to *The Princess Casamassima* for more on James's familiarity with terrorism in the 1880s. See also Paul Avrich, *Anarchist Portraits* (Princeton: Princeton University Press, 1988) and Weiner, "Mike Davis Talks about the 'Heroes of Hell.'"

31. From an 1896 letter to A. C. Benson, quoted in Trilling, *The Liberal Imagination*, 60.

32. James visited Millbank Prison in order to "collect notes" for what would become one of *The Princess*'s opening scenes in December of 1884. He writes of the visit to Thomas Sergeant Perry: "I have been all the morning at Millbank Prison (horrible place) collecting notes for a fiction scene. You see I am quite the Naturalist." Quoted in Edel, *Selected Letters of Henry James*, 148.

33. For more on *The Princess*'s complicated relation to race, nation, and the generic terms of literary naturalism, see Sara Blair, *Henry James and the Writing of Race and Nation* (London: Cambridge University Press, 1996), 90–122.

34. Gilles Deleuze, "He Stuttered," in *Essays Critical and Clinical* (Minneapolis: University of Minnesota Press, 1997), 107. Deleuze goes on to associate the "stuttering of language" to a "growing from the middle" of a word, sentence, paragraph, and so on: "Creative stuttering is what makes language grow from the middle, like grass; it is what makes language a rhizome instead of a tree, what puts language in perpetual disequilibrium" (111). Though Deleuze doesn't mention James in relation to creative stuttering, it would be hard to come up with a better phrase to account for the Jamesian style, a fact apparent both in the rhizomatic expansion that characterizes James's efforts at revision and in the rhetoric of excess that returns again and again in the prefaces; novels, after all, do tend to grow from the middle. It is also an effect that appears with a particular force in relation to political language in *The Princess Casamassima* (and, indeed, in *The Bostonians*).

35. Blair, *Henry James and the Writing of Race and Nation*, 90.

36. Much attention is paid in the novel to the fluid quality of Hyacinth's speech; he passes with odd—and mostly unregistered ease—from English to French, and speaks at once the language of the drawing room—"he had had from his earliest years a natural command of [the h]"—and the language of the people.

37. Walter Benn Michaels, *The Gold Standard and the Logic of Naturalism: American Literature at the Turn of the Century* (Berkeley: University of California Press, 1987), 27.

38. Michaels, *The Gold Standard and the Logic of Naturalism*, 172.

39. Leo Bersani, *A Future for Astyanax: Character and Desire in Literature* (New York: Columbia University Press, 1984), 131.

40. Peter Brooks, *The Melodramatic Imagination: Balzac, Henry James, Melodrama, and the Mode of Excess* (New Haven: Yale University Press, 1995), 173.

41. Quoted in Cargill, "*The Princess Casamassima:* A Critical Reappraisal," 103.

42. See the first few pages of Cargill, "*The Princess Casamassima:* A Critical Reappraisal."

43. Trilling, *The Liberal Imagination*, 86.

44. Friedrich Nietzsche, *On the Genealogy of Morals*, trans. Walter Kaufmann (New York: Vintage, 1967), 73. For what it's worth, *The Princess* and Nietzsche's great work on *ressentiment* are almost exactly contemporary. For more on the relation between anarchism and *ressentiment* see Saul Newman, "Anarchism and the Politics of Ressentiment," *Theory and Event* 4, no. 3 (2000), http://muse.jhu.edu/journals/theory_and_event/v004/4.3newman.html.

45. Gilles Deleuze, *Nietzsche and Philosophy*, trans. Hugh Tomlinson (New York: Columbia University Press, 1983), 116.

46. In this, Hyacinth and James are drawing on a familiar critique not necessarily of revolution itself but of a contradiction within the idea of revolution: "What Robespierre calls Danton's vice is the excessive pleasure in beauty and happiness that he and his friends do not want to relinquish and that the people do not desire any less. Danton thus succumbs not merely to the revolution, but also to the revolutionary victory that he has already gained. He is a traitor not because he joined forces with the king and foreign countries (as the people suspect), but because in the frenzy of destruction he has remained true to the happiness that he would not begrudge to anyone, although he enjoys it before the others do." Szondi's reading of Büchner's *Danton's Death* is instructive here: How might one divide things up without reducing them? Is there a way to reorganize life without erasing the remainder that Szondi calls "happiness"? How, in other words, might a whole thing—painting, person, or state—be torn into strips that would in the end remain equal to or greater than the object from which they came? This, against Hoffendahl, is the revolution Hyacinth wants. Peter Szondi, *An Essay on the Tragic* (Stanford: Stanford University Press, 2002), 97.

47. Sheila Teahan, *The Rhetorical Logic of Henry James* (Baton Rouge: Louisiana State University Press, 1995), 34.

48. Hyacinth's situation might, in that case, be read as a formal and thematic meditation on what Peter Brooks has identified as "Freud's Masterplot": "We are here somewhere near the heart of Freud's masterplot for organic life, and it generates a certain analytic force in its superimposition on fictional plots. What operates in the text through repetition is the death instinct, the drive toward the end. Beyond and under the domination of the pleasure principle is this baseline of plot, its basic 'pulsation,' sensible or audible through the repetitions that take us back in the text. Yet repetition also retards the pleasure principle's search for the gratification of discharge, which is another forward-moving drive of the text." We might see Hyacinth's ethical worry about repetition as a formal contribution to novel theory after Brooks; what does one do with the fact that it often seems as if there are only varieties of repetition? As we shall see, Hyacinth's choices will amount, however problematically, to an argument—to a hope—that one can in novels and in life get outside the masterplot. Peter Brooks, *Reading for the Plot* (Cambridge, MA, and London: Harvard University Press, 1984), 102–3.

49. Lacan, quoted in Slavoj Žižek, *The Sublime Object of Ideology* (London: Verso Books, 1989), 140.

50. Žižek, *The Sublime Object of Ideology*, 142.

51. Although we don't need to tie James materially to either figure in order to register important ideological similarities and differences (these ideas were, as James perceived, "in the air"), it is clear that James would have at least known of both figures in terms of their ideas

as well as of their personalities. "[James] may have met Prince Kropotkin, the theorist of anarchism, at Turgenev's bedside in 1880; he was to know him later—after he had written *The Princess*—in London" (Edel, *Selected Letters of Henry James*, 186). And James would have heard of Bakunin both from Turgenev (the two had lived together in Berlin) and from reports of Bakunin's visit to Boston and New York in 1861, a visit that brought him very close to the James circle (for instance, Bakunin had dinner on November 27 with William James's teacher, Louis Agassiz, whom Bakunin referred to as "an old friend") (Avrich, *Anarchist Portraits*, 21). It is, of course, beyond the scope of both this essay and my expertise to detail exhaustively either the similarities or the differences between Bakunin and Kropotkin. Two ideas, however, are pertinent here: first, while both Bakunin and Kropotkin supported the use of political violence, they had very different ideas about the nature of that violence. While Bakunin saw violence as an essentially creative force ("the urge to destroy is a creative urge"), Kropotkin "wished [revolution] to be as humane [. . .] as possible, with the 'smallest number of victims, and a minimum of mutual embitterment.'" Furthermore, it was to be a *social* revolution, carried out by the masses themselves rather than by any political party or group. Political revolutions, he warned, merely exchange one set of rulers for another without altering the essence of tyranny" (Avrich, *Anarchist Portraits*, 66–67). Second, the two had very different ideas about the institutions of anarchism that have some bearing on *The Princess*. Where Kropotkin dreamed of truly autonomous, popular revolution, Bakunin, under the influence of his protégé Nachaev, "was determined to create his own secret society of conspirators, subject to 'a strict hierarchy and to unconditional obedience'" (Avrich, 12). Organized along the model of "revolutionary fives" (an organization made up of cells of five members, only one of whom has contact with other cells), this structure seems to be the model upon which James draws in *The Princess:* Hyacinth offers a pledge of his "unconditional obedience" ("He had taken a vow of blind obedience, as the Jesuit fathers did to the head of their order") before the other four members of his secret cell: Muniment, Schinkel, Poupin, and Hoffendahl. In this, Hoffendahl and company are at least bureaucratic fellow travelers of Bakunin's World Revolutionary Alliance, Ishutin's Hell, Nachaev's The People's Justice, Blanqui's Society of the Seasons, the Black Hand, and, more recently, Peru's Shining Path.

52. Peter Kropotkin, "Law and Authority," in *Anarchism: A Collection of Revolutionary Writings* (New York: Dover Publications, 2002), 197. Alenka Zupančič finds something very much like this difference at work as an opposition internal to Nietzsche's thought: " . . . Nietzsche himself oscillates between two logics delineating the beginning of the new. He alternates between the notion of the Beginning as what will come (only) after a cataclysmic Event inaugurating a new era, and the Beginning as what starts at midday, in the 'midst of life.' Although both logics are indeed present in Nietzsche's work, the second one is clearly the more prevalent of the two. As a matter of fact, the first logic only really acquires an explicit shape with the onset of Nietzsche's 'madness.' In December 1888, he writes to Brandes: 'We have just entered the great politics, even very great. . . . I am preparing an event that will probably break the history in two parts, so that a new calendar will be needed, where the year 1888 will be the year I.'" Hyacinth and *The Princess* are, in that case, like Nietzsche: they are all motivated by the tension between the desire for the year I and the desire for something ambiguously *more* than that. Alenka Zupančič, *The Shortest Shadow: Nietzsche's Philosophy of the Two* (Cambridge, MA: MIT Press, 2003), 25–26.

53. Kropotkin, "Law and Authority," 204.

54. James's novel sketches out three different ways of thinking about anarchism, terrorism, and their effects. The first, to which Hyacinth clings in the early parts of the novel, is an anarchism underwritten by a messianic temporality; the terrorist attack is important because

it will be or at least analogically model a change to end all changes. The second, which occupies Hyacinth after his aesthetic conversion and resulting depression, is a nihilist anarchism interested in the aleatory act of violence for its own sake; in this version, change is already omnipresent and meaningless, and violence stands more as a recognition of this dumb fact than as any kind of progressive act. The third model is James's contribution to thinking about violence, and what follows will work to account for it.

55. Neil Hertz, *George Eliot's Pulse* (Stanford: Stanford University Press, 2003), 72.

56. Leo Bersani and Ulysse Dutoit, *Forms of Being: Cinema, Aesthetics, Subjectivity* (London: British Film Institute, 2004), 172. Freud, of course, begins *Civilization and Its Discontents* with a discussion of an "oceanic feeling" that "a friend" had brought to his attention in response to his earlier *Future of an Illusion*.

57. Lear, *Happiness, Death, and the Remainder of Life*, 27.

58. Lear, *Happiness, Death, and the Remainder of Life*, 20.

59. While in Paris, Hyacinth visits a number of sites related to the Revolution: "The great legend of the French Revolution, sanguinary and heroic, was more real to him here than anywhere else; and, strangely, what was most present was not its turpitude and horror, but its magnificent energy, the spirit of life that had been in it, not the spirit of death. That shadow was effaced by the modern fairness of fountain and statue . . . " (393). Two things about this passage: first, the Revolution, by now predictably, "works" for Hyacinth because it seems, like Paris itself, less an event than an atmosphere. Second, when he looks at the old sites of the Revolution he sees that they have been neither repeated nor replaced, but rather supplemented with—what else—fountains.

60. With this, we might see James as offering a text that would ask "us to imagine what it would feel like to receive something from time if this did not take the usual form of a disruption of illusion and infliction of the violence of temporal difference, but were also not reducible to the merely temporizing deferral of that violence, to a 'buying of time' and only momentary preservation of experiential blankness." Anne-Lise François, *Open Secrets: The Literature of Uncounted Experience* (Stanford: Stanford University Press, 2007), 46.

61. We might, in other words, see the end of *The Princess* as a moment where the prefaces' confusion about center and middle returns, but with a new and urgent motivation. Where the overlap between center and middle looked there like a mess, here the collapse of center, middle, and end stands as an especially poignant argument against counting too absolutely on what middles we have made.

PART II

Repetitions

FOUR

Everyday Life in Anne Brontë

AMANDA CLAYBAUGH

The Brontës' novels are justly famous for their middles. Nelly Dean's narration in the middle of Emily Brontë's *Wuthering Heights* (1847); the Thornfield episode, flanked by Lowood and Marsh End, in the middle of Charlotte Brontë's *Jane Eyre* (1847)—both serve as keystones to the novels' elaborate architecture. And so, too, does the diary that makes up the middle of Anne Brontë's *Tenant of Wildfell Hall* (1848). More typically, however, the middles of Anne Brontë's novels differ from those of her sisters. While theirs display formal mastery, hers more often offer a space for formal experimentation. In the middle chapters of *Agnes Grey* (1847), indeed even in the middle of *Tenant*'s inset diary, we can see Anne Brontë experimenting to find forms capable of containing everyday life.

The everyday is not a topic we associate with the Brontës, who are better known for embracing the extreme, for depicting rioting laborers and tortured birds, *delirium tremens* and violent assaults, ghosts that haunt the Yorkshire moors, nuns that haunt Belgian schools, and the echoing call of Rochester for Jane. But for the Brontës, at least for Charlotte and Anne Brontë, the ordinary was an important subject as well. Charlotte Brontë was quite explicit about this. In the opening pages of her apprentice novel, *The Professor* (1846; 1857), she announced her commitment to depicting persons who are "plain and homely" and events that are "not exciting, and above all, not marvelous."[1]

In her subsequent novels, Charlotte Brontë would continue to focus on ordinary persons (a governess, a teacher, a neglected parson's niece), but she would abandon her initial focus on ordinary events.

It was Anne Brontë who would make such events her particular subject. In *Agnes Grey*, she focused on the everyday life of a governess, while in *The Tenant of Wildfell Hall*, she focused on the everyday life of a wife. In attempting to depict these events, Anne Brontë confronted the impediments to their depiction. More specifically, she found that the most familiar nineteenth-century plots, the *Bildungsroman* and the courtship plot, were incapable of depicting certain forms of everyday experience, among them work and married life. As a consequence, the familiar forms of narration and narrative break down in the middles of *Agnes Grey* and *The Tenant of Wildfell Hall*, and from their failure we can learn a great deal about what new forms would require.

Agnes Grey and the Work of Governessing

Agnes Grey begins twice, first as a *Bildungsroman*. Despite her shyness and timidity, the novel's eponymous protagonist nurses a secret desire to "go out into the world; to enter upon a new life; to act for myself; to exercise my unused faculties; to try my unknown powers; to earn my own maintenance."[2] Agnes is discouraged from leaving home by her fond parents, who think of her as the baby of the family, incapable of caring for herself. But the convenient failure of her father's investments provides her with the excuse she needs to "go out into the world" and, if not make her fortune exactly, at least contribute to her family's income. And so Agnes becomes a governess, working for several months in one family and then several years in another.

When *Agnes Grey* begins again, nearly halfway through, it begins as a courtship plot, a shift in subject matter that is heralded by a shift in form. The first half of the novel had been devoted to long passages narrating Agnes's isolated consciousness, but now these give way to the extended, and only lightly narrated, dialogues typical of the social world. Agnes's oldest student, a frivolous and vain young woman, has come out into society, and the novel is taken over by the student's stratagems for attending church, visiting cottagers, or shopping in town, all in hopes of meeting an admirer. Agnes is biting in her depiction of these maneuvers, but she accompanies her student all the same, secretly hoping to encounter the virtuous curate with whom she herself is falling in love. In this way, Agnes's own courtship proceeds under the cover of her student's.

In between these two beginnings, however, comes a middle that has no recognizable plot at all. It is in these pages that Anne Brontë attempts to depict the work of teaching. Teaching is a subject all the Brontës knew intimately. Charlotte Brontë worked as a teacher in two schools and as a governess in two families; Anne Brontë, as a governess in two families as well; Branwell Brontë worked as a tutor, in the midst of pursuing other careers, and even the reclusive Emily Brontë worked in two different schools for a time. At one point, the Brontës even considered opening a school of their own. These experiences recur in their novels, particularly in those by Charlotte Brontë. The protagonists of *The Professor* and *Villette* (1853) begin by working in schools and end by opening schools of their own; the protagonist of *Shirley* (1849) dreams of leaving home to teach; and Jane Eyre goes through the full range of educational experiences, from being a student through working as a governess to actually running a school.

But while Charlotte Brontë depicts teaching in each of her novels, she does not depict it primarily as a form of work. To be sure, she does refer, from time to time, to the techniques needed for maintaining order in a large classroom or to the kinds of essay topics that may be assigned a promising student, but she is ultimately less interested in what education entails for the teachers than what it entails for the students. For some, education instills a necessary discipline. Jane Eyre learns to be orderly and attentive in the classrooms at Lowood, and she will go on to teach Adèle Varens to be a proper English girl, just as Lucy Snowe will teach her Belgian students to listen attentively, if not always to tell the truth. But for all students, education creates an occasion for feeling: education prompts the reverential love that Jane Eyre feels for Miss Temple, as well as the struggles for erotic mastery between Lucy Snowe and Paul Emanuel, Shirley Keeldar and Louis Moore, Frances Henri and her professor. (Emily Brontë, too, emphasizes this aspect of teaching when she shows the young Catherine teaching Hareton Earnshaw how to read.) Viewing teaching as an occasion of feeling, Charlotte Brontë finds it onerous only when feeling is denied, as when the governess in *Shirley* is kept at arm's length by her students and their family. The feelings prompted by teaching (sympathy, reverence, affection, desire) are the very stuff of the nineteenth-century novel, and so it is hardly surprising that Charlotte Brontë would find teaching straightforward to depict: she simply inserts those feelings into a genre already given over to the feelings created by courtship and family.

For Anne Brontë, by contrast, teaching is simply a form of work. And work, it turns out, is a subject that the nineteenth-century novel has much more trouble depicting. This claim has been made most powerfully by the theorist Elaine Scarry, who observes that work is a subject for which the novel should have an affinity because work, which she conceives of as the making and repairing of the world, parallels the imaginative world-making entailed by novel-writing. And yet, Scarry emphasizes, work nonetheless resists being depicted in novels; indeed, it is, she shows, "in some fundamental ways... very difficult to represent."[3] We can read the middle of *Agnes Grey* in the light of Scarry's account, which I'll discuss more fully below, but it's also possible to read the novel, I'll be arguing, as offering its own account of why work is so difficult to depict, one that elaborates on Scarry's in interesting ways. To be sure, Anne Brontë is a novelist, not a theorist, but her views can be inferred from her own efforts at depiction—particularly from those efforts that failed. For Brontë, work is not, as it is for Scarry, inherently difficult to depict; rather, it becomes difficult to depict in certain social and literary contexts. In the middle of *Agnes Grey*, Brontë explores those contexts, discovering quite specific impediments to depicting work.

The first impediment that Anne Brontë uncovers is social: there are limits on what workers may properly say. Some workers are not permitted to speak at all, and their silence leads insensitive observers to presume that they have no consciousness, a presumption that both Charlotte and Anne Brontë condemn. In *Shirley*, for instance, the workers to whom the factory owner does not deign to speak appear to him to be indistinguishable from the "machines" with which they work.[4] And in *The Professor*, a clerk is not permitted to ask for holiday or admit that he is tired, and his consequent lack of protest against the conditions of his labor leads an observer to conclude that he is nothing but an "automaton" (*Professor* 67). The word returns in *Agnes Grey* when a thoughtless woman speaks indiscreetly in front of her servants, taking their enforced silence as proof that they are "mere automatons" (*AG* 180).

But Anne Brontë goes farther than Charlotte Brontë in analyzing the limits on workers' speech. She recognizes that in addition to those workers, such as servants or factory hands, who are required to be entirely silent, are others, such as governesses, who are required to speak in certain ways. As a governess, Agnes is limited in what she may say *about* her students, as when her mother warns her not to discuss their faults with their parents and her first employer warns her not to discuss their faults with anyone else. And she is also limited in what she may say *to* her students, as when her second employer reminds her that a governess may not speak as frankly to her charges as a mother may do. More surprisingly, her status as a worker also limits what she might say even when she is at leisure. She notes, with considerable bitterness, that guests of her employers never condescend to speak with her, and she notes as well that she is never drawn into conversation by the young men and women with whom she walks to church. And so her status as a governess deprives her of a gentlewoman's right to engage in conversation. (Charlotte Brontë would make a similar observation in *Villette,* when a teacher complains of being paid no more attention in company than "unobtrusive articles of furniture, chairs of ordinary joiner's work, and carpets of no striking pattern."[5])

Agnes protests against these limits in two different ways. At times, she simply ignores them. She criticizes her students even when she has been told not to, and she refuses to flatter and cajole her students even when she is reminded that doing so would be effective. In ignoring the limits set on her speech, she continually runs the risk of losing her job: it is no coincidence that the day that Agnes exchanges "the greatest number of words" with her employer is also the day that the two of them make their "nearest approach to a quarrel" (*AG* 46). At other times, however, Agnes protests against the limits on her speech by following them more stringently than she need do, refusing to say even the little that she is permitted. She suffers from nausea when riding backwards in the carriage, but does not ask to change her seat; she suffers from chills when walking in the garden, but does not ask to go inside. She is allowed very little time to visit her family, but does not ask for more. And when falsely accused of failing at her job, she does not try to defend herself but instead chooses "to keep silence, and bear all, like a self-convicted culprit" (*AG* 48).

The limits imposed on what workers can say are significant because they shape the novels' narration and, with the narration, the novels' capacity to depict work. For Charlotte Brontë, narration functions to compensate for the limits on characters' speech: as narrators, her protagonists can say to their readers all that they are not permitted, as characters, to say. In *The Professor,* for instance, the clerk does not reply directly to the man who accuses him of being an automaton, but instead informs the novel's readers that he is not "a block, or a piece of furniture, but an acting, thinking, sentient man" (57). Compensatory narration creates a particularly intimate relation between reader and narrator, most famously in the case of *Jane Eyre,* and only in *Villette,* Charlotte Brontë's final novel, does this intimacy falter. Anne Brontë promises a similar relation in the opening pages of *Agnes Grey,* when Agnes informs the readers that she will tell them things that she would "not disclose to the most intimate friend" (*AG* 1), but as the novel goes on a quite different relation takes shape: unlike Charlotte Brontë's narrators, Agnes does not allow her narration to compensate for the limits on her speech. When the subject is courtship, this is a familiar technique that confirms that Agnes is a proper lady. Just as she refuses to "express half the gratitude" she feels to the curate who gives her flowers (*AG* 107), so too she cuts herself off in the middle of a narrated reverie: "And how delightful it would be to—(But no matter what I thought)" (*AG* 110). Such refusals are part of a highly legible code, one that leaves Agnes's readers in no doubt as to her true feelings.⁶

When Agnes is narrating her work as a governess, however, the refusals in her narration are much more difficult to decode. In these passages, Agnes no longer addresses her readers as "intimate friends," but instead takes it for granted that they will be hostile to what she has to say. Indeed, she imagines her readers to be much like her employers, uninterested in her sufferings and easily bored by her concerns. And so Agnes responds to her readers as she responds to her employers, by saying even less than she might. She informs her readers that she will "spare" them a description of her happiness upon returning to her family after months of governessing (*AG* 33); she will not "inflict" upon them an account of her journey to take a second post (*AG* 55); nor will she "bore" them by recounting all that happened in her new situation (*AG* 59).

But even as Agnes claims to be saving her readers from what they would not find interesting, she nonetheless emphasizes its deep interest for her. The scenes she condenses or elides are, she emphasizes, the very ones that she relives in her own mind again and again. In this way, Anne Brontë creates a narrator that is every bit as punitive as the much more notoriously sadistic Lucy Snowe. More importantly, she also manages not merely to record the social impediments to depicting labor but also to reproduce them, placing readers in the uncomfortable position of her heartless employers.

There is a formal impediment to depicting work as well: work does not stop, and it does not vary, and this is one reason why Scarry sees work as fundamentally at odds with narrative.

> Work is action rather than a discrete action: it has no identifiable beginning or end; if it were an exceptional action, or even "an action," it could—like the acts in epic, heroic, or military literature—be easily accommodated in narrative. [But] it is the essential nature of work to be perpetual, repetitive, habitual.⁷

Scarry here places the emphasis on the problem of indiscreteness, on the difficulty of fitting an ongoing process into a bounded work of art. Anne and Charlotte Brontë, by contrast, are more interested in the problem of repetition: the difficulty of making a narrative out of a string of repeated events. The great theorist of repetition in narrative is, of course, Gérard Genette, who observes that the classic nineteenth-century novels depict repeated events, what he calls "the iterative narrative," only when they are subordinated to the novel's primary narrative, the sequence of singular events.⁸ Anne Brontë, I want to argue, is rare among nineteenth-century novelists in exploring what it would mean to make the iterative narrative primary.

When we think of repetitive work, it is most often manual labor that comes to mind; indeed, Charlotte Brontë uses the repetitiveness of handloom labor as a standard against which to measure other forms of labor, describing the curates of the parish in *Shirley* as "heavy with ennui, more cursed with monotony than the toil of the weaver at his loom" (*Shirley* 6–7). But Charlotte and Anne Brontë both recognize that teaching can be equally repetitive. Jane Eyre speaks of her "monotonous life," while Agnes Grey speaks of "weary monotony [and] lonely drudgery" (*AG* 96), and Lucy Snowe despairs when she looks toward a future that is no different from her present circumstances.[9] Charlotte Brontë, however, alludes to the repetitiveness of the teacher's labor without attempting to depict it. It is Anne Brontë who attempts to depict the work that teachers do: Agnes struggles with her students during lessons; they drag her through the mud during recess; she is reprimanded by their father for allowing them to get dirty, and she is forced to listen to a quarrel between the parents over luncheon; then, in the afternoon, it is lessons, mud, and reprimands, all over again. It is not possible to make a narrative of such repetitions, and so Anne Brontë relies on two formal techniques. The first is what Genette would call "ellipsis."[10] Agnes skips years in her narration, noting nothing more than the amount of time that has passed. The second technique is synecdoche, a single instance used to stand in for a series of repeated events. Agnes depicts her first day of governessing, and then says "this ... is a very favourable specimen of a day's proceedings" (*AG* 24). In the place of narrative, we get character portraits, with Agnes taking her students one by one and describing each in turn, a strategy that gives no very clear sense of what it is like when all of them are together. The same thing happens when Agnes begins working in a second family: acknowledging that she cannot give in "minute detail" an account of each of her days, she chooses instead to make a "slight sketch of the different members of the family" as well as a "general view" of the first few years of her employment there (*AG* 59). Narrative is thus replaced by analysis.

In this way, Anne Brontë confronts the formal impediments to depicting work that Scarry had described. But her failed efforts to depict it, in the middle of *Agnes Grey*, throw into relief an aspect of depicting work that Scarry does not discuss: repetition can be managed in relation to a projected end. Viewed against a projected end, seemingly identical events are shown to be different, at least insofar as they hasten or postpone what will ultimately come. We can see a clear example of this in the one attempt Emily Brontë makes to depict an everyday experience. This attempt comes in the fragments of Catherine Earnshaw's diary, which recounts a typically "awful Sunday" of

Catherine and Heathcliff sitting in a frigid attic through a church service that lasts three hours long and then forbidden to play or talk or do anything but sit still through the rest of the day. All of this would be almost as tedious in the reading as it would have been to experience if Catherine had not framed her account of the day with reference to a coming end. "H[eathcliff] and I are going to rebel—we took our initiatory steps this evening."[11] In planning to rebel, Catherine projects an end where there would otherwise be nothing but repetition of the same. And with that end projected, suddenly differences appear between the repetitions. Everything that follows, whether in Catherine's diary or in the novel's own narration, can be understood as either hastening or hindering the ultimate "rebellion."

In *Wuthering Heights,* the end point that manages lack of event must be explicitly named: rebellion. But end points can also be signaled more subtly through the expectations prompted by plot. As soon as a young person sets out in the world, as soon as a young woman reaches a marriageable age, we know that we are reading a *Bildungsroman* or a courtship plot, and we can project where the plots will end. And the structure of the plot throws into relief the differences between seemingly similar events. Put another way, experiences are not repetitive in themselves; they come to seem repetitive only when they are not ordered by familiar plots. *Pride and Prejudice* (1813), for instance, would be nothing more than a sequence of calls, balls, and dinners, if we did not understand that each of these events was either advancing or delaying the marriages that we know will constitute its end. In much the same way, *Père Goriot* (1834) would be a repetitive sequence of visits to the salons of various countesses and baronesses, if we did not understand that each of these visits was moving us closer to or farther from the center of Parisian life.

Anne Brontë does not make this claim explicitly, of course, but we can infer it from the failure of her novel's middle. If Agnes's teaching seems repetitive, indeed so repetitive as to undo narrative, it is because the *Bildungsroman* plot has broken down. Although Agnes sets out in great confidence to make her way in the world, her lack of authority as a governess prevents her *Bildung* from proceeding. There is no possibility for Agnes's own education or advancement, since the best governesses, as Agnes's officious employer informs her, "completely [identify] themselves" with the interests of their students (*AG* 152). Nor is there any possibility that the students will become the subject of a *Bildungsroman* themselves, for their parents are so indulgent, and their governess so disempowered, that they do not improve at all. The student who lies and throws tantrums, the student who torments animals, the student who hangs around the stables and swears, and the student who flirts shamelessly—none of them are persuaded by Agnes to change their behavior at all. And so just as the limits placed on Agnes's speech deform her narration, so too her lack of agency causes the *Bildungsroman* to break down.

Once the *Bildungsroman* breaks down, Anne Brontë must find a new plot. She briefly alludes to one when she imagines, for the only time in the novel, a group of readers willing to hear what she has to say:

> I have not enumerated half of the vexatious propensities of my pupils, or half the troubles resulting from my heavy responsibilities, for fear of trespassing too much upon the reader's patience, as, perhaps, I have already done; but my design, in writing the last few pages, was not to amuse, but to benefit those whom it might concern: he that has no interest in such matters will doubtless have skipped them over with a cursory glance, and perhaps, a malediction against the prolixity of the writer; but, if a parent has, therefore, gathered any useful hint, or an unfortunate governess received thereby the slightest benefit, I am well rewarded for my pains. (*AG* 33–34)

Halfway through, the passage begins to imagine *Agnes Grey* becoming a different kind of novel, a reformist exposé of governessing, much like the many pamphlets and tracts that began to be printed in the 1840s.[12] For such a novel it is easy to project an end, if only one that exists outside the novel itself: readers would learn from Agnes's experiences to rear their children more wisely and treat their governesses more kindly, and each day that Agnes endures brings such "benefits" closer to fulfillment. In this way, the reformist plot not only offers a narrative capable of ordering repetition but also establishes a new relation between Agnes and her imagined readers. For while the passage begins by addressing these readers as indifferent, as people whose "patience" might be easily trespassed upon, it soon addresses them as people who can be relied on to fill in what Agnes herself cannot say: she has "not enumerated half" of her students' "vexatious propensities" nor half of the "troubles" that result, but she relies on her new imagined audience to fill in all that she has not said.

But the reformist plot is dropped as soon as it is imagined, and the middle of *Agnes Grey* goes on for many more pages, until Agnes's student finally comes out and the courtship plot begins. The emergence of the courtship plot brings the depiction of work to an end. Once Agnes's older student has come out, we hear no more of her experiences teaching the younger one. And once Agnes falls in love, even the establishment of a school, that desired culmination in Charlotte Brontë's *Bildungsroman* plots, hardly registers on her at all: Agnes and her mother open a school together, but Agnes tells us nothing about her students or her teaching, only about her sad waiting and wondering whether she would ever hear from the curate again.

In this way, Anne Brontë's adoption of the courtship plot can seem like a disappointing abandonment of more unusual subject matter. Instead of finding a way to depict work, the novel simply stops trying to do so and what follows is a remarkably conventional courtship plot. But as the courtship plot comes to its predetermined end, something unexpected happens: a new representational problem emerges. On the penultimate page of the novel, the curate proposes, Agnes accepts, and then there is a break. When the narration resumes, Agnes acknowledges the break by telling her readers, "Here I pause. My diary, from which I compiled these pages, goes but little farther" (*AG* 197), and then she makes a surprising admission, "I could go on for years" (*AG* 197). With that admission, Anne Brontë emphasizes that marriage does not bring the story of a woman's life to an end. Yet so powerful is the ending imposed by the courtship plot that *Agnes Grey* nonetheless goes on for only one more page after marriage.

This is typical of a Victorian novel, which tends to offer only the briefest of summaries after the protagonist's marriage brings about a satisfactory end. But if Anne Brontë self-consciously conforms to this expectation in her first novel, she would challenge it and write beyond it in her second. And she would do so, I will argue, by making fuller use of a reformist plot.

The Tenant of Wildfell Hall and Everyday Married Life

The middle of *The Tenant of Wildfell Hall* consists of a young woman's diary, and that diary begins as a courtship plot. A young woman named Helen has just returned from her first season in London, and her diary describes the various men whom she met there. She has rejected the proposal of one of these men, on the grounds that he was too old and too serious, but she clearly hopes to be proposed to by another, who is distinguished by dashing good looks and somewhat rakish ways. The rake does propose, and Helen accepts, over the strenuous urgings of her guardian. The two marry in due time, but the narrative does not end there. Instead, Helen's diary goes on where Agnes's diary had stopped, and the middle of *The Tenant of Wildfell Hall* is devoted to Anne Brontë's efforts to depict the experience of married life.

Helen's experience of marriage is not a happy one. Together, she and her husband endure the crushing boredom of country house life when it rains, when hunting season is over, when the guests have stayed too long. Helen finds these experiences quite difficult to depict—and for the same reasons that Agnes had difficulties depicting governessing. Once again, there are social impediments to narration. Just as there had been limits on what a governess could say about her charges, so there are limits on what a wife may say about her husband. These limits are acknowledged quite explicitly by one of Helen's friends, who confides in a letter that she is being forced into marrying a man who terrifies her, but then vows that she will, in the future, not "permit . . . [her]self to utter a word in his dispraise"[13] (*TWH* 211); she later asks that this letter, her one improper utterance, be destroyed. Such discretion is expected of a wife, and Helen abides by the same expectations. Her conception of marriage is quite different from that of her husband, who thinks of wife as a "thing to love one devotedly and to stay at home—to wait upon her husband, and amuse him and minister to his comfort in every possible way, while he chooses to stay with her, and, when he is absent, to attend to his interests, domestic and otherwise, and patiently wait his return" (*TWH* 233). But Helen cannot articulate an alternative to his conception, not even in her own diary, nor can she critique her husband's behavior. He seduces one of their houseguests while Helen is watching and dismisses their son as a "'worthless little idiot'" and a "'senseless, thankless oyster'" (*TWH* 231; 230), but all Helen can say in response is that he is "not a *bad* man" (*TWH* 232), merely a man whose notions of marriage are not her own.

Helen's efforts to depict marriage confront formal impediments as well. Writing beyond the end of the courtship plot, Helen has no way of ordering the events of married life. In the absence of such a form, repetitions become painfully evident. Every spring, her husband abandons her to spend four or five months in London. Every fall, he returns to chafe against their quiet country life. During the day, when he is unable to ride and unwilling to read, he peevishly tries to distract her from the book or the child that absorbs her. In the evening, after dinner, it is the same routine of events all over again. Unable to make a narrative out of these events, Helen resorts to ellipsis, as Agnes had done. She writes only when something new has happened, and so she allows first weeks and then months—once, a full year—to elapse between one entry and the next.

In these ways, Helen's diary reaches an impasse, which is breached only when new plots emerge. These plots begin when Helen's husband begins to drink. Helen's diary soon becomes the record of the profanity, immorality, and violence that ensue when her husband and his friends go on another spree. Drunkenness was not an unprecedented subject for the nineteenth-century novel, but it was not often depicted in such detail. Contemporary reviewers were thus shocked by *The Tenant of Wildfell Hall*. A reviewer for the *Spectator* observed that its subject matter was too "coarse and disagreeable" for the novel itself ever to be "attractive."[14] A reviewer from the *Englishwoman's Journal* speculated that it was only out of "duty" that the novel's author had taken up the "ugly task" of depicting drunkenness, while a reviewer from the *North American Review* presumed quite the opposite, that *The Tenant of Wildfell Hall* was written by an author who takes "morose satisfaction in developing a full and complete science of human brutality"—the same author, the reviewer went on to speculate, who had also written *Wuthering Heights* and the "offensive but powerful portions" of *Jane Eyre*.[15]

Anne Brontë responded to these criticisms in the preface she published with the novel's second edition. Here, she defended her decision to depict drunkenness in such detail:

> I find myself censured for depicting con amore, with "a morbid love of the coarse, if not of the brutal," scenes which, I will venture to say, have not been more painful for the most fastidious of my critics to read, than they were for me to describe. I may have gone too far, in which case I shall be careful not to trouble myself or my readers in the same way again; but when we have to do with vice and vicious characters, I maintain it is better to depict them as they really are than as they would wish to appear . . . and if I have warned one rash youth from following in their steps, or prevented one thoughtless girl from falling into the very natural error of my heroine, the book has not been written in vain. (*TWH* 3–4)

In this preface, Anne Brontë, whose father had founded the temperance society in their parish, imagines that her novel will have a similar reformist effect. And this view of the novel has since been codified. In the preface to the 1900 Haworth edition of the Brontës' works, Mary (Mrs. Humphry) Ward insists that "the book's truth, so far as it is true, is scarcely the truth of the imagination"; she writes that "it is rather the truth of a tract or report."[16] And subsequent generations of critics have read *The Tenant of Wildfell Hall* as a major work of temperance fiction.[17]

Charlotte Brontë would reinforce this reading of the novel as self-consciously reformist by adding that her sister's impulse to rescue drunkards came from real life. Reflecting on Anne Brontë's career after her death, Charlotte Brontë identified the choice of subject as an "entire mistake," but excused that mistake on the grounds of biography. Charlotte Brontë reveals that Anne Brontë had "been called on to contemplate, near at hand and for a long time, the terrible effects of talents misused and faculties and abused."[18] This was a guarded reference to Branwell Brontë, who was descending into alcoholism and drug addiction while Anne Brontë was working on *The Tenant of Wildfell Hall*. Nor was Anne Brontë alone in registering her brother's decline in her work. All of the novels published by the Brontës touch on it in some way.

Hindley Earnshaw drinks himself to death in *Wuthering Heights*, as does John Reed in *Jane Eyre*. In *Villette*, Lucy Snowe is hired to replace a nursery maid discovered with gin on her breath, while Jane Eyre attributes the strange noises coming from the attic to the bottle of porter in Grace Poole's hand, and in *Shirley* the fatuous curates grow repulsively "hilarious" over their post-dinner glass of wine (9), while the more admirable characters find no charm in the "wretched black bottle" (127). In *The Professor*, the protagonist explicitly identifies himself as someone who does not drink liquor or even wine, and Agnes Grey is quick to criticize the upper-class men who drink "great quantities of wine" and even some brandy and water (*AG* 43).

That Anne Brontë was distressed by her brother's drinking, that she wished to prevent others from the same fate—this is reason enough to explain why Helen's husband starts drinking in the middle of *Tenant of Wildfell Hall*. And yet, I want to suggest that there is another reason as well. The husband's drinking sets in motion a plot capable of resolving the difficulties of depicting married life. With respect to narration, a husband's drunkenness frees his wife from the limits on what a wife may properly say. When her husband begins to drink, Helen begins to complain. It is only after her husband returns from a four-month sojourn in London entirely enervated by drink that Helen can, for the first time, openly criticize his behavior, first to herself and later to him. The fact that he has drunk to excess in London licenses her to admit that she would prefer that he stay with her at home; the fact that it is drink that has destroyed his health licenses her to question his insistence that she care for him, "wait upon" him, "amuse" him, "minister to his comfort," as he would like. In this way, his drunkenness enables a range of criticisms that go much farther than drinking. Indeed, Helen first chooses to discuss her husband's drinking with him on the night that she witnesses him flirting with one of their guests. Even she admits that the flirtation is "'not referable to wine'" (*TWH* 223), and yet it is the wine that justifies her in making the other complaint.

The husband's drunkenness also brings with it alternate plots. These are the plots of temperance reform. The nineteenth-century temperance movement was, quite simply, a storytelling reform. In the eighteenth century, temperance had been an elite cause, promoted by a handful of medical men and ministers, who made scientific and religious arguments. Thus Benjamin Rush's "thermometer," which aligned various moral and physical consequences with the intrinsic "hotness" of a particular drink, or Joseph Livesey's chemical demonstrations that there was no nutritious content to alcohol. But temperance became a mass social movement only after it was reconceptualized in terms of plots. Two were important. The first, which I call the cautionary temperance tale, unfolds the inevitable consequences of drink: from the first occasion of drunkenness, or from the first exposure to spirits, or even from the very first taste of alcohol follows an unyielding trajectory of moral, physical, and economic decline, ending in death. This is the plot that Branwell Brontë would follow, and the plot that Helen's husband follows as well.

Alongside this plot is a second one, which I call the temperance conversion plot. This plot begins the same way, but then takes a turn: the drunkard becomes convinced of his danger, renounces drink, and converts to sobriety. Both of these plots percolated in Victorian fiction over the course of the century, rising from the stories told by drunkards in meetings, through anonymous tracts circulated by reformers and then didactic short stories written by such authors as Sarah Stickney Ellis, better known for her conduct books, finally reaching the works of such canonical authors as Charles Dickens, George Eliot—and Anne Brontë.

Anne Brontë's characters are aware of these plots—and aware as well of the specific ends these plots project. Helen is envisioning a temperance conversion plot every time she pleads with her husband to give up drink before it is too late, while her husband alludes to the end of the cautionary temperance tale when he callously refers to Helen's father, early in their marriage, as having "'dr[u]nk himself to death'" (*TWH* 256). In light of these two ends, death and reform, a series of otherwise repetitive actions begin to constitute a narrative. Each new bout of drinking leaves Helen's husband a little more fallen and brings him a little closer to death. And each conversation that Helen has with the least depraved of her husband's friends brings that friend a bit closer to forever renouncing drink. In this way, the relentless fall of Helen's husband, paralleled by the possible reformation of his friend, brings order to the middle of *The Tenant of Wildfell Hall*.

Helen's husband starts to drink, then, in part because Anne Brontë was distressed by drinking and in part because she was experimenting with new forms capable of depicting married life. The latter motive is thrown into relief by the fact that the temperance plot is not the only one to emerge. It is shadowed by an adultery plot. Such plots are the most common way in which the nineteenth-century novel, at least prior to George Eliot and Henry James, managed to "go on" past the marriage that ends the courtship plot. In *Wuthering Heights,* for instance, Cathy's story continues past her marriage only because she is still in love with another man, and in *Agnes Grey,* the adultery is even more explicit. Here, adultery is enacted by Agnes's student, whose machinations during courtship had provided a cover for Agnes's own desires. The student is soon engaged, more quickly than Agnes herself, but then, to Agnes's horror, the engagement does not stop her flirtations with other men.

Nor does her marriage. Taken to London after her marriage, the student flirts so scandalously that her husband sends her back to the country to live in permanent seclusion with his family. She is left with no one but Agnes to visit her in the country house that has become a prison. This is the cautionary example of what it would mean, in a courtship plot, to "go on" beyond marriage.

In *The Tenant of Wildfell Hall*, adultery returns, brought into the novel through the schemes of Helen's husband, who first seduces the wife of a friend and later installs his mistress as a governess. But the possibility of adultery is more richly emplotted around Helen herself. She is pursued, and is sometimes even tempted, by the most cultured of her husband's friends. She invariably rejects his advances, of course, but adultery need not be committed for the plot to perform its functions. The first function is licensing Helen to articulate her reservations about her husband; her would-be lover catalogues the husband's faults as a way of winning Helen's favor, and Helen, while assiduous in rejecting the lover's advances, is much less quick to silence his criticisms. The second function is throwing into relief the differences between Helen's otherwise repetitive days, with a good day being one in which her husband is absent and she manages to evade her suitor, and a bad day, one in which she is waylaid and courted by one or abused by the other.

The formal motivation behind the temperance plot is also revealed in the fact that the plot ends up having little substantive effect. We can gauge the plot's effect as the novel moves from the inset diary to the frame narrative, where the diary becomes a text to be read. The frame story begins in a small farming village, with the arrival of a mysterious widow and child, who will prove to be Helen and her son. Helen's difference from the villagers is marked explicitly as a difference in attitudes toward drink. They welcome her by offering her young son a glass of wine, he shrinks from it in disgust, and Helen explains that she has trained him to be repelled by wine. The villages are shocked by this, none more so than a young gentleman farmer, a self-professed "beau." He argues that Helen's policy will deprive her son of the manliness that comes from encountering and triumphing over temptation. Helen is not persuaded, and the two part on bad terms. Over time, however, the "beau" falls in love with Helen and tries to court her. She demurs, he persists, until finally she decisively rejects his proposals, giving him her diary in order to explain her reasons. Reading this diary, which makes up the middle of the novel, the suitor learns that she is not a widow, but in fact a still-married woman, who has fled her husband because of his brutality, his adultery, and his treatment of their child.

But her suitor does not, significantly, read her diary as a cautionary temperance tale. At no point does he imagine that the consequences of Helen's husband's drinking might constitute any warning about his own. He reads the diary, but he is not reformed. To be sure, the suitor tends to be fatuous and obtuse, but he is not entirely wrong in his reading. For the drinking of the suitor is, like Helen's own advocacy of temperance, a topic that the novel suddenly and entirely abandons toward its end. We see this after Helen's husband dies and she and the suitor are finally free to marry. Helen, who had lived through and fled from the drunkenness of one husband, marries another without insisting that he stop drinking or even discussing whether he should. Moreover, she and the suitor never resolve the question over which they had first argued, about whether or not she was foolish in forbidding her young son to drink. Whatever Anne Brontë's own commitment to temperance might have been, Helen's commitment to it has been entirely forgotten.

Anne Brontë registers this point as well through a doubling of characters. Helen's first and second husbands take their place alongside other pairings in the Brontës' novels, such as the two Mrs. Rochesters and the two Catherines. These pairings tend to measure some kind of change, with the second Mrs. Rochester learning to contain the rebellion expressed by the first or Catherine Linton learning to love more wisely and happily than Catherine Heathcliff had done. But the pairing of Helen's two husbands shows no change at all. Not only does the second husband believe, as the first had done, that drinking is the prerogative of manliness, but he, too, is the cosseted son of an indulgent mother; he, too, behaves irreverently in church; and he, even more than Helen's first husband, responds to provocations with violence. The parallels are quite precise, and they suggest that Anne Brontë recognizes that not only has temperance reform not achieved its ends, but it never will.

Conclusion

Anne Brontë has always been the neglected Brontë sister. On the occasion of Charlotte Brontë's death, one reviewer wrote, "of Anne Brontë, known as Acton Bell, we have scarce a remark to make."[19] And the few remarks this reviewer did make were hardly flattering: *Agnes Grey*, he said, is a "commonplace book" by a "common-place person."[20] This would be the view of Anne Brontë until recently, when a handful of critics began to appreciate her novels.[21] But she still stands in the shadows of her sisters. It is not my purpose here to argue that Anne Brontë is their equal, although I do want to highlight the fact that she grappled with formal problems that did not interest Emily Brontë and that Charlotte Brontë would evade. Rather, I want to suggest that Anne

Brontë's novels, particularly their middles, offer us an occasion for reflecting on narrative and plot.

Agnes Grey and *The Tenant of Wildfell Hall* illustrate a fundamental truth about narrative, one that can often be difficult to teach. Narrative is a sequence of events, but it is a sequence, as theorists from Gotthold Lessing to Peter Brooks and J. Hillis Miller have argued, characterized by both sameness and difference.[22] Some things must repeat, most commonly characters, so that the sequence of events will be recognizable as a sequence, and others must be different, so as to create a sense of change and causality. Usually, this is done so deftly that it can be difficult to show how the effect is achieved. But in the middles of Anne Brontë's novels, we see what happens when there is not enough difference, when the work of teaching, or the state of married life, seems like more and more of the same. We can use these middles to show our students what narrative requires by showing them what happens when those requirements are not met.

At the same time, these failures, and the experiments Anne Brontë takes to rectify them, prompt us, I would argue, to develop new ways of thinking about plot. Much has been said about the two defining plots of the nineteenth century, the *Bildungsroman* and the courtship plot, and the most distinguished theorists of these plots, Franco Moretti and D. A. Miller, have shown how their forms, particularly their endings, reinforce their ideology.[23] What Anne Brontë's use of the temperance plot shows us, however, is that the form of familiar plots can be used for purposes quite other than what their ideology suggests. Anne Brontë, at least, was committed to the ideology of temperance reform, even though she used its plots for purely formal ends. But other authors, I have elsewhere argued, used the plots of various reform movements to emplot a range of experiences that have nothing to do with the reform's actual ideology.[24] What Anne Brontë's middles suggest, then, is that plots need to be understood as recognizable forms, ones that can be emptied of their substantive content and replaced with content of a quite different kind.

And finally, Anne Brontë's middles remind us that these seemingly abstract problems of narrative and plot present themselves in specific cultural contexts. Narration, in these novels, is deformed by what actual persons, workers and wives, are permitted to say. And familiar plots depend on social privilege, as when Agnes is unable to enact the *Bildungsroman* she has so hopefully projected because she is denied the agency that the plot presumes. In this way, Anne Brontë also contributes to a developing narrative theory attentive to cultural realities.

Notes

1. Charlotte Brontë, *The Professor* (1846; 1857; London: Penguin Books, 1948), 37, 47.
2. Anne Brontë, *Agnes Grey* (1847; London: Oxford World's Classics, 1988), 9. All further references to this edition are marked in the text as "*AG.*"
3. Elaine Scarry, *Resisting Representation* (Oxford: Oxford University Press, 1994), 60.
4. Charlotte Brontë, *Shirley* (1849; London: Penguin Books, 2006), 70.
5. Charlotte Brontë, *Villette* (1853; London: Penguin Books, 1985), 102.
6. For a fuller discussion on social codes of propriety and their effect on female narration, see Alison Case, *Plotting Women: Gender and Narration in the Eighteenth- and Nineteenth-Century British Novel* (Charlottesville: University of Virginia Press, 1999).
7. Scarry, *Resisting Representation*, 65. The other reason, which Scarry elaborates in a footnote (87n), is that work is fundamentally social, rather than individual, and so at odds with novelistic character.
8. Gerard Genette, *Narrative Discourse: An Essay in Method* (1972; Ithaca: Cornell University Press, 1980), 117.
9. Charlotte Brontë, *Jane Eyre* (1847; London: Oxford World's Classics, 2008), 115.
10. Genette, *Narrative Discourse*, 106.
11. Emily Bronte, *Wuthering Heights* (1847; New York: Norton, 2003), 16. Cited in text as "*WH.*"
12. For a fuller discussion of these governess writings, see Mary Poovey, *Uneven Developments: The Ideological Work of Gender in Mid-Victorian England* (Chicago: University of Chicago Press, 1988), 131.
13. Anne Brontë, *The Tenant of Wildfell Hall*, ed. Herbert Rosengarten (1848; New York: Oxford University Press, 1993), 211. All further references to this edition are marked as "*TWH.*"
14. Review of *Wuthering Heights* and *Agnes Grey*, *The Spectator*, December 18, 1847. Reprinted in *The Brontës: The Critical Heritage*, ed. Miria M. Allot (London: Routledge, 1974), 217.
15. "The Three Sisters," *Englishwoman's Journal*, January–February 1860; "Novels of the Season," *North American Review*, October 1848. Reprinted in *The Brontë Sisters: Critical Assessments*, vol. 1, ed. Eleanor McNees (London: Helm Information, 1996), 213, 155.
16. Mrs. Humphry Ward, "Preface," *The Tenant of Wildfell Hall* (1848; New York: Harper Brothers, 1900), xv.
17. See, for instance, Marianne Thormahlen, "The Villain of *Wildfell Hall:* Aspects and Prospects of Arthur Huntingdon," *The Modern Language Review* 88, no. 4 (October 1993): 831–41.
18. Charlotte Brontë, "Biographical Notice of Ellis and Acton Bell." Reprinted in *The Brontë Sisters: Critical Assessments*, 56.
19. Peter Bayne, "Currer Bell," *Hogg's Instructor*, May 1855. Reprinted in *The Brontë Sisters: Critical Assessments*, 173.
20. *Englishwoman's Journal*, 223. Reprinted in *The Brontë Sisters: Critical Assessments*, 223.
21. Particularly distinguished is Rachel K. Carnell's essay "Feminism and the Public Sphere in Anne Brontë's *The Tenant of Wildfell Hall*," *Nineteenth-Century Literature* 53, no. 1 (June 1998): 1–24.
22. Gotthold Lessing, *Laocoon: An Essay on the Limits of Painting and Poetry* (Baltimore: Johns Hopkins University Press, 1984); Peter Brooks, *Reading for the Plot: Design and Intention in Narrative* (Cambridge, MA, and London: Harvard University Press, 1984); J. Hillis Miller,

"Ariadne's Thread: Repetition and the Narrative Line," *Critical Inquiry* 3, no. 1 (Autumn 1976): 68.

23. Franco Moretti, *The Way of the World: The* Bildungsroman *in European Culture* (London: Verso, 1987); D. A. Miller, *Narrative and Its Discontents: Problems of Closure in the Traditional Novel* (Princeton: Princeton University Press, 1981).

24. Amanda Claybaugh, *The Novel of Purpose: Literature and Social Reform in the Anglo-American World* (Ithaca: Cornell University Press, 2007).

FIVE

The Clerk's Tale

Characterizing the Middle in *Dombey and Son*

SUZANNE DALY

Dombey and Son has a complex relation to the idea of the middle. It is generally considered to be the first novel of Dickens's middle period, that historic stretch which also encompasses *David Copperfield, Bleak House, Hard Times,* and *Little Dorrit*. Written and published in serial form between 1846 and 1848—just at mid-century—it appeared as a book in 1848, a year of revolution and rupture throughout Europe that triggered a reaction in England toward the middle-class values of reform and regulation.[1] Finally, *Dombey and Son* is not generally considered to be in the first rank of Dickens's oeuvre; it is, in a word, a middling novel. What I wish to consider, however, is the way in which the narrative middle, and specifically Walter Gay's absence from the middle, speaks to the way Dickens conceives and characterizes the middle class.

Fred Kaplan tells us that in writing *Dombey and Son*, Dickens created "for the first time in his career an overall plan, revealing a coherence and cohesiveness from the beginning of writing the book."[2] Yet the narrative arc is frequently understood to have been somewhat irregularly plotted.[3] Rather than skillfully interweaving the stories of several characters as he does in his late-period novel *Our Mutual Friend*, or foregrounding a single character's history as in the earlier *Oliver Twist*, Dickens begins by making Paul Dombey the focus of attention (the novel begins with his birth), and then kills him off at age nine in the novel's sixteenth chapter. With forty-six more chapters to go,

Dickens must create a new dilatory space, or space of suspense; to create, in effect, life after death.[4] He does so in part by seeming to kill one of Dombey's clerks, Walter Gay (although only the most naïve of readers could fail to anticipate his return) and by allowing another Dombey employee, Carker the Manager, to appropriate an alarming level of power and influence in both the Dombey firm and the narrative as a whole. The novel's middle takes up the increasingly dramatic ways in which Paul's wealthy and powerful father, in his pride and arrogant blindness, fails in his duties both to the family and the firm that bear the name of Dombey—the "house" as both domicile and place of trade. Yet even as Dombey unwittingly destroys these two communities, his despised and rejected daughter Florence gradually knits together a social structure that will eventually regenerate both spaces. Her role, however, remains domestic; it is through Walter Gay, the boy who eventually becomes her husband, that change and regeneration are effected at the novel's end. In order to perform these tasks, though, Walter must disappear in the novel's middle section so as to avoid the taint that his clerkship in the House of Dombey and Son would confer on him and that would paradoxically unfit him, in Dickens's terms, eventually to rebuild it.

Among mid-Victorian novels, *Dombey and Son* is something of an anomaly in that the character that brings the story to a close is entirely absent from its middle. It could be argued that the novel contains two false starts: first Paul's plot, then Walter's, is curtailed, and this double curtailment may account for critics' sense that the novel's architectonics are faulty. This somewhat aberrant narrative structure, however, allows us to see two things about the function of Victorian novels' middle sections: first, that in the middle, ideology is frequently worked out through characterization and not simply through plot, and second, that this ideologically inflected character-building-through-repetition is often precisely what drives the plot itself. In other words, a plausible plot depends upon the reader's willingness to accept that certain characters will behave in certain ways, and the way that a given character is constructed signals its standing within the novel's moral universe. Furthermore, Walter's odd absence would appear to be an apt example of what Alex Woloch explains is the interplay of form and content in the way that characters are apportioned space in the novel; he writes, "the very formal terms of the socionarrative matrix—inclusion and exclusion, hierarchy and stratification, abstraction, utility, functionality and effacement—are continually manifested as themes, concerns and 'stories' of the novels themselves" (20).[5]

The novel's first sixteen chapters largely concern Dombey's ambitions for his small son and the ways in which his "sense of property"[6] in him is violated by Paul's other attachments, particularly to his sister Florence and to Walter.

After Paul's death, Dombey and Florence increasingly come to represent two opposing poles around which the narrative is structured; despite Florence's meek, passive nature and her desperate love for her father (or possibly because of it), Dombey loathes her. The circle of acquaintance each attracts provides a running commentary on their respective moral status: Florence attracts the pure of heart, while her father attracts hangers-on, hypocrites, and scheming social climbers who take advantage of his delusions of omnipotence. Whereas Dombey's circle is composed of people of family, a military officer, and capitalists like himself, the middle way of Victorian society as well as the values we are accustomed to think of as quintessentially Dickensian and "middle-class"—hard work, loyalty, frugality, dedication to family—are embodied in *Dombey and Son* primarily by those who constellate around Florence: a railroad worker and former miner; his wife, a wet nurse; a sailor; and finally, by Walter, a clerk, and his uncle and guardian, the owner of a ships'-instrument shop. None of these characters by any means fits the accepted definition of "middle class."[7]

Curiously, the story's hero and villain, the figures to whom Florence and Dombey are most closely connected, are, or were, both clerks in the House of Dombey and Son. James Carker, Dombey's malevolent manager who sets out after Paul's death to destroy both the Dombey firm and the Dombey family, has begun as a clerk and worked his way up to be Dombey's second-in-command when the novel opens. Walter Gay, the boy whom Florence eventually marries, also begins at the bottom of the clerkship ladder. Dombey, however, tormented by his son's affection for Walter, sends his clerk to Barbados on a ship suggestively named the *Son and Heir* to work in one of his counting-houses. Walter is shipwrecked on the voyage out and is believed drowned throughout most of the novel, but he has in fact been picked up by a China trader and hired by his rescuers. Offstage, Walter quickly advances with this new employer, and when he returns to England at last he is appointed "to a post of great trust and confidence . . . mounting up the ladder with the greatest expedition" in his unnamed company (974). The metaphor of the ladder, much used by Dickens with regard to clerks, points at his ambivalence toward these social and economic climbers.[8] To be truly middle class in Dickens's universe is to be not only "solid," but static; it is a state one inhabits without having to attain it.

Who, then, were these Victorian clerks, the crucial but shadowy actors in *Dombey and Son,* and what did their presence signify to Dickens and his readers? Dickens's own father, John Dickens, was a clerk in a navy payroll office who aspired above his station, which was not working class, but not quite middle class either.[9] In her study of the Victorian lower middle class, Arlene Young cites Geoffrey Crossick's argument that the term "lower middle class" was coming into being just at mid-century to describe "the conflation of two broad occupational groups—the old *petit bourgeoisie* of shopkeepers and small businessmen and the new and burgeoning army of urban white-collar workers who manned the expanding service sector of the Victorian economy." Yet she claims that these two groups "fit uncomfortably together for the purposes of historical . . . analysis" because, among other things, the *petit bourgeoisie* was

> an old and established group, with a history and traditions, while the urban white-collar worker was a relatively new phenomenon without a comparable history, tradition, or established niche within society. There had obviously been people doing similar kinds of clerical work before the mid nineteenth century, but not in the numbers nor in the settings of large urban offices that became common in the second half of the century.[10]

The urban clerk as a type, in other words, was a newcomer, and like other newcomers, Young writes, "he was despised" (484).

Despised and, it would seem, feared. Yet this is hardly obvious from much mid-Victorian literature, in which clerks tend to be pathetic rather than despicable, coded as insignificant and powerless, and stereotyped in opposition to their swearing, brawling, drinking, and often animalistic working-class counterparts. Clerks are, in Young's description, "pale, haggard, and dull, the pathetic and overworked but contemptible denizens of dusty, cramped offices."[11] For a clerk who is typical in this respect, we need look no further than Bob Cratchit in Dickens's *Christmas Carol*. Cratchit, moreover, is not only pathetic, he is trapped in a job that offers no hope of advancement. When Scrooge undergoes his secular conversion and embraces the spirit of Christmas, Cratchit receives better benefits to be sure—he is given a raise, days off, a heated office, and even health care for Tiny Tim—but he will never be promoted.[12] Yet despite the fact that clerks were for the most part relatively powerless and dependent, clerks on several different levels were frequently read as interlopers. At the upper level, many sons of the prosperous middle class began their careers in business as clerks with the understanding that they did so in order to learn the trade "from the bottom up" and would advance rapidly. William Poole in 1878 cites a complaint about this type of clerk in his *Clerk's Grievance*, "youths who, by the aid of patronage or family influence—the crowning curses of clerkship—monopolize most if not all of the best appointments to which clerks aspire. They are usually the fortunate sons of parents who move in the upper middle class of society . . . with a few worthy exceptions they are the youths who lack either brains or taste for the course of study necessary to fit them for scientific pursuits."[13]

Even at lower levels, clerkships could be contaminated by the taint of influence; through a system less clear-cut than the old methods of placing apprentices, clerks could find jobs through family or business connections. In *Dombey and Son*, Walter's uncle Solomon Gills, an elderly ships'-instrument maker, lives on "the ghost of [his] business—its substance . . . vanished long ago" (94), yet he obtains for Walter a post at Dombey and Son through the "fragment of [an] old connexion" (94) to the firm. Clerks also sought employment by placing and answering newspaper advertisements, and curiously, both the old and new ways of job-seeking—the private and the public—told against them in the popular imagination.

But the predominant fear was that clerks, through a combination of limited education and extensive exposure to their social superiors, would adopt the superficial appearance of middle-class businessmen and, what was worse, begin to aspire above their station. Here, Uriah Heep rather than Bob Crachit is the paradigmatic figure. As Franco Moretti notes:

> English society in the eighteenth and nineteenth centuries, despite the Industrial Revolution and Chartism, is by far the most stable in Europe, and proud to be so. Its value-system is decidedly stable, and stability itself is seen as a value, and as one of the strongest ones at that. In this framework, the notion of social mobility cannot evoke the certainly ambiguous but fascinating and vital figures of Julien Sorel, Rastignac, or Bel-Ami. It has rather the bestial and slimy face of Uriah Heep, the feeble and snobbish behavior of Pip.[14]

Or, we might add, the "sly civility"[15] of Carker the Manager. In Carker, Dickens crystallizes popular prejudices about clerks-on-the-make; after Paul's death, Carker gains control of Dombey's firm and, eventually, of his new wife. To gain revenge on Dombey for years of high-handed treatment and what he describes as "slavery" (854), Carker secretly speculates beyond the firm's capacities, bankrupting it, and then runs off with Mrs. Dombey before the ruin comes to light. Carker is thus associated with finance capital and speculation rather than the more "honest" practice of importing and exporting, or buying and selling, on which the house was founded. Carker also personifies mid-century fears that ambitious clerks with too much access to their betters would desire to become gentlemen themselves. In his book on Victorian clerks, David Lockwood cites a nineteenth-century employer who claims that the primary reason that clerks want to be clerks is that their position affords them the opportunity to imitate their "masters": "They call themselves their masters' equals, and demand recognition as such. And in dress, assumption, everything within their power, they follow this up, affording themselves much gratification, and realizing substantial advantage from the nature of their vassalage."[16] In this reading, young men are at once vassals and independent economic actors who freely choose their occupations, and those who choose clerkship do so because it appeals to their ambition to be gentlemen (an ambition that, needless to say, they can never fulfill); as Lockwood writes, "Because of the actual conditions of their employment, the dress, speech, and outward mannerisms of clerical gentlemanliness were often an exaggerated and perverted form of the real thing" (31).[17] Both Young and Lockwood note that much of the distaste for "the clerk" was voiced in terms of his dress, which was deemed to lack both the honesty of working-class garb and the sober propriety of the middle-class business suit. The clerk was a flashy, degraded copy of the original.

Dickens takes pains to demonstrate the multifarious ways in which Dombey's manager transgresses his rightful station; Carker imitates Dombey's dress in a manner that is at once obsequious and slyly mocking, his home is too luxurious and tasteful and his horse too expensive. He reads many languages and plays many games well. The oil painting of his discarded mistress that he prominently displays in his home suggests his desire to fashion himself as a rake, a subject-position incompatible with clerking. Even his much remarked-upon teeth, stunningly white and even, are clearly better than they have any right to be. His aberrant rise is an indictment of Dombey's blindness; it marks the way in which a corrupted order has failed to reproduce itself properly and has thus allowed a malignant outsider, a defective imitation, to gain a foothold. Dickens, however, aborts the subplot in which Carker seems to be stalking Florence, apparently with an eye toward marrying her; his doing so suggests that this was a narrative thread he preferred not to follow to its logical conclusion. After Paul's death, when Dombey has gone to Bath with Bagstock and been introduced to Edith Granger (but before he has proposed), Carker the Manager "[takes] the liberty," as he later tells Dombey, of waiting on Florence when she is away from home visiting the Skettles family. After enlisting Rob the Grinder to spy on the Wooden Midshipman's shop and report on Florence's movements, he intercepts Florence as she is walking with her hosts, introduces himself (significantly, she does not recognize him), and asks if he might bring a message to Dombey from Florence, knowing well that the prospect of sending an unsolicited message to her father terrifies her. Upon seeing him, Florence is "sensible of an inclination to shiver" (429); when he leaves, after whispering to her that there is no news of Walter's ship, she shudders violently. Carker delivers Florence's message of dear love to her father with a "wolf's face . . . with even the hot tongue revealing itself through the stretched mouth" (442) that passes for a smile. In the same exchange, he suggests to Dombey that Walter's loss is fortunate because Florence was in danger of becoming too attached to him, as she is "confiding and young [and] perhaps hardly proud enough, for your daughter" (443). We later learn that Carker has paid two more visits to Florence, in which he has

> assumed a confidence between himself and her—a right on his part to be mysterious and stealthy, in telling her that the ship was still unheard of—a kind of mildly restrained power and authority over her—that made her wonder, and caused her great uneasiness. She had no means of repelling it, or of freeing herself from the web that he was gradually winding around her; for that would have required some art and knowledge of the world, opposed to such address as his; and Florence had none. . . . This conduct on the part of Mr. Carker, and her habit of often considering it with wonder and uneasiness, began to invest him with an uncomfortable fascination in Florence's thoughts. (476–77)

With his visits, Carker usurps yet another of Dombey's prerogatives: the right to terrorize Florence. Clearly, Carker is here being cast in the role of seducer whose game is either to gain control of Dombey the firm by marrying Florence or to destroy Dombey the man by ruining her.[18] Yet by the time this game is revealed in the narrative, in chapter twenty-eight, Carker has already abandoned it; Dombey's impending marriage both upends Carker's plans for Florence and gives him a new instrument of revenge: Edith Granger, whose uncanny resemblance to Alice Brown, the woman in the painting, gives the pursuit greater interest. Unlike Florence, Edith possesses the ability to comprehend if not to resist Carker, and Florence, herself safe, is left to observe their struggle.

Yet Carker the Manager ultimately fails to produce what George Eliot ironically called "that copy of himself which seemed so urgently required of a man—to the sonneteers of the sixteenth century,"[19] that is to say, to reproduce; his line will die with him, whereas Walter's will live on. Walter, as a clerk, is a copyist, as was Carker the Manager, but he is not the stereotypical "bad copy" of the master that defines mid-century clerkdom; rather, he proves to be the missing link between his uncle, the petit-bourgeois shopkeeper Sol Gills, and his father-in-law, the merchant-capitalist Dombey. It is Dombey himself who performs his roles as head of the house imperfectly and produces defective copies of himself in both his son and his manager. Florence, conversely, copies middle-class virtue in any form she finds it, but here her legendary passivity is counteracted by her instinctive knowledge of *what and whom* (and what aspects of whom) to copy. She copies her working-class friends because they are virtuous, but their virtue is grounded in their acceptance of their class status; their lack of social ambition manifests as a lack of motivation to misbehave. Copying, then, is crucial on many levels to the work of both characterization and plot in the narrative middle; the author produces characterization by repeating salient traits (Dombey is haughty, Florence is meek, Carker is sneaky) in different circumstances, and this repetition reveals the tension between that which is repeated comfortably, out of habit, by those characters who belong to a certain way of life, and that which is copied anxiously (and inevitably badly) by those striving to climb the ladder of success or interact with their higher-ups. Thus Dickens carves out an uncomfortable dichotomy between those who repeat what is familiar to them, a birthright, and those who copy what they don't fully understand, whether they're copying clothing, words, or manners. Performing middle-class status is revealed to be analogous to the process of characterization itself: both depend on repeated iterations of a stable set of behaviors in order to clarify and solidify identity. Whereas plot depends on uncertainty, confusion, and change, characterization by repetition provides a key to the labyrinth of plot in that it allows the reader to predict the actors' behavior. And middle-class characters in mid-Victorian novels are identifiable as such only to the degree that they are shown comfortably repeating certain actions, easily inhabiting certain spaces, and using certain language.

Judith Butler has famously discussed this sort of copying (the copying that constitutes all social identity-formation) as a repetition for which there exists no original, and herein we begin to see the origins of the novel's disciplinary function as adumbrated by D. A. Miller in *The Novel and the Police*: characters in novels are repetitions without originals insofar as they represent the murky and endlessly iterated class positions that exist outside the novel, but characters are also textual worlds unto themselves that are formed through the repetition of language alone. In other words, novelistic characterization can always claim its own origins (however spuriously) in the words of authors who in turn may be content to allow readers to infer that they are "drawing from life." Characters, then, regardless of what literary or real-life antecedents they may possess, are brought to life, discrete and original, simply by being named, over and over, as who and what they are. It is only when readers mistake textual effects for actual people that they understand characters as models to be followed rather than instantiations of literary technique. Thus Dickens's concern with his characters' morality: he wants readers to be clear as to which characters' behavior they should themselves strive to copy, even if he can only do so by punishing wrongdoers extravagantly.

Walter Gay's absence is in striking contrast to Carker's increased prominence in the novel's middle. When he goes off to sea in chapter nineteen, Walter is still a boy, his honest and romantic nature untainted despite the fact that his guardians compare him to Dick Whittington and speak openly of his making a financially advantageous match with his master's daughter.[20] Upon his return in chapter forty-nine, Walter's significant characteristics (loyalty, industry, intelligence) are virtually unchanged; this blank space in the narrative middle allows us retrospectively to imagine the ship as a space of play and adventure that has the salutary effect of maturing without corrupting him. In readings of *Dombey and Son,* Rajeswari Sunder Rajan and Suvendrini Perera have filled in this blank for us; the water, as much as the building in the City, is the locus of international commerce on which Dombey's fortune (as well as his pride) is founded.[21] In Dickens's terms, however, the sea functions as an undefined elsewhere that keeps Walter safe, productive, and dead to the corrupt and disintegrating world of the Dombeys. To Paul Dombey, the ocean waves speak of his impending death, which signifies for him a release from pain and a reunion with his dead mother; to Florence, newly married to Walter, the waves speak of love. The ocean is thus figured as an aporetic space filled with the desires of those who encounter and impose meaning upon it. Walter's commercial successes on the high seas, however, are apparently non-narratable; Dan Bivona and Roger B. Henkle have observed

> how strange it is that that the great "plot," the central narrative paradigm of male bourgeois life, is so rarely told [in the mid-Victorian novel]: the story of the man rising in the business world, whetting himself on competition, defining his subjectivity by the competitive process itself. . . . This is the denied element in the representation of the middle class male.[22]

This is so in Dickens, they argue, because "Dickens can never fully mediate the immense psychic attraction the competitive struggle has for him" at a time when capitalist competition was "socially constructed in terms of the deferral of pleasure that is innate to the middle class ethos."[23] The "shipwreck plot" thus allows Dickens to bring Walter back at once exactly the same and completely different.

Walter's narrative death is predicated on what Dombey perceives to be an act of usurpation on Walter's part: bitterly jealous of his son's love for Walter, Dombey seizes an opportunity to exile his clerk to a post in Barbados. And while Dombey comes to regret his act, in the novel's terms he is hardly wrong to fear a clerk's influence. Not only is Carker the Manager malevolent, but Walter does in fact manage by the novel's end to surpass even Carker's ambitions for replacing Dombey: he marries Dombey's daughter, takes over Dombey's firm, and produces the heir who will inherit all but the (now tainted) Dombey name. It could be argued that the narrative logic for banishing Walter has to do with protecting him from the poisonous quality of the firm of Dombey and Son; after all, it is the space that produces not only Carker the Manager but also his disgraced brother Carker the Junior, a clerk who was caught stealing early in his career and was kept on, on the lowest rung of the clerkship ladder, as both a perpetual punishment and an example to the other clerks. (Dombey imagines that permitting the bad Carker's brother to rise to the lofty position of Manager attests to his own benevolence; the joke is that Carker the Junior, his ambition beaten out of him, is a model of virtue.) I wish to argue, however, that there is something more at stake here. To be dead to the world for thirty chapters is in this context to be cleansed of the taint of clerkship and social climbing that would otherwise cling to the character. Death and narrative, as Peter Brooks has argued, are deeply intertwined; it is only with a person's (or a character's) death that his or her life retrospectively takes on a narrative form with a beginning, middle, and end.[24] Walter's apparent death allows him to be reborn unchanged in character yet transformed in status and occupation; all that was really drowned at sea was his identity as a clerk. He has, in effect, two plots, one as a clerk, the other as Florence's fiancé and then husband, inheritor of his uncle's wealth and restorer of the Dombey fortune. The only connection between the two is his unwavering love for Florence, which was conceived in his childhood. Franco Moretti has observed that "in the English novels the most significant experiences are not those that alter but those which confirm the choices made by childhood innocence" (182). Walter's absence permits him to retain an attachment to Florence that is purely emotional and untainted by self-interest.

A death at sea is, for the survivors at home, like the death of a character in a novel in that it is a death without a corpse, a disembodied kind of death. It has no material reality, but is rather the story of a death. It is marked by the absence of a living body rather than the presence of a dead one. Walter's death at sea, his shipwreck and drowning, mean that for thirty chapters he is no longer bodied forth by the text; he can neither affect nor be acted upon directly by the events in the novel. The presumed-dead plot is hardly new to Dickens; it is seen in Shakespeare's comedies, perhaps most notably in *Twelfth Night*, and Dickens uses it to great effect in *Our Mutual Friend*. Yet unlike John Harmon/John Rokesmith, Walter Gay does not lead a double life in the pages of the novel. He simply disappears. This was not Dickens's original plan for Walter; Forster's *Life of Charles Dickens* quotes Dickens's letter, which accompanied the manuscript of the first four chapters of *Dombey*:

> About the boy, who appears in the last chapter of the first number, I think it would be a good thing to disappoint all the expectations that chapter seems to raise of his happy connection with the story and the heroine, and to show him gradually and naturally trailing away, from that love of adventure and boyish light-heartedness, into negligence, idleness, dissipation, dishonesty, and ruin. To show, in short, that common, every-day, miserable declension of which we know so much in our ordinary life; to exhibit something of the philosophy of it, in great temptations and an easy nature; and to show how the good turns into bad, by degrees. If I kept some little notion of Florence always at the bottom of it, I think it might be made very powerful and very useful. What do you think? Do you think it may be done, without making people angry?[25]

From the beginning, then, Dickens had doubts about making Walter Gay the hero of his story. Yet in abandoning the story of Walter's fall, Dickens decided to give him no story at all. I have referred to Walter Gay and Carker the Manager as the novel's hero and villain respectively, and to some degree this is true, especially if we read the novel as possessing a melodramatic structure: Carker imperils the heroine (and her family's business) and Walter rescues them. From a narratological standpoint, however, characterizing Walter as a hero seems more questionable. Mieke Bal has written that the term "hero" has acquired so many problematic and contradictory features that "it is better left alone."[26] Yet, she argues, "the problem of the hero has ideological relevance, if only because of the connotations of the concept itself. . . . The suspicion that the choice of a hero and of the features attributed to him or her betrays an ideological position is a reason not to ignore the problem but rather to study it."[27] She lists the ways in which the hero is often distinguished from other characters:

- qualification: comprehensive information about appearance, psychology, motivation, past
- distribution: the hero occurs often in the story, his or her presence is felt at important moments in the fabula
- independence: the hero can occur alone or hold monologues
- function: certain actions are those of the hero alone: s/he makes agreements, vanquishes opponents, unmasks traitors, etc.
- relations: s/he maintains relations with the largest number of characters[28]

By these criteria, the only character in *Dombey and Son* who could plausibly be considered a hero is Florence, although her vanquishing of her father's hatred is hardly an act of conventional heroism. In contrast to Florence, Walter has no antecedents and no inner life, and he is conspicuously absent in the novel's unfolding. Bal argues, following Hillis Miller, that characterization is largely achieved through a process of repetition and accumulation.[29] We are told early on that Walter is cheerful, loving, adventurous, and industrious, but these characteristics are neither repeated nor reinforced in the way that Carker's malevolence, Dombey's pride, or Florence's loving humility are. It is only after Walter's return that the reader is told that he is unchanged, that his virtues have allowed him to advance with his new employers. Furthermore, this lack of characterological change points to another problem in conceiving Walter as the hero: he is a static character. Of all the novel's major characters, only Dombey himself is changed through suffering and repentance; Walter merely returns to take up where he left off with Florence. Ironically, whereas Dombey goes bankrupt and deprives Florence of her patrimony, Walter's uncle, the shopkeeper Sol Gills, turns out to be a successful capitalist; he realizes a belated return on some old investments and provides Walter with the money to rebuild the house of Dombey. The reader is thus spared the spectacle of Walter ascending the ladder; the fact that his ascent takes place in a geographic and narrative elsewhere leaves the reader free to ignore the implications of that ascent. What little Dickens reveals about Walter's change in fortune (his new company makes him a supercargo before promoting him to an unspecified higher position) is framed merely as virtue rewarded.

The novel's end (for narrative middles inevitably give way to endings) marks the restoration of order in the terms of the old story—the interloper Carker is cast out and ritually punished (in this case by being flattened by a train) and the worthy outsider Walter, having earned his status through a series of trials, takes his place in the social system the regeneration of which he will now effect. For despite Miss Tox's famous pronouncements, Dombey and Son is most emphatically *not* "a daughter after all." It is a son-in-law and a grandson, a new and improved little Paul. The social system in question, however, is not so much the family as the family business; the moral center is, finally, figured as a mercantile system that can only be conflated with the newly reconstituted family by virtue of its having been displaced onto the shoulders of Carker the Manager throughout the novel's middle.

Notes

1. For an influential discussion of the Victorian fear of revolution, see Walter E. Houghton, *The Victorian Frame of Mind, 1830–1870* (1957; New Haven: Yale University Press, 1985), 54–58.

2. Fred Kaplan, *Dickens: A Biography* (New York: William Morrow & Co., 1988), 206.

Kaplan writes that with *Dombey and Son,* Dickens "became a more careful, self-conscious craftsman, with a controlling overview inherent in the inception and the initial plans" (221).

3. An early example of this line of criticism is George Gissing's comment in *Critical Studies of the Works of Charles Dickens* that it is "impossible to avoid the reflection that the death of Dombey's son and heir marks the end of a complete story . . . and that the narrative of the later part is ill-constructed" (New York: Haskell House, 1965, 90). Although Kathleen Tillotson argues in *Novels of the Eighteen-Forties* that "*Dombey and Son* stands out from among Dickens' novels as the earliest example of responsible and successful planning" (Oxford: Oxford University Press, 1956, 157), she and John Butt note in *Dickens at Work* that the device of interweaving home and office "wears thin after Paul's death" (London: Methuen, 1956, 96). In his article "Managing the House in *Dombey and Son:* Dickens and the Uses of Analogy," Andrew Elfenbein describes Paul's plot as a "curtailed *Bildungsroman*" (*Studies in Philology* 92 [1995]: 361–82; 365).

4. I borrow this term from Roland Barthes; see *S/Z,* trans. Richard Miller (New York: Hill and Wang, 1974), 75–76. See also Peter Brooks, *Reading for the Plot: Design and Intention in Narrative* (1984; New York: Vintage, 1985), 92.

5. Alex Woloch, *The One vs. the Many: Minor Characters and the Space of the Protagonist in the Novel* (Princeton: Princeton University Press, 2003).

6. Charles Dickens, *Dombey and Son,* ed. Peter Fairclough (1848; New York: Penguin, 1985). All further citations are noted in the text. The passage I quote above is one of those originally "cancelled by Dickens in the proof stage, because of space limitations posed by serial publication" (35) and restored in the Penguin edition. Other editors have not chosen to restore these passages, so readers of, for example, Alan Horsman's Oxford edition will not find them.

7. It is perhaps easiest to define the middle classes negatively, although even here we run into difficulties; in general, the jobless poor, manual laborers, factory workers, and servants at one end of the spectrum were not middle-class, and at the other, the aristocracy and possessors of hereditary land-based wealth were not. Beyond that, the boundaries blur. The category "middle class" could include professionals as well as merchants and business owners, all of whom were likely to draw distinctions between one another's social statuses. A nearly mystical calculus of occupation, income, education, and family background mediated not only class status but the possibility of mobility in either direction.

8. See, for example, Dickens's description of the Carker brothers on page 239: "The younger brother's post was at the top of the official ladder; the elder brother's at the bottom. The elder brother never gained a stave, or raised his foot to mount one."

9. For a brief sketch of John Dickens's history, see Kaplan, *Dickens: A Biography,* 18–19, 20–21. Kaplan describes Dickens's parents as "people aspiring to retain their lower-middle-class gentility" (31) and notes that "In Dombey senior, [Dickens] created a version of John Dickens transformed into a self-contained monster of personal pride and love of self" (217).

10. Arlene Young, "Virtue Domesticated: Dickens and the Lower Middle Class," *Victorian Studies* 39 (1996): 483–511; 484. See also Young's *Culture, Class, and Gender in the Victorian Novel: Gentlemen, Gents, and Working Women* (New York: St. Martin's, 1999).

11. Young, *Culture, Class, and Gender in the Victorian Novel,* 58.

12. Charles Dickens, *A Christmas Carol,* ed. Richard Kelly (Peterborough, Ontario: Broadview, 2003), 123.

13. Poole, *The Clerk's Grievance* (1878), cited in David Lockwood, *The Blackcoated Worker: A Study in Class Consciousness,* 2nd ed. (Oxford: Clarendon, 1989), 25.

14. Moretti, *The Way of the World: The* Bildungsroman *in European Culture* (London: Verso, 1987), 184. It is significant but not surprising that in *David Copperfield,* Uriah Heep serves as clerk to Mr. Wickfield, and in *Great Expectations,* Pip becomes a clerk in Herbert's firm, Clarriker and Company, after the collapse of his prospects.

15. For this term see Homi Bhabha, *The Location of Culture* (London: Routledge, 1984), 93–101.

16. Lockwood, *The Blackcoated Worker,* 30–31.

17. Tootle, on the other hand, is allowed to rise in the world and even learn to read as long as he remains a railroad worker, unpolished and faintly ridiculous.

18. Dickens restages this plot in *David Copperfield;* Uriah Heep, Wickfield's apprentice, nearly succeeds in taking over Wickfield's law practice and forcing Wickfield's daughter Agnes to marry him. In both cases, the daughter functions as the means by which control over the family, as opposed to the firm, would be gained, but she is also the father's surrogate who would be made to suffer for his (real or imagined) abuse of authority.

19. George Eliot, *Middlemarch,* book three, chapter twenty-nine.

20. For an exhaustive treatment of the Dick Whittington theme in Dickens's novels, see Patrick Parrinder, "'Turn Again, Dick Whittington!': Dickens, Wordsworth, and the Boundaries of the City," *Victorian Literature and Culture* 32 (2004): 407–19.

21. In *Reaches of Empire: The English Novel from Edgeworth to Dickens* (New York: Columbia University Press, 1991), chapter three, Perera argues that "Dickens' cartography locates the novel's opposing forces, the House of Dombey and the Wooden Midshipman's shop . . . on the meeting ground of the East India Docks. . . . The doctrine of empire represented in East India House encompasses the spirit of romance and adventure that enraptures Walter Gay and his quixotic naval guardians, Uncle Sol and Captain Cuttle. At the same time, empire is the incontrovertible image of Dombey's solipsism" (62). See also Rajeswari Sunder Rajan, "'The Shadow of that Expatriated Prince': The Exorbitant Native of *Dombey and Son,*" *Victorian Literature and Culture* 19 (1991): 85–106.

22. Dan Bivona and Roger B. Henkle, *The Imagination of Class: Masculinity and the Victorian Urban Poor* (Columbus: The Ohio State University Press, 2006), 13.

23. Bivona and Henkle, *The Imagination of Class,* 14.

24. Brooks, *Reading for the Plot,* 95. Brooks here cites Walter Benjamin's "The Storyteller": "[a man's life] first assumes transmissible form at the moment of his death." Benjamin, *Illuminations,* trans. Harry Zohn (New York: Schocken, 1969), 95.

25. John Forster, *Life of Charles Dickens,* vol. 2 (London: J. M. Dent, 1966), 21. Dickens subsequently used Walter's abandoned narrative trajectory as Richard Carstone's plot in *Bleak House.*

26. Mieke Bal, *Narratology: Introduction to the Theory of Narrative,* 2nd ed. (Toronto: University of Toronto Press, 1997), 131.

27. Bal, *Narratology,* 132.

28. Bal, *Narratology.*

29. Bal, *Narratology,* 125–26. See also J. Hillis Miller, *Fiction and Repetition: Seven English Novels* (Cambridge, MA: Harvard University Press, 1982).

SIX

Pendennis's Stasis and Journalism's Work

AMANPAL GARCHA

In *The History of Pendennis*'s middle—to be precise, in chapter thirty-six of the novel's seventy-five chapters—Thackeray depicts the hero busily working at his occupation as a journalist. His work is highly significant in his plot's progression: Pen's journalism allows him to make a respectable living in London, propelling the literary career that brings him success by the novel's end. In representing it, though, Thackeray constructs this work as standing opposed to two principles important to plottedness: novelty and change. Journalism denies Pen's creative impulses, forcing Pen to repeat himself rather than to produce something new and forward-looking.

> Let us be allowed to pass over a few months of the history of Mr. Arthur Pendennis's lifetime, during the which, many events may have occurred which were more interesting and exciting to himself, than they would be likely to prove to the reader of his present memoirs. We left him, in his last chapter, regularly entered upon his business as a professional writer, or literary hack, as Mr. Warrington chooses to style himself and his friend; and we know how the life of any hack, legal or literary, in a curacy, or in a marching regiment, or at a merchant's desk, is dull of routine and tedious of description. One day's labour resembles another much too closely. A literary man has often to work for his bread against time, or against his will, or in spite of his health, or

of his indolence, or of his repugnance to the subject on which he is called to exert himself, just like any other daily toiler. When you want to make money by Pegasus (as he must, perhaps, who has no other saleable property), farewell poetry and aerial flights: Pegasus only rises now like Mr. Green's balloon, at periods advertised beforehand, when the spectators' money has been paid. Pegasus trots in harness, over the stony pavement, and pulls a cart or a cab behind him. Often Pegasus does his work with panting sides and trembling knees, and not seldom gets a cut of the whip from his driver.[1]

Somewhat paradoxically, Pen's writing is a key to his narrative of self-transformation even as it possesses qualities of sterility and stasis.

In depicting hackwork's mechanical repetitiveness, Thackeray does more than just represent stasis. He also aesthetically produces it, as this long, meditative passage is one of the many that interrupt—and thus stop—*Pendennis*'s narrative flow. Nineteenth-century realist narratives create such flow in part by representing (in their plots) a more or less sequential series of causally related occurrences; these occurrences give rise in turn to uncertainties about the events' meaning, uncertainties that the narratives implicitly promise to resolve. As several novel theorists have observed, realistic narratives—with their temporally sequential organization and attempts to create meaningful progress—assert a philosophical idea: that for individual people and, perhaps, Western culture more generally, time moves forward in an organized, purposeful manner. Yet much of Thackeray's late fiction is characterized by a near-surfeit of narratorial commentary. This commentary creates in *Pendennis* a pronounced sense of digressiveness and, more drastically, in *The Virginians*, a kind of diffusive "bagginess," as John Sutherland writes, that Thackeray himself recognized as a "drag" on the novel's story.[2] This diffusive stasis is not unique to Thackeray's novels, as most Victorian fiction contains elements—including long descriptions—that slow or stop narrative. Some type of repetitiveness, moreover, is intrinsic to all narrative. Still, Thackeray's novels present a puzzle in terms of their extraordinary emphasis on stasis and repetition both in their content, as in the above passage, and in their form.

As Thackeray depicts hackwork's changelessness, this undifferentiated repetition inevitably seems sterile and boring. Thackeray's discourse, though, which is itself repetitive in its insistence on hackwork's routinization, is an important source of his novels' appeal. Victorian readers received *Pendennis* very well, making it one of Thackeray's most financially successful literary endeavors. These same readers made *The Newcomes* very popular and purchased *The Virginians*, a novel now considered almost unreadable owing to its discursiveness, in fairly large numbers.[3] Readers now often regard stasis—the suspension of narrative progress—as a heavy aesthetic liability, yet Thackeray's fiction shows that, in his novels, it was an important element in appealing to his audience. To put the puzzle another way, while today's readers look for novelistic middles that incite desire by producing suspense or presenting interesting subplots, Victorian readers happily consumed the static, digressive text with which Thackeray fills his volumes—text that emphasizes a present lack of change rather than gesturing towards a more meaningful future.

This text owes its appeal, in part, to the value modern capitalism, and the modern culture that capitalism helped create, places on changefulness and, in particular, on the production of newness. Journalism, Pen's occupation, constitutes one of the most important agents in establishing the value of newness, as it daily trumpets the significance of the "news" it publishes. Pen must labor so relentlessly because journalism demands new text daily, and he must compromise his creativity because journalism emphasizes quickness of production over quality. Fundamentally based on the principle of always creating something new and different to sell to its readers, journalism helped create the Victorians' sense of themselves as inhabiting a time of headlong change. It crystallizes the principles of nineteenth-century modernity, which, as Jürgen Habermas argues, place an extraordinary emphasis on "the new," "the transitory, the elusive and the ephemeral, [and] the very celebration of dynamism."[4]

In its depiction of this phenomenon of modern culture—an industrialized journalism that profited from its newly expanded abilities to produce novelty and circulate it throughout England—the passage about Pen's hackwork in *Pendennis* does not, of course, indulge in the sensationalism or striking judgments that produce the effect of novelty and thus sustain journalism. Rather, Thackeray's passage provides an antidote to the overstimulating, constant change journalism presents to readers. The narrator's melancholic overview of the hack's work as meaningless, because of its repetitive labor and its identity with other occupations, transforms journalism, the producer of newness, into a banal institution based on *sameness*. This depiction of an occupation that helped define modern culture eases the anxiety intrinsic to a society that saw itself in terms of constant change. At an earlier point in *Pendennis*, Warrington presents journalism's practices in a much different way that accentuates the ways the press participates in this modern culture of newness. During a nighttime walk, Warrington directs Pen to look at the lighted-up newspaper offices that hold the press's "great engine" that "never sleeps." Through Warrington's commentary, Thackeray depicts the offices as acutely responsive to even the slightest political and commercial activity:

Yonder journal has an agent, at this minute, giving bribes at Madrid; and another inspecting the price of potatoes at Covent Garden. Look! Here comes the Foreign Express galloping in. They will be able to give news to Downing Street tomorrow: funds will rise or fall, fortunes be made or lost. (391)

In contrast to this representation of journalism's bewildering, constant activity, as the press captures and transmits the political and economic fields' rapid goings-on, the narrator's earlier commentary on Pen's journalism shows the press as a bastion of reassuring stasis. While prices rise and fall and foreign news gallops its way to shake London's financial markets, Pen's work is the same day to day—and moreover, it is like that of "any hack, legal or literary, in a curacy, or in a marching regiment, or at a merchant's desk." With the press's explosive growth in the first half of the nineteenth century and its importance to British culture, both as a metaphor for that culture's valuing of change and as an agent in creating its sense of changefulness, journalism is an appropriate vehicle in a Victorian *Bildungsroman* for the hero's success in the world. Yet Thackeray's melancholic depiction of Pen's hackwork represents this vehicle as one that is characterized more by its inability to move—Pegasus, after all, stands on its "trembling legs" and rarely leaves the ground—than its manifestation of modern values.

Later in chapter thirty-six, we learn that Pen's writing for the *Pall Mall Gazette*, the journal that employs him, has been recognized for its "pert lines" and its "flippant, witty, and amusing" quality (450). Reviewers attributed the same qualities to Thackeray's own early journalism, which he collected in *The Paris Sketch Book*, published in 1840. *The Spectator* called the *Sketch Book* "a collection of clever and smart papers, of the better kind of light magazine articles," but cautioned prospective buyers that the "flippant touch-and-go style of magazine-writing, where commonplace labours to appear dashing and brilliant, is not fit . . . for continuous reading."[5] The difficulty of hack writing does not in fact arise from the author's submission to a regime in which originality and "wit" must give way to the essentially bureaucratic style that Pen might adopt as a consequence of his "dull routine." Instead, Pen must consistently produce texts that seem new and out of the ordinary: texts that consistently read as "flippant" and "amusing."

In describing Pen's hack style, Thackeray's adoption of the terms that a reviewer used to represent his own early journalistic writing shows, for one thing, that this middle, routine period in Pen's history constitutes an attempt by Thackeray to reflect on his own early career. The idea of "flippant" routinization also represents a compression of two ways of imagining the time of the modern market. On the one hand, this rushed time demands flippancy, a way of articulating ideas or language on the spur of the moment that makes them seem interesting, clever, and new. This demand for novelty creates never-ending attempts at reinvention. On the other hand, routinization, while dreary, is a less daunting characterization of this time, as routine implies a reassuring, if dull, repetition of acts and consistency of identity. If Pen's and Thackeray's journalism submits to modern time through its labored flippancy, Thackeray's meditation on journalistic work transforms journalism's attempt at constant newness into work that involves a more reassuringly stable, static consistency.

As his sketches show, Thackeray experienced modernity's far from stable rush of time when he was a journalist. He struggled through the editorship of *The National Standard*, a periodical he bought in 1833, and after he lost his inheritance, he produced a column every few days for *The Constitutional* and eventually regularly authored more substantial pieces for *Fraser's*, *The Times*, and other periodicals.[6] The chief fault he found with editing *The National Standard*, he wrote to his mother in 1833, "is that I am but ill disposed after writing & reading so much to read another syllable or to write another line."[7] Yet he also wrote of

> another evil [which] I complain of, that this system of newspaper writing spoils one for every other kind of writing; I am unwilling now more than ever, to write letters to my friends, & always find myself attempting to make a pert critical point, at the end of a sentence.[8]

The habitual, inevitable "pert critical point" that the "system of newspaper writing" produces: in *On Television*, Pierre Bourdieu argues that "the fear of being boring and anxiety about being amusing at all costs" rules the journalistic field, in which content must quickly and constantly be produced and must be directed toward consumers' short attention span. A field defined by overwhelming competition from other programs, media, and entertainment sources naturally veers toward "polemics over rigorous argument" and a "readiness to denounce or indict" instead of to analyze.[9] Similarly, Thackeray's pert, critical style comes from writing material in an overcrowded, fast-moving field, in which quick, striking judgments delivered with a knowing air could capture readers' attention. In *Pendennis*, Thackeray depicts Pen writing mostly literary and theater reviews, delivering "a little whipping" to poets and actors "whom he tried at his literary assize" (451). Pen's punishing style emphasizes harshness and bite over thoughtful moderation—hence his reputation for flippancy and wit, not reason. *Pendennis* implicitly connects Pen's propensity for "whipping" with his constant, writing, just as in his letters Thackeray connects his ever-present labor with his reflexive production of "pert, critical point[s]," as the necessity for creating abundant copy inevitably results in sharp, stinging judgments. Instead of methodical analysis, "polemics"; instead of reasoning, a "readiness to denounce or indict": quickly produced and consumed media give rise to an aggressive style.

For Thackeray, this necessary reliance on aggressive judgmentalism helped ensure the relative shortness of his early journalistic articles. Again, Pen's career provides a useful parallel, as he writes the bulk of his long novel before his career as a hack writer and composes short reviews and dispatches in his workaday London life. As James Mill writes in an 1824 essay titled "Periodical Literature," because magazines and newspapers "must sell immediately," journalists strive for "immediate effect, of unpostponed popularity, of the applause of the moment."[10] The stress that such immediacy places upon writers produces both an aggressively judgmental style—for such flippant judgmentalism creates an instant and entertaining, through unfounded, clarity—and pieces that do not require readers' sustained, long-term attention. Thackeray's choice of "sketches" to denominate his journalistic pieces testifies to their shortness: the title of "sketch book" suggests the works' fragmentary form and Thackeray's own self-consciousness about their diminutiveness. The hack journalist's emphasis on witty judgments, moreover, also enforced a limitation on articles' lengths. Since such wit's purpose lay in conveying clarity and authority, length can only create complexity and nuance, which the hack writer avoids: if irony and flippancy tend toward the "pure" form of the perfectly condensed aphorism, they avoid longer forms such as the sprawling, multiplot novel. Indeed, a lengthy excess of wit results in nonsense and tiresomeness—a point made by *The Paris Sketch Book*'s reviewer, as he states that "the flippant touch-and-go style of magazine-writing . . . is not fit . . . for continuous reading." In its striving for immediate "effect" and for aggressive, aphoristic clarity, such wit opposes itself to the *duration* that invites "continuous reading."

A close, direct relationship exists between the quick, whiplike judgments that define the hack writer's stock-in-trade and *Pendennis*'s meditative, discursive passages: besides—and in part because of—their reliance on a distanced, almost affectless ironic mode, they both militate against the absorption and emotional investment that compelling plots create and that would facilitate continuous reading. This opposition to continuity occurs on several, interrelated levels. First, on the level of *function:* both hack writing and *Pendennis*'s narratorial asides seek to evaluate their objects of representation, not to produce a narrative about them. In journalistic pieces, this evaluation expresses itself explicitly and obviously: Thackeray, for instance, includes in *The Paris Sketch Book* several of his reviews evaluating literature and visual art. In *Pendennis*'s meditative asides, this evaluation expresses itself more subtly: in the passage about Pen's labors, the narrator treats Pen's routine with an apparent lack of sentimentality, exposing its drudgery and devaluing it in relation to Pen's own assessment, which would have found it "more interesting and exciting" than it "would be likely to prove to the readers of his present memoirs." In both cases, the writing functions to enforce a clear judgment, not to occupy the reader with the suspenseful uncertainties that create a plot. Second, on the level of *affect:* both types of writing adopt—and lead readers to adopt—a relationship of ironic distance to the objects represented, a relationship characterized by distance and a lack of sentimentality. While this writing creates affective disinvestment, plot compels readers to surrender themselves and their emotions to characters and events. Third, on the level of *form:* both journalistic articles and *Pendennis*'s asides take the form of discursive, essayistic exposition, not storytelling.

These different levels on which these texts resist "continuous reading" add up to a manifestation of a different *temporality* from plot. On the one hand, this temporality is that of a succession of instants: the separate moments of harsh judgment that reviews display and the distinct insights *Pendennis*'s asides relate. These texts assert their essayistic points one after another, at best creating logical or rhetorical connections between them but not connecting them through reference to a continuous, temporal progression. On the other, this temporality thus creates an abstraction from time: unaffected and wholly authoritative, these essayistic texts seem to speak from a position in which time has ceased to matter. In *Pendennis,* these asides do not just constitute a form of narratorial discourse that interrupts and slows plot; they manifest a temporality alien to plot. Thackeray uses this form to discuss the rigors of hack writing, transforming this labor from one that tries to create an endless succession of "new" instants to a more dreary, but less anxious, repetitiveness.

Thackeray's own hack writing, which he published in periodicals and in *The Paris Sketch Book,* helped produce the style of these asides and, more generally, his ironic, disaffected narrative voice. Thackeray wrote *Pendennis* well after he had escaped the pressures of hack journalism, but the atemporal, essayistic, judgmental style produced by this journalism constitutes one of this novel's central components. Critics who identify the *longeurs* that bog *Pendennis* down point to an essentially antiplot discourse within the novel: the discourse of the world-weary, apparently absolutely experienced, ironic commentator, whose voice hack journalists created to remove themselves and their readers phantasmatically from the quick-moving capitalist market's pressures.

Despite its assumed knowingness, this voice expresses itself through a principle of incompletion. *Pendennis*'s middle expresses this incompletion not only through its numerous interruptions for narratorial asides but also through its attenuated, anticlimactic plotlines themselves: this discourse does not just periodically stop the plot, it invades the very logic of the plot itself, substituting evenness for pronounced narrative tension. To understand this invasion, it is useful to examine another example of narratorial digression, this one from the same chapter about Pen's life in London but discussing Major Pendennis's encounter with the Duke of Wellington in Green Park.

> Old Pendennis, whose likeness to his Grace has been remarked, began to imitate him unconsciously, after they had parted, speaking with curt sentences, after the manner of the great man. We have all of us, no doubt, met with more than one military officer who has so imitated the manner of a certain great captain of the age; and has, perhaps, changed his own natural character and disposition, because Fate had endowed him with an aquiline nose. In like manner have we not seen many another man pride himself on having a tall forehead and supposed likeness to Mr. Canning? many another go through life swelling with self-gratification on account of an imagined resemblance (we say "imagined," because that anybody should be *really* like that most beautiful and perfect of men is impossible) to the great and revered George IV: many third parties, who wore low necks to their dresses because they fancied that Lord Byron and themselves were similar in appearance: and has not the grave closed but lately upon poor Tom Bickerstaff, who having no more imagination than Mr. Joseph Hume, looked in the glass and fancied himself like Shakespeare? shaved his forehead so as farther to resemble the immortal bard, wrote tragedies incessantly, and died perfectly crazy—actually perished of his forehead? These or similar freaks of vanity most people who have frequented the world must have seen in their experience. Pen laughed in his roguish sleeve at the manner in which his uncle began to imitate the great man from whom they had just parted: but Mr. Pen was as vain in his own way, perhaps, as the elder gentleman, and strutted, with a very consequential air of his own, by the major's side. (462)

Formally, this passage resembles the earlier one in its length and its digressiveness in relation to the main characters' plot actions: just as the narrator abstractly meditates on the nature of hack work, rather than focusing on the specific vicissitudes of Pen's story, he generally discusses the nature of vanity and imitation, distancing himself considerably from the Major's and Pen's actions.

This passage also asserts a similar basic point about English society: its propensity for unfulfilling, repetitive behavior. While in Pen's case this repetition manifests itself in the dull routine of periodical writing, in the Major's it takes the form of aping his betters. Nineteenth-century realistic novels usually create idiosyncratic main characters, but in these two passages, the emphasis on repetition ends up lessening the distinctiveness of the characters the narrator portrays. By taking Pen's life in London and portraying it as essentially the same as that of any "hack," Thackeray negates the individuality of Pen's experiences and thus of Pen himself. Similarly, by portraying the Major's impulse to imitate the Duke of Wellington as one shared by a wide variety of people—military, political, literary—Thackeray asserts the Major's similarity to just about everyone else, at the very moment when an idiosyncratic aspect of his character threatens to become apparent. In both Pen's and the Major's cases, of course, Thackeray's insistence on the characters' imitative actions—Pen's hack drudgery, in which every writing effort resembles the last, and the Major's aping of the Duke's style—helps to repudiate their distinctiveness as characters, since they seem bent on denying their own individuality. Thackeray's extensive meditations on these characters' essential similarity to others and on their imitative actions, however, reveal an intention forcibly to counteract whatever distinctiveness they have accrued through the narrative's course, not simply to reveal a "truth" of their characters or of Englishmen generally.

In *Pendennis,* the common appearance of these discursive, deindividualizing meditations thus militates against the plots' and the characters' completeness—not by fragmenting narrative time, event, or character but instead by blurring the differences by which they might be recognized in their integrity. Critics have noted Thackeray's tendency in *Pendennis* and other works to assert his stories' and characters' undifferentiated quality, ascribing it variously to his stringently "realistic" vision of society, his irony, his assumption of an economically and socially "sophisticated" voice, and his assimilation of characteristically Victorian ideas about memory and psychology.[11] These meditations certainly create the effects that critics have identified and analyzed: Thackeray's discursiveness does advance a stringently unsentimental, ironic view of the world, just as it asserts an unmistakable snobbery and demonstrates its affinities with associationist psychological theories. Thackeray's profound engagement with Victorian journalism, especially in his career's early years, when he developed his style and overall aesthetic, suggests that this discursiveness's roots do not just lie in philosophical realism or, precisely, in Victorian class divisions or theories of the mind. Instead, these roots lie in the processes and practices of hack journalism and the capitalistic pressures that made the journalistic field a crystallization of modern culture's rushed temporality. Thackeray's narratorial voice, skeptical of authentic experience and individuality, articulates a discourse acutely self-conscious about the impossibility of achieving "full" meaningfulness: the acts, phenomena, and characters it depicts blend into the social background, and as they threaten to gain integrity, this discourse enforces their lack of differentiation.

No better description of Thackeray's hack journalism: a discourse that stakes its most robust truth-claims on its self-consciousness about its content's essential meaninglessness. Thackeray's letters reveal his struggles to keep up with the demands of periodical writing but only obliquely show his understanding of how he managed to produce the large amount of text required of him. Passages in *The Paris Sketch Book* more clearly announce his view of his own production as often compromised by close imitation of another work or even outright plagiarism. The "Advertisement" to the first edition sets the tone:

> About half of the sketches in these volumes have already appeared in print, in various periodical works. A part of the text of one tale, and the plots of two others, have been borrowed from French originals; the other stories, which are, in the main, true, have been written upon facts and characters that came within the Author's observation during a residence in Paris.[12]

Rather than beginning with an assertion of the volume's novelty or distinctiveness, qualities referenced by the last clause, with its mention of the writings' grounding in the "Author's observation," Thackeray instead characterizes the volume as to some degree superfluous: many articles "have already appeared in print," and three tales have been partly "borrowed from French originals."

In one of the sketches, "On Some French Fashionable Novels," Thackeray more aggressively makes this characterization:

> On the title-page of these volumes the reader has, doubtless, remarked, that among the pieces introduced, some are announced as "copies" and "compositions." Many of the histories have, accordingly, been neatly stolen from the collections of French authors (and mutilated, according to the old saying, so that their owners should not know them).[13]

Thackeray achieves a rigorously "realistic," unsentimental effect with this passage, admitting to his own lazy derivativeness in putting together the *Sketch Book*. He relies on similar admissions often in his early career. On beginning his editorship of *The National Standard*, he addresses readers by refusing to assert his publication's objectivity or lack of "puffery." Other publications "boast that they are perfectly independent of all considerations extraneous to the sheet in which they write," Thackeray proclaims, "but none that we know of reduce that boast to practice: we therefore boast not at all. We promise nothing, and, if our readers expect nothing more, they will assuredly not be disappointed."[14] As in the *Sketch Book*, his hard-nosed realism becomes ostentatiously—indeed, unrealistically—self-flagellating: no reader buys a periodical honestly expecting "nothing," and regardless of how deficient *The National Standard*'s prose is, either in its quality or its objectivity, the prose still amounts to *something*.

While modern critics, reading these passages through a lens ground by poststructuralist theory, undoubtedly see in them a refreshing recognition of texts' essential meaninglessness generally or the journalistic text's commodified hollowness in particular, they in fact constitute a rhetorical strategy aimed at creating the *effect* of truth-telling, even at the expense of obvious truth (such as the fact that readers would not read *The National Standard* expecting "nothing"). Thackeray also uses this strategy in *Pendennis*, denying Pen's and the Major's idiosyncrasies in favor of "realistically" representing Pen's undifferentiatedly laborious days in London and the Major's supposedly very common habit of imitation. As in his early writing, Thackeray produces a sense of his discourse's truth at the expense of the full meaningfulness of the discourse's referent. His proclamation of his sketches as "stolen" and "mutilated" "copies" establishes its candor by characterizing his stories as, essentially, fakes. Likewise, in *The National Standard*, he declares his editorial integrity by reducing the papers' articles to puffed-up nothingness. By the time Thackeray writes *Pendennis*, this self-critique takes a different form, as his realism depends on the destruction of one of the novel's most important aspects, the depiction of distinctive characters.[15] To establish the narratorial persona as a clear-eyed truth-teller, he turns against his own imaginative creations, depicting Pen and the Major as "copies" (and copiers), just as surely as his *Sketch Book*'s stories.

Through the course of the narrative, the reader may have been seduced into sharing the characters' own illusions of distinctiveness, but Thackeray's narrator asserts that such illusions disguise his characters' absolute derivativeness. This assertion, of course, makes the narrator seem to possess an extremely firm grasp of truth. It also, however, endangers the narrative's capacity to keep the reader's interest alive. In his reading of Jane Austen's work, D. A. Miller has theorized that literary style "can only emerge at the expense of substance"—that style "is incompatible with, even corrosive of" content.[16] *Pendennis*'s narrator constructs his truth-telling style explicitly in opposition to the novel's narrative "substance," denying the characters their specific motivations, personalities, and stories in order to secure his perspicacity. As Pen leaves the small world of Chatteris and his immediate family for Oxbridge, the narrator steps in to negate Pen's idiosyncratic response to this moment of excitement, reducing Pen's story to an insignificant iteration of "every man's":

> Every man, however brief or inglorious may have been his academical career, must remember with kindness and tenderness the old University comrades and days. The young man's life is just beginning: the boy's leading strings are cut, and he has all the novel delights and dignities of freedom. He has no ideas of cares yet, or of bad health, or of roguery, or poverty, or tomorrow's disappointment. The play has not been acted so often as to make him tired. Though the after-drink, as we mechanically go on repeating it, is stale and bitter, how pure and brilliant was that first sparkling draught of pleasure! (200)

Again, the narrator's melancholic, jaded remarks counteract the novel's narrative drive in several ways: first, the narratorial digression interrupts and thus slows the plot's progress, as the reader gets a meditation on the nature of university experience in general rather than an account of Pen's particular story; second, it denies the interesting uniqueness of Pen's experience by characterizing it as a cliché, one that "every" university man has had; third, it aims to annihilate the very novelty of the "delights and dignities of freedom" that it reports by contextualizing that novelty within an entire lifetime of "bad health," "poverty," and the "stale and bitter" taste that results from "mechanically . . . repeating" the debauches that Pen has yet to enjoy. The result: whatever narrative desire the plot has incited by Pen's adventurous departure to Oxbridge, this narratorial remark all but destroys, as the narrator tells the reader that it is a rather insignificant iteration of pleasure in a depressing cycle of dissipation.

The annihilation of narrative desire occurs to secure the narrator's melancholy identity as a man whose experience provides him with a clear, unaffected view of otherwise exciting and emotionally rich events in Pen's career. While this narratorial digression, like the ones about Pen's literary labors and the Major's imitative behavior, diminishes the narrative's integrity by interrupting the plot's progression and destroying a main character's distinctiveness, it augments the narrator's "wholeness." Pen and his story bleed into "every man's," but the narrator refines his identity as an older, unsentimental gentleman who has privileged insight into Englishmen's lives and self-deceiving foibles. *Pendennis*'s narrative becomes incompletely realized, not just because it has been fragmented and interrupted by the narrator's discourse but also, and more profoundly, because that discourse destroys the narrative's "edges"—the borders that differentiate Pen's (and, often, other characters') identity from any or every other man's story. Its incompletion becomes an effect of its capaciousness: once Pen's and the Major's stories become all "men's," the reader cannot experience the characters as possessing an immanent, whole self that the narrative represents and unfolds. Thackeray's narrator instead transfers this complete identity onto himself, and his unique possession of truthfulness both evidences and seems to be the result of his realized self—an older, jaded club man who apprehends with crystal clarity the truths of his own and others' lives.

Again, Thackeray produces the narrator's truthfulness as an *effect*. He puts forth the melancholic view of Pen, the Major, and "every man" as living lives determined by indistinguishable, mechanical repetition to create out of the narrator's discourse a textual element of "full," replete meaning. Thackeray's early writing reveals this effect's origin in the temporal and material difficulties of the journalistic field. In *The National Standard* and *The Paris Sketch Book*, he creates a reliably authoritative voice by debasing much of his own writing as a cynical, mechanical response to, essentially, the need for filler. The same dynamic results, as he portrays the bulk of his work as meaningless so that his voice gains a sense of honesty and "completeness." Alison Byerly argues that Thackeray denominated his short works "sketches" in order to associate them with Romantic qualities of spontaneity and artistic authenticity, even though they were created under the industrialized journalistic field's alienating conditions.[17] In fact, almost precisely the opposite is true. Designating his articles as incomplete "sketches" chiefly serves to assert their lack of significance or meaningfulness, accentuating their status as works that do not show the author's full commitment. The "sketch" designation does not detract from but rather *adds to* Thackeray's presentation of the works as reprinted, "mutilated," and stolen articles, collected and published for the sake of easy profit. He calls his works sketches not to mystify these works as the expressions of fleeting Romantic inspiration, but rather to establish the realism of his worldly voice in its acute awareness of the compromises intrinsic to the commodified field of artistic production.

Thackeray's singling out of the *Sketch Book*'s stories as particularly compromised, having in part been plagiarized from foreign originals, connects his cynicism about his early journalism with *Pendennis*'s narrative effects. As in the *Sketch Book,* in *Pendennis,* Thackeray's plots and their elements constitute the principal targets for his realistic voice. Early in his career, Thackeray produced mainly news articles, essays, and reviews for *The National Standard, The Constitutional* and the other periodicals for which he wrote, composing primarily plotless discourse resembling the essayistic, critical parts of his later novels. Stories did not make up the most significant portion of Thackeray's initial works: Thackeray did not predominantly write in a plotted form, and he attacked the stories he did write as "copies." In "The Devil to Pay—A Sketch," a work appearing in *The National Standard* and most probably written by Thackeray, the author reveals psychological and material reasons for

Thackeray's marginalization of plot. The short piece tells of a hack writer harassed by a "printer's devil," in the form of a small demon who comes repeatedly to the writer's door in the middle of the night requesting "more copy." Despite the author's attempts to satisfy the devil with writing, the "haunting spirit" is "back again in a minute for more," demanding "'Cop. copy! . . . copy! copy!'" until the author must lock him out in order get a moment's rest.[18] Whether written by Thackeray or not, "The Devil to Pay" captures the atmosphere of constant demand that Thackeray represents elsewhere as characteristic of the journalistic trade.[19] This trade, requiring relentless and repetitive writing, creates a temporality antithetical to plottedness: a succession of intense, critical instants, in which the writer must produce, not progressive, meaningful narrative. In his journalism, as in *Pendennis*, Thackeray refers to this laborious temporality and presents two different ways of transforming it into imaginatively satisfying, meaningful discourse: one, by placing this repetitive labor in a plot, as in Pen's *Bildung* story, in which his journalistic career is, in part, made the stuff of adventure and eventual triumph; and two, by commenting on this exhausting labor from a vantage point essentially beyond time and work, when "the play has . . . been acted so often" that the labor seems absolutely routine, repetitive, and insignificant.

This second strategy dominates in Thackeray's early works and in *Pendennis*. In the *Sketch Book,* Thackeray's stories, especially "The Painter's Bargain" and "The Gambler's Death," refer to and make plots out of the financial pressure on creative workers to produce profitable goods. Yet Thackeray's cynical voice, manifested in the plotless essays and reviews, occupies a far greater number of pages. In *Pendennis,* the novel's middle plots Pen's career as a hack journalist, meaningfully—and somewhat triumphantly—stringing together his writing efforts into a story of eventual success as a novelist. As in the stories about beleaguered artists in the *Sketch Book,* though, Thackeray constructs this plot with pronounced anticlimactic, deflationary aspects. Like the figure in "A Painter's Bargain," Pen appears as a mediocre artist who abandons whatever romantic impulses he possesses in the course of his rise. Thackeray's melancholic voice thus reinforces the disillusioning effects of his plots. His voice's formal and ideological importance, however, goes beyond these effects. Thackeray emphasizes this voice so strongly—in *Pendennis,* by interspersing so many long, discursive narratorial meditations—because it offers a much more satisfying compensatory response to the relentless pressures he felt to produce text. By depicting the working life as so repetitive, this voice allows Thackeray and his readers imaginatively to occupy an unalienated position, in which worry, labor, and the need or desire to achieve success exist as matters of easy routine—a routine, moreover, that has already been completed in the past.[20] If plots make workaday pressures meaningful by offering the prospect of a successful career *in the future,* Thackeray's clubby voice advances the fantasy of monetary success and epistemological certainty as *wholly present,* immanent in every melancholic line and remark.

This compensatory fantasy explains Thackeray's decision to market works that include a large amount of plotless text and readers' decisions—somewhat baffling today—to buy and consume them. His plots' subjects attest to the large place constant work occupied in middle- and even upper-class lives and imaginations, as such work came to characterize labor in "legal or literary" fields and "in a curacy, or in a marching regiment, or at a merchant's desk"—or, in short, in a growing number of occupations and professions.[21] His plots respond to the anxiety created by such labor by offering readers a promise of eventual, measured success in the course of such labor. The large amount of plotless text, however, allowed readers to indulge in a much more potent and immediate fantasy of escaping such alienating labor altogether and sharing the Thackerayan narrator's position beyond work, experience, and desire. In short, while his plots assert that industrialized, laborious time might eventually become meaningful, his narratorial voice asserts the idea that one may occupy a position outside of time altogether, in the timelessness borne of repetition that provides the narrator a perspective on his own and "every man's" stories and in the temporal stasis that this plotless discourse creates.

Thackeray's voice shows obvious marks of class privilege, an aspect of his discursive "pert critical points" that remains consistent throughout his career, as his clubby personas flaunt their knowledge, education, and apparent leisured life of dissipation. As Joseph Litvak argues in reference to *Vanity Fair,* his characteristic irony betrays a sophistication that makes his narrators seem outside and above labor and laboring classes.[22] These upper-class markings belie Gordon Ray's often-cited conclusion that Thackeray's writing helped transform the identity of the English gentleman from an aristocratic to a middle-class ideal.[23] Among the most potent fantasies put forth by *Pendennis* and Thackeray's early work, in fact, is that of enjoying the perfect leisure of the apparently economically secure authorial persona, who presents himself as no longer affected by the excitements and stresses of the time that the laboring middle classes inhabited.

Pendennis's long middle in particular, with its anticlimactic urban plots and its extensive stretches of disillusioned, demystifying narratorial discourse, exhibits the potency of this fantasy, as the excitements that modern literary theory associates with narrative give way to inaction, stasis, and discursiveness. While we may expect that novelistic middles explore, frustrate, multiply, and above all seek to intensify readers' desires for narrative ends and meaning, in fact, *Pendennis*'s offers an escape from the rigors of plot and its time altogether. This escape, moreover, does not "subvert" or challenge the structured time of middle-class labor that the novel's middle takes as its subject. Instead, as Thackeray's development of his discursive, leisured voice during the period when he most suffered under the constant pressure to produce more text suggests, it offers phantasmatic *compensation* for submitting to this demanding temporal regime and a phantasmatic escape from it. While asserting that modern life and work are full of the most repetitive of routines, Thackeray creates an ideal of stasis and stability out of what otherwise seems like an exhausting, alienating rush of constant change.

Notes

1. William Makepeace Thackeray, *The History of Pendennis* (Oxford: Oxford University Press, 1994), 450. This edition is hereafter cited parenthetically in the text by page number.

2. For an assessment of *Pendennis*'s digressiveness, see J. R. Findlay, "Review of *Pendennis* in the *Scotsman*, 18 December 1850," in *Thackeray: The Critical Heritage*, ed. Geoffrey Tillotson (London: Routledge and Kegan Paul, 1968), 96. See also John Sutherland, *Thackeray at Work* (London: Athlone, 1974), 90–93.

3. Peter Shillingsburg, *Pegasus in Harness: Victorian Publishing and William Makepeace Thackeray* (Charlottesville and London: University of Virginia Press, 1992), 76–79.

4. Jürgen Habermas, "Modernity—An Incomplete Project," trans. Seyla Ben-Habib, in *The Anti-Aesthetic*, ed. Hal Foster (Port Townsend, WA: Bay Press, 1983), 4–5.

5. "Unsigned Review of *The Paris Sketch Book*, the *Spectator*," in *Thackeray: The Critical Heritage*, 25.

6. See Edgar Harden, *A Checklist of Contributions by William Makepeace Thackeray to Newspapers, Periodicals, Books, and Serial Part Issues, 1828–1864* (Victoria: University of Victoria Press, 1996) for an extensive list of Thackeray's early pieces and the periodicals in which they were published.

7. Thackeray to Mrs. Carmichael-Smyth, September 6, 1833, in *The Letters and Private Papers of William Makepeace Thackeray*, ed. Gordon Ray, 4 vols. (Cambridge: Cambridge University Press, 1945), 1:270.

8. Thackeray to Mrs. Carmichael-Smyth, September 6, 1833, *Letters*, 1:264.

9. Pierre Bourdieu, *On Television*, trans. Priscilla Parkhurst Ferguson (New York: New Press, 1999), 2–3.

10. James Mill, "Periodical Literature," *Westminster Review* 1 (1824): 207.

11. For these accounts of Thackeray's deflationary, distanced, and undifferentiating narrative techniques, see George Levine, *The Realistic Imagination: English Fiction from Frankenstein to Lady Chatterly* (Chicago: University of Chicago Press, 1981), 131–81; Joseph Litvak, *Strange Gourmets: Sophistication, Theory and the Novel* (Durham: Duke University Press, 1997), 55–76; and Nicholas Dames, *Amnesiac Selves: Nostalgia, Forgetting, and British Fiction, 1810–1870* (Oxford: Oxford University Press, 2001), 135–45. *Thackeray: The Critical Heritage*, contains numerous entries discussing Thackeray's characteristic irony.

12. William Makepeace Thackeray, "Advertisement" to *The Paris Sketch Book of Mr. M. A.*

Titmarsh (1840), in *The Complete Works of William Makepeace Thackeray*, 24 vols. (New York: Charles Scribner's, 1911), vol. 12.

13. Thackeray, *The Paris Sketch Book*, 116.

14. William Makepeace Thackeray, "Address," *The National Standard*, December 28, 1833, 397.

15. For the definitive study on characters' distinctiveness, its importance to the history of the English novel, and its relationship to capitalist ideologies, see Deidre Shauna Lynch, *The Economy of Character: Novels, Market Culture, and the Business of Inner Meaning* (Chicago: University of Chicago Press, 1998).

16. D. A. Miller, *Jane Austen, or The Secret of Style* (Princeton: Princeton University Press, 2005), 17.

17. Alison Byerly, "Effortless Art: The Sketch in Nineteenth-Century Painting and Literature," *Criticism* 41 (1999): 349–64.

18. William Makepeace Thackeray (?), "The Devil to Pay—A Sketch," *The National Standard*, January 18, 1834, 44.

19. There is some disagreement about whether this sketch was actually written by Thackeray. While W. T. Spencer includes it in his volume of *Mr. Thackeray's Writings in "The National Standard" and "Constitutional"* (1899), the more recent bibliography compiled by Edgar Harden does not list it, presumably because there is no direct evidence that Thackeray was the author. Yet not only do the initials appended at the end of the sketch, "T. M.," suggest both an inversion of "Makepeace Thackeray" as well as Thackeray's eventual pen name Titmarsh, but the motif of the Devil is treated in a similar fashion as in several other of Thackeray's early sketches, such as "A Painter's Bargain" and "The Devil's Wager."

20. See Levine, *Realistic Imagination*, 180, for a different interpretation of Thackeray's adoption of this "memorial" mode.

21. There are numerous good critical accounts of the growth of the "professional" in the nineteenth century. Two in particular have informed this study: Jennifer Ruth, "Mental Capital, Industrial Time, and the Professional in *David Copperfield*," *Novel: A Forum on Fiction* 32 (1999): 303–30; and W. J. Reader, *Professional Men: The Rise of the Professional Classes in Nineteenth-Century England* (New York: Basic, 1966).

22. Litvak, *Strange Gourmets*, 63.

23. Gordon Ray, *Thackeray: The Uses of Adversity, 1811–1846* (New York: McGraw-Hill, 1955), 13.

PART III

Suspensions

SEVEN

Dilatory Description and the Pleasures of Accumulation

Toward a History of Novelistic Length[1]

AMY M. KING

> With regard to novels, I should like to see one undertaken without any plot at all.[2]
>
> —Mary Russell Mitford

Midway through Jane Austen's *Emma* (1816), the title character finds herself waiting for a friend. Bored, her continually spurred inner narratives temporarily stilled, Emma begins to look outward at a street scene:

> Mr. Perry walking hastily by, Mr. William Cox letting himself in at the office door, Mr. Cole's carriage horses returning from exercise, or a stray letter-boy on an obstinate mule, were the liveliest objects she could presume to expect; and when her eyes fell only on the butcher with his tray, a tidy old woman traveling homewards from shop with her full basket, two curs quarrelling over a dirty bone, and a string of dawdling children round the baker's little bow-window eyeing the gingerbread, she knew she had no reason to complain, and was amused enough; quite enough still to stand at the door. A mind lively and at ease, can do with seeing nothing, and can see nothing that does not answer.[3]

The moment's insistent ordinariness, its absence of a narrative principle, its sheer focus on the small detail—what mystery, what clue or hidden drama, might these banal notations be shadowing?—present us with a curious paradox. It is a sign of Emma's essential moral health; her ability to closely observe without spinning narrative is a sign of a "mind lively and at ease." It is also a potential danger, as too much of such winningly quotidian detail might bring the novel itself to a halt. In this scene, as in others, Austen stages in *Emma* a dialectic that would go on to have a determining, if less openly advertised, presence in the nineteenth-century British novel: an ethical value to stilled observation without a principle of closure, and a fear that such minute observation might endanger from within the narrative drive of the text that values that observation.

With this dialectic in mind, I want to investigate what I believe to be the religio-ethical basis—and discursive forms—of the observational habits that this scene in *Emma* foregrounds. To do so, I will turn to two of Austen's geographical and temporal near-neighbors: the late-eighteenth-century Hampshire naturalist Gilbert White, and the early-nineteenth-century Berkshire prose artist Mary Russell Mitford. In the discursive practices of White's perennially popular *The Natural History and Antiquities of Selborne* (1789), and the lay observations, or what I will call the "paranaturalism," of Mitford's *Our Village* (1824–32), which were, alongside Dickens's *Pickwick Papers*, among the nineteenth century's most popular sketch narratives, we can detect the trace and formation of both an ethics of close observation and a set of descriptive modes premised upon dilation of detail and delaying narrative drive. The novel's descriptive operations and the ethics of close observation recall what John H. Brooke has called the *theology of nature* that implicitly undergirded much naturalist observation through mid-century: a worldview that saw nature as divinely created and the study of nature as a form of reverence, or a devotional exercise (and not explicitly a means to prove the existence of God).[4]

In absorbing the theology of nature's emphasis on observation as a devotional exercise, I argue in the larger work from which this essay comes that the nineteenth-century British novel, and especially its long narrative middles and extended practices of observation, has a religio-ethical basis at the level of what we might think of as its genetic code.[5] If *Emma*'s peculiar fascination for later nineteenth-century novelists was its neoclassical equilibrium between narrative drive and luxurious detail, we might, with White's and Mitford's examples in mind, understand better why the nineteenth-century novel usually sacrificed any hunt for a similar equilibrium to a desire for more dilation, more detail.

Long, detailed description is, after all, as problematic for classic narrative theory and novel theory as it is in *Emma*. Most canonical theories of realism—

those articulated by Peter Brooks, Roland Barthes, René Girard, and Fredric Jameson most notably—center on desire: the reader's desire to get to the end of the reading experience, the protagonist's desire to get to some goal.[6] And that can make their accounts of realist fiction seem oddly foreshortened, as if there is only a beginning and an end to a novel, with the inconsequential middle to be gotten over. We might alternately consider the different kinds of readerly interest generated by lingering in narrative moments of protracted description: descriptive *pause* as opposed to plot. Novel theory, in its well-intentioned dedication to the abstractions of form, nevertheless neglects the single page or even paragraph that owes little or nothing to the advancement of plot but that instead might even be said to still narrative progress. In other words, what drops out of this dominant critical tradition is description—not only the fact of it, but precisely how in the reading experience description works against the headlong thrust towards closure.[7] The long descriptive excursus, which lingers and dilates rather than presses on towards closure, constitutes an important and undertheorized portion of nineteenth-century British narrative. These descriptive pauses, constituted by what I term "dilatory description," have the perceptual effect (in reading) of stilling time. It is my belief that the experience of reading in the lengthy, sometimes still, middle of the nineteenth-century British novel should prompt us to think less about the operations of plot and more about the stillness of descriptive pause; it should also prompt us to consider that the pleasures of pause may claim us despite its frustration of desire.

Novelistic length, as Catherine Gallagher has suggested, has generally been inconsequential to narratology; citing Mieke Bal, Gallagher points out that "since the relation of parts to each other is the relevant question, the length of the novel ceases to count; the internal patterning of *The Last Chronicle of Barset* may be set down as concisely as that of *The Turn of the Screw*. Nothing in this sort of temporal analysis would help us develop a concept of length."[8] In considering length as a feature of narrative middles, this essay suggests the following historical origin for nineteenth-century novelistic length: a set of late-eighteenth-century and early-nineteenth-century descriptive practices that reflect an orientation towards the natural world stemming from the *theology of nature*, which saw the observation of nature as a devotional exercise. It is my contention that the formalist questions about novelistic length are best understood if we contextualize them with other prose genres (such as narrative natural histories), especially those genres that were as anxious as the novel was in the nineteenth century to apprehend and represent the everyday world. Narrative natural history was also rhetorically invested in describing the quotidian and the real, which was productive in that genre of description and length, and I argue that the novel of everyday life shared natural history's descriptive operations.

These genres, these descriptive practices, share a kind of self-appointed localism: White's is a parochial natural history and Mitford's is a village-chronicle. The fictional genre that is most closely related to these genres is the novel of everyday life, in particular the novels of Elizabeth Gaskell and Anthony Trollope, but not limited to them. That their localism, as recent work on Mitford and White has shown, must also be understood within a set of broader national and colonial contexts is an issue to which this essay will return. What might be called the "bounded ecologies" of Mitford, White, and the novel of everyday life take in what we have thought of as generically different narratives, but which share a common descriptive propensity towards dilation within their self-styled local context. The chronotope, to employ Bakhtin's term, of these narratives is bounded and rural daily life, by which I mean to suggest their spatial demarcation and their temporal ongoingness.[9] These bounded ecologies have in common descriptions of nature that are protracted, detailed, and positively valued; it is the larger claim of this essay that this kind of reverence for description is the function of the theology of nature, which, as Aileen Fyfe in *Science and Salvation* suggests, describes the close links between the investigation of nature and religion until the middle of the century. There were, as Jonathan Topham has shown, multiple "natural theologies" in the first half of the nineteenth century—and, more broadly speaking, something we might call a generally held consensus that nature was divinely created.[10] That description may have been perceived as a form of devotion might help us better understand length and dilatoriness.

White's and Mitford's projects are observational texts that model and originate a rationale for dilatory description and a quotidian thematics, both of which have length as their formal by-product. The formal links between White's narrative natural history and Mitford's sketch narration have yet to be sufficiently theorized, though they have been linked since Raymond Williams by the common literary landscape that they share with Austen; White and Austen lived, at different moments, in abutting parishes, and with Mitford shared a common geography of roughly thirty square miles in northern Hampshire and southern Berkshire. My claim for Mitford's and White's importance to the history of novelistic length does not rest on their common geography with Austen. Their importance instead rests in the confluence I am arguing for between what I term the bounded ecologies of native natural history (White's being the seminal example) and the nineteenth-century novel. Specifically, I am interested in the curious formal feature that Mitford's and White's texts share and that provides a template for the dilatory description that pervades some iterations of the nineteenth-century novel: individual descriptions within the natural histories are protracted and detailed, while the texts as a whole are fragmented by their structures (in Mitford's case the sketch, and in White's, the epistolary form). The perceptual effect of verisimilitude as well as length produced by the individual descriptions is then contested by frequently recurring closure.

It may seem perverse to claim that dilatory description issues not from an uninterrupted long narrative form, but rather from a set of sketches and letters that only accumulatively produce long narratives. But seen another way, this formal feature of native natural histories might provide a key to understanding nineteenth-century novelistic length as an approved consequence of the merits of extended (even dilatory) description and quotidian subjects. Like the natural histories that accumulate length gradually amidst a state of frequently recurring closure, the individual building blocks of description in the long middle of the nineteenth-century novel seem to interrupt and close down the progress of the narrative, even as they exponentially add to the length of the narrative. These dilatory descriptions, as well as the thematic influence of the quotidian (within a bounded ecology that also finds its cognate in native natural history), might seem at first simply a hindrance to narrative momentum, but their accumulative power is far more intrinsic to these narratives than mere digression: these formal features contribute not only to the formal property of length but also to what we might call the pleasures of the middle in the nineteenth-century British novel.

To press the historical claim (perhaps into vulgarity): these narrative modes emerged in the earliest decades of the nineteenth century, when the novel's propensity towards protracted length was beginning to take shape. It is perhaps important to acknowledge directly that the narratives written by White and Mitford are generically different as a whole from the novels that we often take to be metonymic of the long nineteenth-century British novel: White's 110 letters are no match in volume to Dickens, Thackeray, or Eliot, and it is important to state unequivocally that there is an obvious and important generic distinction between a natural history and, say, a *Bildungsroman*. My point is not so much that the natural histories look much like novels at all, but rather that certain nineteenth-century British novels share with these natural histories a common feature: description that is protracted and detailed, where the lingering in protracted description is positively inflected. The elongated descriptive passages of the natural world with which any reader of Eliot's *Adam Bede*, for instance, is familiar may be understood as a kind of cognate to the dilatory description that one finds subsumes the entirety of White's and Mitford's texts. And even though Anthony Trollope's novels in the Barsetshire series do not mimic natural history's description of the natural world as Eliot's *Adam Bede* does, they mimic the principle of everyday observation of a bounded locale that is so central to the native natural historical mode of White and Mitford. There is a spectrum, one might argue, within the nineteenth-century British novel in the degree to which novels work with a kind of narrative desire that is significantly different from natural histories; nevertheless, even nineteenth-century British novels that are highly invested in the machinations of plot may have learned from those histories the value of positively inflected lingering in protracted description and observation of the local and the quotidian.

One of the primary burdens of this argument will be to demonstrate that descriptive pause is derived generally from an observational impetus generated by natural theology, both in its direct application, as with White, and as it was popularly filtered and further secularized, as in Mitford. These heterogeneous prose pieces reflect in varying ways the general diffusion of the belief system of natural theology. The idea that knowledge of God is drawn from nature, as opposed to revelation, is the center of natural theology; as a result, observational projects of the natural world have the exalted purpose of demonstrating the inherent beneficence of God, of uncovering the mystery of a created universe. Thus to observe carefully and particularly, and to dilate upon that observation, had a built-in justification, for to observe the natural world was to demonstrate, as the title of John Ray's 1691 volume posits, "the wisdom of God manifested in the works of creation."[11] In other words: there is an underlying principle or belief system that engenders bounded observational projects such as Mitford's narrative sketches and White's natural history. Here I will be most concerned with how natural theology, however overt or implicit, provided religio-ethical justification for the expansion of minute acts of observation into lengthy, and narratively static, descriptive prose. That the study of nature could be a pleasure *and* an act of piety might go some distance in explaining the cultural diffusion and persistence of the tenets and rhetoric of natural theology deeper into the nineteenth century than we sometimes tell ourselves. Indeed, the nineteenth-century British novel might be understood as the site in which, despite the novel's inherent secular intentions, the secularization of this particular kind of piety—observation and description of the everyday of God's creation—occurred. The bounded ecologies of White and Mitford function as a textual bridge between natural theology and the secular realist tradition of the nineteenth-century British novel, and point us towards a large claim: the ethical justification for and practice of description in the nineteenth-century British novel derives from the importance placed on quotidian observation by natural history informed by the theology of nature.

To return to the example of Austen with which we began: *Emma* might serve as a cautionary lesson not heeded by a less economical nineteenth-century narrative tradition. Some of Austen's most vivid characters—Miss Bates, the endless talker, and Mr. Woodhouse, the hypochondriacal homebody—practice localism and dilation upon detail in such a way that they threaten both the rationality and progression of the narrative. Austen's almost excessive transcription of Miss Bates's speech seems a formal experiment in how much realist detail a novel can handle before it becomes a hindrance to narrative progression and interest. There is another lesson, however, embedded in *Emma*: Mr. Knightley is the novel's close and accurate observer of the natural world, agrarian and otherwise, as well as of its inhabitants, and he models for Emma an alternative to what D. A. Miller has called her "novelizing imagination."[12] If Emma is the figure who generates narrative in what is otherwise a rather still local place, Mr. Knightley is the figure who suggests how a restricted locale can generate observations that are anything but incidental. The potential danger that Austen seems to have perceived in dilatory description—that it was an abettor of novelistic realism, an ethical desideratum, and at the same time a potential hindrance to narrative momentum—is one that the nineteenth-century British novel more often ignored as it took up the charge of White and Mitford.

Gilbert White, Natural Theology, and Description

Natural theology—the theology based on reasoning from natural or observable facts rather than from revelation—is commonly understood as having developed coextensively with the "new science" of Galileo and Newton.[13] It informed most natural history at least until the appearance of Charles Darwin's *Origin of Species* (1859), and, as such scholars as Peter Bowler, Frank Turner, and Bernard Lightman have shown, natural theology was not eclipsed by a naturalistic understanding of evolution for more than fifty years after Darwin's seminal publication.[14] British natural theology's classical age extended from the middle of the seventeenth century to the end of the nineteenth century, which is generally understood as the period that marks the demise of natural theology as the social grounding for the investigation of nature. Scientists and popularizers of science deep into the nineteenth century continued to use (in varying degrees) natural theology to provide a rationale for their scientific work and its contribution to the society that supported that work.[15] As Frank Turner argues, "it may very well be that only as a secular or temporal theodicy replaced the religiously grounded social vision associated with traditional natural theology could scientists pursue the investigation of nature without reference to the divine."[16]

It is not my claim that with the advent of Darwin and the eventual turn in professional science away from the natural theological worldview that the nineteenth-century British novel thus ceased to be long; length obviously remains a dominant formal feature beyond the 1860s. As I suggest above, we make too much of the supposed watershed moment of 1859—natural theology created a representation of nature that made it possible (for Darwin and others to follow) to easily substitute the hand of nature for the hand of God, and that image of nature and the strategies and reasons for representing the world did not change overnight.[17] My point here is to work carefully against an older teleological approach that would tell this story as one of progress away from a traditional theological worldview to the liberal ideas achieved by Darwin; I do not wish to construct a teleological relationship between the nineteenth-century British novel and these natural histories insofar as one could then claim that, with the gradual shift away from natural theology, the novel correspondingly shifted. Rather, I would emphasize that nineteenth-century British novels learned from the narrative mode of natural history in the earliest decades of the century, when the propensity towards length (as well as detailed description) began to take shape. The genre of the novel learned from those histories the value of positively inflected lingering in protracted description, and observation of the everyday, and it was not a lesson that was suddenly lost on the nineteenth-century British novel when the process of replacing natural theology with a secular theodicy began to evolve in the second half of the century.

The rational observation of nature was made legitimate by natural theology, a shared theological paradigm that saw the study of nature as revelatory of a divine presence and the act of creation. Natural theology was so pervasive that, as Colin Jager has suggested, it "frequently operated less than explicitly, an assumed background to any theological discussion rather than a proposition that needed continued demonstration: one need simply refer to the beautiful complexity of the natural world, and one's listeners could link it to its divine source."[18] One sees the discursive impact of natural theology in literary forms as well, least surprisingly perhaps in Gilbert White's *The Natural History of Selborne*, a natural history whose parameters were limited to the single parish of Selborne. White's text has almost always enjoyed interest; it has never gone out of print, and is considered British natural history's "one literary classic, universally acknowledged . . . (apart from the *Origin of Species*) its one native sacred text."[19] Originally published in 1789, it was not until an 1827 reprint that it became widely successful; it has since gone through some two hundred editions. What remains is an epistolary natural history, consisting of 110 letters, most of which are short in pages even as embedded descriptions within them expand in meticulous detail on specific objects. Although the letters have returning themes—swallows, in particular, are a favorite—there is neither a sense of *telos* nor an overarching ordering scheme; the *telos,* if one can call it that, confined to the goings and comings of a thirty-year-old tortoise (itself surely an emblem for the text's deliberateness) that White marks across four discrete letters. It is only in one letter late in the text that White can almost be said to achieve a kind of end-directed narrative, which might be attributed to the fact that the particular weather phenomenon he describes in it—the "remarkable frost of January 1776 so singular and so striking"—has a built-in beginning and end.[20]

For White, the influence of natural theology is obvious and expressed; the writing of his bounded ecology, the act of (as he referred to himself and others) "stationary men," found not only its ethical *raison d'être* but its technical propensity towards minute dilated description in natural theology. In his advertisement to the book, White states that "if the writer should at all appear to have induced any of his readers to play a more ready attention to the wonders of the Creation, too frequently overlooked as common occurrences; or if he should by any means, through his researches, have lent an helping hand towards the enlargement of the boundaries of historical and topographical knowledge . . . his purpose will be fully answered" (7–8). But even White's natural theology by and large operates tacitly rather than explicitly, for generally his text is taken up with the particulars of description of the natural world, and not with theological questions.[21] Certainly White's observations of the natural world were intended to infer the existence and characteristics of God, but the study of nature's design born of faith mingled easily, and could in fact be entirely expressed by, a "rational" or empiricist study. White's text, to some extent devoted to ornithology, is capacious enough to devote attention to a wide variety of natural phenomena and rural practices; its primary mode is descriptive rather than synthetic. When he does invoke a theological impetus for observation, his rhetoric is unexceptional: "we may advance this extraordinary provision of nature as a new instance of the wisdom of God in the creation" (53). On another occasion he invokes natural theology as best expressed by the faith of a child listening to the calls of birds: "we remember a little girl who, as she was going to bed, used to remark on such an occurrence, in the true spirit of physico-theology, that the rooks were saying their prayers; and yet this child was much too young to be aware that the scriptures have said of the Deity—that 'he feedeth the ravens who call upon him'" (235). And yet it is not in these discrete and rare citations of natural theology that one best traces the influence of natural theology upon White's project, but rather in the formal features of his naturalist description.

An example, in which White describes the house martin's nesting habits:

> After so much labour is bestowed in erecting a mansion, as Nature seldom works in vain, martins will breed on for several years together in the same nest, where it happens to be well sheltered and secure from the injuries of weather. The shell or crust of the nest is a sort of rustic-work full of knobs and protuberances on the outside: nor is the inside of those that I have examined smoothed with an exactness at all; but it is rendered soft and warm, and fit for incubation, by a lining of small straws, grasses, and feathers; and sometimes by a bed of moss interwoven with wool. In this nest they tread, or gendered, frequently during the time of building; and the hen lays from three to five white eggs.
>
> At first when the young are hatched, and are in a naked and helpless condition, the parent birds, with tender assiduity, carry out what comes away with their young. Were it not for this affectionate cleanliness the nestlings would soon be burnt up and destroyed in so deep and hollow a nest, by their own caustic excrement. In the quadruped creation the same neat precaution is made use of; particularly among dogs and cats, where the dams lick away what proceeds from their young. But in birds there seems to be a particular provision, that the dung of nestlings is enveloped in a tough kind of jelly, and therefore is the easier conveyed off without soiling or daubing. Yet, as nature is cleanly in all her ways, the young perform this office for themselves in a little time by thrusting their tails out at the aperture of their nest. As the young of small birds presently arrive at their ἡλιχία or full growth, they soon become impatient at confinement, and sit all day with their heads out at the orifice, where the dams, by clinging to the nest, supply them with food from morning to night. For a time the young are fed on the wing by their parents; but the feat is done by so quick and almost perceptible a sleight, that a person must have attended very exactly to their motions before he would be able to perceive it. (136–37)

The beneficial contrivances of nature that White is at pains to point out are a tacit but nevertheless legible testimony to a divine creator. That the description dilates to include such details as the lining of the nest suggests more than a writer who is sure of his reader's indulgence; rather, here detail is justified by it being further testimony to the harmony and variety found in nature: the nest is used in successive years, as "nature seldom works in vain." The lengthiness of the description is a formal consequence of the value placed on observed detail, which the passage directly invokes: "the feat is done by so quick and almost perceptible a sleight, that a person must have attended very exactly to their motions before he would be able to perceive it." In attending carefully to the details of nature, White gains knowledge not only of house martins but of God; in recording that observation, the description has a religio-ethical purpose derived from natural theology's emphasis on observation of the natural world.

The broad discourse of natural theology, operating both diffusely and explicitly, therefore provided impetus for acts of observation that could be construed as reverence. White, who spent twenty-five years making daily records of his specific locale (he stopped only ten days before his death), is especially interesting seen in this light.[22] The journal recorded eleven different kinds of observations, including the collection of weather conditions (such as temperature and barometic pressure) and the observation of plants and animals within one's locality. Although the late eighteenth century saw what Alan Bewell has described as an explosion of colonial natures that came from expeditions such as Cook's, White's example displays an observational project of a different, even contrary, scale than those natural history expeditions that took in vast new parts of the globe.[23] White's project, like the regional histories that came before his (most notably, Robert Plot's *Natural History of Oxfordshire* in 1677), turned inward to Selborne, a parish in "the extreme eastern corner of the county of Hampshire," which he described additionally as a "vast district" whose circumference would take three days to walk (19).

White's observational project participates in a cosmopolitan natural history even as it remains, in fact, scaled to the local and the particular.[24] Observation of far-flung natures complemented and informed observation of local natures; one of the two naturalists to whom White addresses his letters in *Selborne* is Thomas Pennant, whose *Indian Zoology* (1769) and *Arctic Zoology* (1784) are the converse of White's in terms of scale and geography if not in method. The more extravagantly ambitious naturalists of the period, such as Alexander von Humboldt or Joseph Banks, also were understood to be testifying to the "wonders of creation." In an age in which natural history and imperial ambitions and travel were intertwined, White's localism represents a cosmopolitan methodology with a radically different scale.[25] The far-flung colonial histories from beyond British shores, unlike native natural histories of which White's is the seminal example, produced macroscopic modes of observation; as a model of observation—of the parish, or restricted locale—White's localism provided an alternative scale more akin to British novelistic discourse (especially the novel of everyday life).

In placing an absolute value on observation, natural theology generates a narrative mode that I would term "purposeful focusing," one that has an underlying religio-ethical impulse in its claim to the divine. The production of detail by purposeful focusing would be inevitable, as we will see it was for White. The proliferation of details testified to the observational dictum, but it would also—and this is key—have the secondary effect of testifying to the truth claim of the narrative or the sense of the "real" in the text. Naturalist studies such as White's could be so purposeful in their observation, so intent in their focusing, that details proliferated to the point of superfluity, or what Roland Barthes refers to as "narrative luxury," which is essential to the *effet du réel* in a text.[26] White's own claims to verisimilitude rest, as do many nineteenth-century British novels, in the claim that the observation is close; he makes the further claim that he is getting a truer picture even though he is observing a more restricted locale, as if to say that to observe a small area is to get a greater sense of the whole: "Selborne parish alone can and has exhibited at times more than half the birds that are ever seen in all Sweden; the former has produced more than one hundred and twenty species, the latter only two hundred and twenty-one. Let me add also that it has shewn near half the species that were ever known in Great-Britain" (90).

As we will see, the effect of looking so closely and purposefully at specific objects in nature is twofold: the forward momentum of the narrative comes almost to a halt under the detail proliferation, even as the reality effect coheres because of what Barthes refers to as the luxuriousness, or superfluity, of detail. In a sense, the narrative's forward momentum is sacrificed to the instantiation of reality. And yet as we will see in White and Mitford, the texts do not suffer for the sense of narrative pause or stillness produced by purposeful focusing, but rather model for nineteenth-century British novels a kind of positively inflected *lingering* in protracted description. Considering the popularity of White's and Mitford's texts, we need to consider that they do not succeed despite their neglect of the advancement of plot but because of that neglect—that they depend upon a different kind of desire, one based in the lingering in observed details that the text requires us to *see,* and not in the headlong thrust towards closure or some kind of secret knowledge. Knowledge, in naturalist description, is not deferred or held back; it is instead immediate, and constantly accumulating, producing the formal feature of length.

The sense of *pause* in much of White's prose is the effect of a general naturalist procedure: the need to look, and describe, at protracted leisure. If the temporality of perception in natural history tends to produce stilled description, two of White's practices are more unique and specifically influential to nineteenth-century natural histories: a first-person vantage point and, complementarily, a geographical restriction to the supposed range of that first-person observer. In an age that saw the attempt at universal natural histories (such as those by the Comte de Buffon and Oliver Goldsmith) or natural histories that took in large parts of the globe, White's restricted locale distinguished him.[27] An important consequence follows: White's ability to apprehend much of the bounded natural world under his purview expands his subject matter beyond natural "wonders" to the banality of the everyday. He concerns himself, for instance, with the depths of wells, the parish's fossils and soils, the abundance of hedgehogs and hares, a neat echo in one area, the severe frost of January 1776, the frugal Hampshire practice of dipping rushes in fat and using them in lieu of candles, the locale's hearthstones, even the effect of deforestation on the taste of the district's wood pigeons. Not only does the boundedness of White's study expand his subject matter, but it also enables more focused observations and more extensive descriptions within the context of the quotidian.

White's prose both dilates—it protracts, lengthens, or extends in time— and is dilatory: it seems to linger, or even describes the act of lingering, causing the sensation of delay or stillness. In other words, the "dilatory description" that is born of White's observational task and theological rationale produces a prose style whose detail is protracted to the point of stalled momentum. A further quotation from White may make this point more clear:

> Those that are abroad on evenings after it is dark, in spring and summer, frequently hear a nocturnal bird passing by on the wing, and repeating often a short quick note. This bird I have remarked myself, but never could make out till lately. I am assured now that that is the Stone-curlew (*charadrius oedicnemus*). Some of them pass over or near my house almost every evening after it is dark, from the uplands of the hill and North field, away down towards Dorton; where, among the streams and meadows, they find a greater plenty of food. Birds that fly by night are obliged to be noisy; their notes often repeated become signals or watchwords to keep them together, that they may not stray or lose each other in the dark.
>
> The evening proceedings and manoeuvres of the rooks are curious and amusing in the autumn. Just before dusk they return in long strings from the foraging of the day, and rendezvous by thousands over Selborne-down, where they wheel round in the air, and sport and dive in a playful manner, all the while exerting their voices, and making a loud cawing, which, being blended and softened by the distance that we at the village are below them, becomes a confused noise or chiding; or rather a pleasing murmur, very engaging to the imagination, and not unlike the cry of a pack of hounds in hollow, echoing woods, or the rushing of the wind in tall trees, or the tumbling of the tide upon a pebbly shore. When this ceremony is over, with the last gleam of day, they retire to the deep beechen woods of Tisted and Ropley. (234–35)

Natural theology is built into the temper of the passage; as Colin Jager writes in reference to the workings of natural theology, the "harmony-amid-variety of a beautiful scene . . . transparently inspired in the beholder a 'natural' feeling for the divinity behind it."[28] Here the stone-curlew and the crow alike are under his observational eye, though neither requires him to go to great lengths to see them. That the prose expands and lengthens under the pressure of an even more exaggerated localist gaze—at home, in the evening—is telling, for it suggests the general relationship between bounded observation, dilatory description, and prose length. In extrapolating from the call of the crow to a number of different images, the descriptive possibilities ramify; the call is a "confused noise or chiding," or a "pleasing murmur," and likened to the sound of three separate natural possibilities: hounds in an echoing wood, or wind in tall trees, or the sound of the tide on a pebbly seashore. That they are actually rooks (crows) and not any of these three possibilities is temporarily lost under the weight of the passage's dilatoriness. It is only in the final moment of the passage, when the "last gleam of day" is invoked, that the literal natural object returns to our view, and closes down the passage: what else to say, except the sun has set and the crows have left? Dilatory description works against closure. And yet is it not the case that the passage's investment is in the middle, the protracted moment of quotidian observation, and not in the emblematic sun's setting?

The recording of everyday detail led White to a formal choice more in line with the fiction of his day than more normative natural histories. In eschewing chapters that separated out and organized natural observations (such as "Of Insects," "Of Plants," "Of Rocks"), White instead employed the more typically novelistic structure of the epistolary.[29] It is as if White refused to get caught in conceptual systems of organization, but preferred the verisimilitude of embedded entangled naturalist description over the boundaries of abstract categories; he is able to integrate natural wonders with everyday observations and practices, the effect of which is to make his concerns seem embedded in an environment and his observations sometimes like the novelistic recording of everyday life. In terms of scientific history, this is what makes White the first "ecologist," a word, however, that first appears much later, in 1873; in terms of literary history, this is what makes White's prose one important model upon which the dilatoriness of nineteenth-century realist description is based.[30]

To speak to the larger issue: to the extent that description is the building block of narrative length, it is from the almost undivided middleness of White's descriptive prose that the expansiveness of nineteenth-century realist description is begotten. That middleness is thematically expressed by what Stuart Peterfreund has called White's "sense of the ecological wholeness and interactivity of the world," but formally enacted by a refusal to generate categories.[31] One entomological description is here exemplary:

> There is a small long shining fly in these parts very troublesome to the housewife, by getting into the chimneys, and laying its eggs in the bacon while it is drying: these eggs produce maggots called *jumpers,* which, harbouring in the gammons and best part of the hogs, eat down to the bone, and make great waste. This fly I suspect to be a variety of the *musca putris* of Linnaeus: it is to be seen in the summer in farm-kitchens on the bacon-racks and about the mantle-pieces, and on the ceilings. (78–79)

Even if the novel of the late eighteenth century had not sufficiently evolved to encompass, as it would by Thomas Hardy's moment, the everyday details of butchered pigs and how they might be spoiled, White's naturalist text anticipates those realist effects as well as a later-nineteenth-century ecological sense. Linnaeus's classification (the *musca putris*) is invoked, but unlike Linnaeus White's prose is descriptive and contextually embedded. White's employment of local observation, his generation of detail, and his prescient ecological sense invokes a set of resources that we have been taught to think of as exclusively novelistic, but which seem rather to be the consequences of natural theology's ethics of description.

White's commentary on his own methodology produces something close to what we might recognize as a theory of description relevant to the nineteenth-century British novel: a full description comes from being fixed in one place, actively engaged in the observation of manners, and willing to use a rich language field to describe what is observed. White writes that "faunists . . . are too apt to acquiesce in bare descriptions, and a few synonyms: the reason is plain; because all that may be done at home in a man's study, but the investigation of the life and conversation of animals, is a concern of much more trouble and difficulty, and is not to be attained but by the active and inquisitive, and by those that reside much in the country" (125–26). Inquisitive observation of the natural world, and a desire to manufacture descriptions that are more than "bare" and without "synonyms"—a rich language field—produce what he understands as better observation and description. That he, not unlike a novelist, sees himself as a recorder of the life and manners of animals, and no mere cataloguer of the natural world, is patent.

If readerly interest in White's description can be explained by reference to its consanguinity with fictional description, what can we say about the pleasure associated with this kind of narrative? White's text seems to demand a different conception of readerly desire than one premised upon occult or secret knowledges that are deferred until an ending, for it generates interest because of its stillness (and impediment to narrative progress) not despite this feature. We should ask rather: what is the interest associated with pause rather than plot? In the broadest formation, as I suggested earlier, the pleasure in reading White is engendered by the *effet du réel*, produced as it is by a superfluity of detail. More specifically, however, the particular kind of interest attached to texts such as White's—those that are suffused with dilatory description, such as, notably, long novels of the nineteenth century—seems generated by what I will call accumulative pleasure. The pleasures of accumulation make dilatory description signally inappropriate for normative narrative theories, which tend to assume, along the baseline model of the detective plot, that the function of narrative is to winnow detail into retrospective categories of significance and insignificance (i.e., the clue and the red herring). No such winnowing occurs in descriptive practices such as White's that are premised on the absolute equality of all genuine details, and where the ongoing pleasure depends not on a game of hermeneutics (which detail will signify?) but on the sheer desire for *more:* more detail, more knowledge, in a horizon that is, theoretically at least, infinite. The pleasures implied by White's descriptive practices may in fact suggest that detective fiction is a misleading model through which to theorize nineteenth-century realist narrative, that pause (not just plot) figures in the pleasure of reading in the middle, and that there is a religio-ethical imperative, derived from natural theology, built into the genetic code of description.

It might be useful to turn here at the close of this discussion of White to examples from the nineteenth-century novel, insofar as the connections I am trying to draw between natural history and the nineteenth-century novel imply not only a shared technique but also a shared "worldview." Elizabeth Gaskell's *Wives and Daughters* (1866) and *Sylvia's Lovers* (1863) provide particularly strong examples of the way in which the nineteenth-century novel and natural history might dovetail, especially in their mutual commitment to the everyday and detailed descriptions, and the reverence for a created world which I claim is behind each discursive project. That they are narratives driven by pleasure in the pause associated with the long middle of the nineteenth-century novel seems clear—nothing much happens in *Wives and Daughters,* and to the extent that *Sylvia's Lovers* devolves at times into melodramatic plots, it often anticipates the later *Wives and Daughters'* total grounding in description of the everyday bounded ecology of the local place. Gaskell's literary observational style (dilatory description and commitment to the everyday as subject matter) mimics the practice of natural history informed by natural theology and suggests a shared worldview. There is reverence, I argue, in Gaskell's commitment to dilatory description, the everyday, and the length that ensues, although in the case of Gaskell's fictions we see an overt engagement with theological issues. In Gaskell's late fictions in particular, the description of everydayness is a form of reverence, where the very act of paying attention to and observing the world (the work of the nineteenth-century novelist, and of realism in the novel of everyday life in particular) bespeaks a faith that to do so is to testify to God's existence.

Sylvia's Lovers is a novel that takes great pains to describe the knowable world; its brief turn away from what I will refer to as the microhabitat of Monkshaven to the heroic landscape of Turkey (in the section devoted to the Siege of Acre) has tended to obscure the contribution of the rest of the novel, for it has tended to be read as an artistic lapse rather than, as I understand it, as an intentional generic contrast to the descriptive detail of Monkshaven. The novel is steeped in a literary observational style that seems to mimic the practice of natural history informed by natural theology; the long, almost digressive passages of description of the natural world around Monkshaven seem, in light of the implied concept of natural history through the Quakers, to invoke natural history as a model for narrative. Examples abound of description of the natural landscape:

> The coast on that part of the island to which this story refers is bordered by rocks and cliffs. The inland country immediately adjacent to the coast is level, flat, and bleak; it is only where the long stretch of dyke-enclosed fields terminates abruptly in a sheer descent, and the stranger sees the ocean creeping up the sands far below him, that he is aware on how great an elevation he has been. Here and there, as I have said, a cleft in the level land (thus running out into the sea in steep promontories) occurs—what they would call a "chine" in the Isle of Wight; but instead of the soft south wind stealing up the woody ravine, as it does there, the eastern breeze comes piping shrill and clear along these northern chasms, keeping the trees that venture to grow on the sides down to the mere height of scrubby brushwood.[32]

Description of the natural landscape is accompanied by similar attention to the human aspect of that ecology, as in the following passage:

> The farmhouse lay in the shelter of a very slight green hollow scarcely scooped out of the pasture field by which it was surrounded; the short crisp turf came creeping up to the very door and windows, without any attempt at a yard or garden, or any nearer enclosure of the buildings than the stone dyke that formed the boundary of the field itself. The buildings were long and low, in order to avoid the rough violence of the winds that swept over that wild,

bleak spot, both in winter and summer. It was well for the inhabitants of that house that coal was extremely cheap; otherwise a southerner might have imagined that they could never have survived the cutting of the bitter gales that piped all round, and seemed to seek out every crevice for admission into the house. (*Sylvia's Lovers* 35)

The detail in these passages are not exceptional moments in the novel, but are instead almost typical. And, like George Eliot's *Adam Bede,* with which *Sylvia's Lovers* has much affinity, these long descriptions of the natural world are part of a more general commitment to the presentation of an entire world both natural and social, and in particular the everyday workings and details of place and person.

Wives and Daughters, even more so than *Sylvia's Lovers,* is a novel made up almost entirely of middles. Recourse to description of the natural world and the social ecology of village life is strongly reminiscent of Mary Mitford's work, as well as more generally the ethic of close and detailed description unencumbered by narrative momentum that is so constitutive of natural history. To make a more specific point: the value that natural history places on "observation" is mirrored by *Wives and Daughters.* One of the best examples of this occurs in chapter thirty-three, when Gaskell's own observational powers and commitment to the description of natural detail appear side by side with the letter awarding Roger the scientific travel-fellowship; the letter says that he had "great natural powers of comparison and classification of facts; he had shown himself to be an observer of the fine and accurate kind."[33] The scene evoked seems to rely upon the same observational mantle:

> It was one of those still and lovely autumn days when the red and yellow leaves are hanging-pegs to dewy, brilliant gossamer-webs; when the hedges are full of trailing brambles, loaded with ripe blackberries; when the air is full of farewell whistles and pipes of birds, clear and short—not the long full-throated warbles of spring; when the whirr of the partridge's wing is heard in the stubble-fields, as the sharp hoof-blows fall on the paved lanes; when here and there a leaf floats and flutters down to the ground, although there is not a single breath of wind. The country surgeon felt the beauty of the seasons more than most men. (*Wives and Daughters* 382)

The observer (here, Dr. Gibson) is present in the scene, and the details that are enumerated reveal a sensitivity to the process of observation akin to a naturalist. In *Wives and Daughters* those people who are strong observers are distinguished from those who cannot see the truth; it is no accident that Roger

Hamley's great error of judgment manifests itself as a failure of observation, one in which he cannot see the truth about a woman (Cynthia) but rather only a series of trite poetic images: she was a "a polar star, high up in the heavens, and so on, and so on; for with all a lover's quickness of imagination and triteness of fancy, he called her a star, a flower, a nymph, a witch, an angel, or a mermaid, a nightingale, a siren . . . " (388). The capacity to observe is equated in the novel with the capacity for truth—qualities most consistently present in Molly, the novel's heroine, rather than the man of science. Detailed and indeed dilatory observation of the everyday, Gaskell's work seems to imply, is as much the province of the novelist as the scientist.

Mitford and Novelistic Dilation

The most obvious link between White's *Selborne* and Mitford's *Our Village* is scale: the bounded ecology, or what Mitford appreciatively calls the "confined locality," of her southern Berkshire town of Three-Mile-Cross echoing in its self-consciously limited space the small parish that White used to establish the notational practices of native natural history.[34] Invoking White and Austen right from the start—"nothing is so delightful as to sit down in a country village in one of Miss Austen's delicious novels, quite sure before we leave it to become intimate with every spot and every person it contains; or to ramble with Mr. White over his own parish of Selborne, and form a friendship with the fields and coppices, as well as with the birds, mice and squirrels who inhabit them" (1. 2)—Mitford, in linking her Berkshire to their Hampshire, establishes for literary history a geographical zone with a definable character: a paradigm, rooted in the western and southwestern Home Counties, of bounded and local ecological spaces.[35] Not appreciated or understood in the context of naturalist writing, Mitford needs to be reconceived as a bridge between narrative natural history and the novel form, not least because she herself understood her work as the blending of the description of the natural and the social. One key way we might see this in *Our Village* is her use of the term "habitat," which in the early nineteenth century was still a specialist term from natural history. The word had not yet evolved to become a maker of the social in nature, but Mitford employs it in her blending of description of the natural world and the social world of the village (2. 46).[36]

But in moving from White to Mitford we move from naturalist writing to what I will call paranaturalism: a fictional style willing to use the capacious descriptive practices of White's *Selborne* in the service of delineating a human community as well as copious natural scenes. Mitford for this reason—as well as her contemporary popularity and how celebrated she was by some of the most important literary figures of the day—needs to be returned to a more central place in the story of early-nineteenth-century literature. Mitford's capacious descriptive practices of the social and the natural worlds (her "paranaturalism") in *Our Village* needs to be understood as a bridge genre between natural history and the nineteenth-century British novel. As expansive as any natural history—*Our Village*'s 1,500 pages and five volumes make White's 101 letters seem austere by comparison—Mitford's sketches engage a social ecology that presages the thematic concerns of the later realist novel. The starkest possible lesson of Mitford's paranaturalism is that dilated, and dilatory, description is as necessary to social narratives as to natural ones. White had claimed that "that district produces the greatest variety which is the most examined" (51), and Mitford applies that lesson of geographical restriction and descriptive expansion to the social organism of village life in a text that is as close as possible to a continuous series of descriptive middles.

The shift from natural to social ecology, however, by no means erases the impact of natural theology or obviates the necessity for continued attention to nature. The overt rhetoric of natural theology within *Our Village* is subdued, but beneath the text's observational practices rests the common intellectual background of natural theologies, expressed though an intellectual context in which it operated more as a kind of tacit backdrop to representations of nature than as an explicit rhetoric. Mitford's demonstrable reverence for nature suggests the way in which natural theology through the Romantic period and beyond shaded into pantheism—this, I would argue, reflects the way in which what Aileen Fyfe has described as a theological understanding of nature persists in the first half of the nineteenth century and in varied discursive forms.[37] To observe and describe, whether in an intentionally and explicitly reverent way (such as White), or whether under the general sway that to observe and describe is an affirmative act (as in Mitford): these are possible expressions under the large tent of the theology of nature. Indeed natural theology, as a pervasive background to discourses about nature at least until Darwin, legitimated and perhaps lent ethical weight to Mitford's local naturalist observation; in claiming, as she does in the preface to *Our Village*'s first volume, that her "descriptions" were written "with the closest and most resolute fidelity to the place and the people," Mitford also invokes the tell-tale language of natural theology: "She has painted, as they appeared to her, their little frailties and their many virtues, under an intense and thankful conviction, that in every condition of life goodness and happiness may be found by those who seek them, and never more surely than in the fresh air, the shade, and the sunshine of nature" (1. v–vi). Here the realist claim and natural theology's emphasis on an observable divinity at work in the natural world collude. Her descriptions are formed by the commitment to close fidelity and a "conviction" that in observing nature the "goodness" of the divine is intuited. Here we have perhaps the most direct trace of the formal connection between descriptive verisimilitude and the observational dictum in natural theology. In other words, realism gets its ethical impetus and its inclination towards dilated description from the legitimacy enjoyed by observers "never more surely than in the fresh air, the shade, and the sunshine of nature."

Our Village returns continually and never apologetically to the minute and local description of the local natural world, as if a license for dilating upon this subject had been tacitly granted. It is important to understand that *Our Village* does not claim to be a natural history, and is in fact a kind of accumulation of various different prose stylings and genres, one of which, crucially for my purposes, is a kind of amateur naturalist observation. A statistical page-count of the first three volumes of *Our Village* reveals the following: 25 percent of the text is devoted to observation of nature. There is a falling-off in the final two volumes, but still some 20 percent of the entire five-volume *Our Village* is devoted to naturalist observation.[38] This has gone generally unrecognized in writing on Mitford, which tends not to discriminate between the different narrative practices embedded within the whole, and which then recruits the whole for discussions variously of the idyll, enclosure, and the image formation of England as rural ideal.[39] I am instead revisiting *Our Village* as a partially paranaturalist text, and provide an alternative account of what Franco Moretti, in his recent analysis of *Our Village,* calls "decorative": "for each page devoted to agricultural labour, there must be twenty on flowers and trees, described with meticulous precision. If urban readers are made to share the village's perception of space, then, it is also true that this space has been thoroughly gentrified; as if Mitford had traveled forward in time, and discovered what city-dwellers will want to find in the countryside during a brief week-end visit."[40] Moretti's otherwise astonishing mapping of the social geography and buried politics of *Our Village* is hard-pressed to understand Mitford's fascination with nature as anything other than the prerogative of the urban elite.

I understand this preponderance of pages devoted to "flowers and trees" differently, as the enthused narrative product of a particular kind of amateur and female observer of nature. Outside of the normal structures that codify and categorize work as "naturalist" or "scientific," *Our Village* has simply gone unrecognized for what to some extent it is: a narrative instantiation of an everyday, amateur, and essentially uncredited naturalist.[41] To understand *Our Village* in ecological terms and not only as Moretti does, in Marxist terms, is to historicize these popular sketches through a lens other than the national or political; it is to suggest as well that Mitford was engaged in a kind of amateur natural history or sensibility (not unlike many of her moment), and that her descriptive practices were informed by those observational styles and dicta. The significance of this distinction to the form of the novel seems important: if we do not understand Mitford simply as a purveyor of English rural myth-making then we must begin to take account of her five volumes of sketches in other, more formalist ways. To my purpose, we find in Mitford's text a link between narrative naturalist description and the fiction that was to follow.

Embedded as they are within a generically heterogeneous compilation, the paranaturalist portions of *Our Village* have gone unnoticed, not least because she was no gentleman of science. Contextualist histories of science have shown how science takes place not just in privileged recognized sites of inquiry but also in amateur and even unrecognized contexts, and have called for "a greater plurality of the sites for the making and reproduction of scientific knowledge" as well as a broader sense of what constitutes scientific activity, including natural history.[42] A more plural sense of the sites of natural history extends to portions of Mitford's text, especially descriptive passages devoted to botanical detail, which are conversant with vernacular terms. The distinction between a self-proclaimed naturalist and a less tutored, peripatetic observer of nature is, however, relevant, not least because Mitford and White themselves would insist on the distinction.[43] Mitford certainly avoids claiming herself as a naturalist, but she does think of herself, like the "bird-catcher" in the sketch of the same name, as someone possessed of a feeling for nature: "there is about it much of the peculiar and characteristic beauty which almost all natural phenomena exhibit to those who have themselves that faculty, oftener claimed than possessed, a genuine feeling of nature" (3. 255).[44] The "genuine feeling of nature" that Mitford possesses, alongside her local residence in the country, make her a habitual, if amateur, observer of the natural world.

Examples of Mitford writing in the vein of an amateur naturalist abound; the following examples are more representative than exceptional. In "Walks in the Country. The Shaw" Mitford notes the particular names of the trees and flowers, including the "wild scabious, or, as the country people call it, the gipsy-rose" (4. 87). In "Lost and Found," Mitford loses herself in a beech-wood coppice; and tries to "count the countless varieties of woodland-moss" (3. 310). On other occasions, she is more particular about the numerous varieties under her gaze:

> The Shaw, leading to Hannah Bint's habitation, is . . . a very pretty mixture of wood and coppice; that is to say, a track of thirty or forty acres covered with fine growing timber—ash, and oak, and elm—very regularly planted; and

interspersed here and there with large patches of underwood, hazel, maple, birch, holly, and hawthorn, woven into almost impenetrable thickets by long wreaths of the bramble, the briony, the briar-rose, or by the pliant and twisting garlands of the honeysuckle. In other parts, the Shaw is quite clear of its bosky undergrowth, and clothed only with large beds of feathery fern, or carpets of flowers, primroses, orchises, cowslips, ground-ivy, crane's bill, cotton-grass, Solomon's seal, and forget-me-not . . . the variety is much greater than I have enumerated . . . the soil so different in different parts, that the sylvan flora is unusually extensive and complete. (4. 100–1)

At other times Mitford does a fair job at approximating in her prose the work of a botanist: "oh look! Look! I am sure that this is the wood-sorrel! Look at the pendent white flower, shaped like a snowdrop and veined with purple streaks, and the beautiful trefoil leaves folded like heart . . . we began gathering, leaves, blossoms, roots and all, for the plant is so fragile that it will not brook separation" (2. 101–2). She has a naturalist's eye for descriptive detail and respect for the work of other naturalists, including Gilbert White; her naturalist leanings, like White's, almost manifest in her gardening—in one sketch, she sets out to find "a particular sort of mould" for compost for her geraniums (5. 185). What is clear is that Mitford's presentation of nature as almost uniformly beneficent suggests that her descriptions function under the sign of natural theology.

The heterogeneity of Mitford's text make the claims I have advanced specific to only portions of it (namely, the paranaturalist descriptions). Undeniably much of the social ecology—her presentation of village life, and its inhabitants—of *Our Village* could be construed as idyll, and certainly in these portions of the text Mitford's position as a narrator between two (differently classed) worlds makes those portions of *Our Village* congruent with the genre of idyll. Nevertheless, what the unexpurgated Mitford reveals is that Mitford's descriptive modes are far less indebted to the picturesque and the idyllic/pastoral than some of her most prominent commentators have supposed.[45] Mitford's expansion on the natural scenes around her cannot be contained by the vocabulary of the picturesque, for too much of *Our Village* turns on specific observations of a natural object or place and depends upon a mode, familiar from White, of local attentive observation. This is a mode of attention that Mitford herself urges upon her readers: she recommends drawing flowers as her friend does (she achieves a "wonderful verisimilitude") as a pastime that encourages the ethical value of truth: "and, above all, it fosters and sharpens the habit of observation and the love of truth. How much of what is excellent in art, in literature, in conversation, and in conduct, is comprised in that little word!" (3. 138). Here we can see an allusion to what Mitford sees her own art as performing: the approach to truth through the habit of natural observation and description.

Put another way, the dilatory description produced by these attentive acts of observation emanate from an observational dictum coming from natural theology, and not only, I would argue, from a conservative desire to falsely preserve hierarchical social structures.[46] It is in the series of sketches titled "Walks in the Country" (a genre that appears in the first four volumes) that Mitford's reverence for nature is established; these walks in the country have varying destinations or natural objects, but share a general sunniness and appreciation for the beneficence of nature that suggests what we might think of as a digested natural theology. The following example is from volume one, "Walks in the Country. Violeting":

> March 27th.—It is a dull grey morning, with a dewy feeling in the air; fresh, but not windy; cool, but not cold;—the very day for a person newly arrived from the heat, the glare, the noise, and the fever of London, to plunge into the remotest labyrinths of the country, and regain the repose of mind, the calmness of heart, which has been lost in that great Babel. I must go violeting—it is a necessity—and I must go alone: the sound of a voice, even my Lizzy's . . . would disturb the serenity of feeling which I am trying to recover. (1. 102)

When Mitford arrives at her destination—after a walk that takes her across a broad social and natural ecology, including the parish workhouse with its flowerless garden (not a rose tree or a currant bush!) and the bean-setters "stooping for six, eight, ten hours a day, drilling holes in the earth with a little stick, and then dropping in the beans one by one"—she encounters a bank of violets (1. 104). The scene is recuperative of energy lost in London, as she had forecasted, but also evocative of the divine:

> Ah! I smell them already—their exquisite perfume steams and lingers in this moist heavy air. Through this little gate, and along the green south bank of this green wheat-field, and they burst upon me, the lovely violets, in tenfold loveliness! The ground is covered with them, white and purple, enamelling the short dewy grass, looking but the more vividly coloured under the dull, leaden sky. There they lie by hundreds, thousands. In former years I have used to watch them from the time the tiny green bud, till one or two stole into bloom. They never came on me before in such sudden and luxuriant glory of simple beauty,—and I do really owe one pure and genuine pleasure to feverish

London! How beautifully they are placed too, on this sloping bank, with the palm branches waving over them, full of early bees, and mixing their honeyed scent with the more delicate violet odour! How transparent and smooth and lusty are the branches, full of sap and life! And there, just by the old mossy root, is a superb tuft of primroses, with a yellow butterfly floating over them, and looking like a flower lifted up by the air. What happiness to sit on this turfy knoll, and fill my basket with blossoms! What a renewal of heart and mind! To sit in such a scene of peace and sweetness is again to be fearless and gay and gentle as a child. Then it is that thought becomes poetry, and feeling religion. Then it is that we are happy and good. Oh that my whole life could pass so, floating on blissful and innocent sensation, enjoying in peace and gratitude the common blessings of nature, thankful above all for the simple habits, the healthful temperament, which render them so dear! (1. 105–6)

The harmony, variety, and abundance of the natural scene evokes for Mitford religious feelings that seem "natural" in that they are inspired by the scene of nature. Mitford *in situ* is a describer whose dilations seem inspired by the reverence she accords the natural objects (here, violets) under her observation.

The localness of *Our Village* is perhaps its most self-evident theme, considering that both the title and her preface announce, as it were, a particular chronotope: "the writer may at least claim the merit of . . . that local and personal familiarity, which only a long residence in one neighbourhood could have enabled her to attain" (1. v). Nevertheless, as both Franco Moretti and Elizabeth Helsinger have profitably shown, the text participates in larger political and cultural discourses through its representational choices; for instance, the sketch "The Incendiary" makes a brief but telling reference to the rick-burning in Berkshire following the armed uprisings in 1830 that the text had all but suppressed. Perhaps even more central to the localness of Mitford's text is the fact that she lives in an unenclosed parish, which allows for freer movement and opportunities for observation; this, Moretti claims, "reverses the direction of history" by making her readers experience the world "according to the older viewpoint."[47] Certainly Mitford's text may have had the effect of occluding the changes being wrought by enclosure, but it is also a historical fact that her observational vantage point was then unenclosed, which is a bit of good fortune to which she draws her reader's attention in the aforementioned "Violeting," one of her most canonical and anthologized sketches. Although Moretti sees Mitford's country walks purely as a practice of leisure—which to some extent they are, considering that she records herself walking by people engaged in field work—we might also consider that Mitford was naturalizing as necessary labor, to gather material for writing. In part a Grub Street hack needing to support her penurious family, Mitford was tapping into what David Allen in *The Naturalist in Britain* describes as a hungry new publishing market for natural history from the 1820s.[48]

Mitford was part of the literary culture, that is, and not just retroactively part of the process of mythmaking; this is important when we consider her possible contribution to the question of length and nineteenth-century narrative, because her work, if considered through a formalist and ecological lens, is at least an intriguing bridge between the description of the natural world (the purview of natural history) and the description of the social world (the territory of the novel). *Our Village*, like *The Natural History of Selborne*, embodies a localness that is in part a self-styling, but which nevertheless has an earnestness about it; in both cases, the boundedness of their subjects—the environs of a parish and a village—in combination with the observational dictum of natural theology produce what is almost a surfeit of description.

This surfeit produces a narrative practice that defeats normative critical approaches to fiction. One of the difficulties of analyzing Mitford's text is its sheer length: not only the fifteen hundred pages of sketches, but also the way many of the sketches dilate under the observational dictum that drives them. In one (not atypical) sketch titled "The Freshwater Fisherman," the plot of the courtship story between the fisherman and his bride is subjugated to a discussion of the Loddon, Kennet, and Thames rivers; the ratio of courtship to river, or plot and description, is 2 to 5. Moreover, it is difficult to abstract and abridge the relevant moment in Mitford given the length of descriptions and the accumulation of details that are lent little if any hierarchy; that is, our typical critical protocol of condensing text into quotable units, based in large part on the citation of lyric poetry, is defeated.[49] The following is an example of the way that Mitford's prose dilates under the pressure of observation, though admittedly, and symptomatically, this abstract from some eleven pages of description does not adequately capture the dilatoriness of the prose:

> Never was water more exquisitely tricky—now darting over the bright pebbles, sparkling and flashing in the light with a bubbling music, as sweet and wild as the song of the wood-lark; now stretching quietly along, giving back the rich tufts of the golden marsh-marigolds which grow on its margin; now sweeping round a fine reach of green grass, rising steeply into a high mound, a mimic promontory, whilst the other side sinks softly away, like some tiny bay, and the water flows between, so clear, so wide, so shallow, that Lizzy, longing for adventure, is sure she could cross unwetted; now dashing through two sand-banks, a torrent deep and narrow . . . now sleeping, half-hidden, beneath the alders, and hawthorns, and wild roses, with which the banks are

so profusely and variously fringed, whilst flags, lilies, and other aquatic plants almost cover the surface of the stream. In good truth, it is a beautiful brook, and one that Izaak Walton might have sitten by and loved, for trout are there; we see them as they dart up the stream, and hear and start at the sudden plunge when they spring to the surface for the summer flies. (1. 136–37)

The passage is also footnoted, in which she refers to "a curious circumstance in natural history" in which she thought she was observing a bunch of flowers, which turned out to be "several clusters of dragon-flies, just emerged from their deformed chrysalis state, and still torpid and motionless from the wetness of their filmy wings" (1. 136). Mitford's under-recognized orientation as a naturalist contributes here and throughout many portions of *Our Village* to description that goes on and on—stilling the text, and contributing literally and perceptually to its length. The effect of looking this closely and purposefully at this meadow and stream is twofold: the forward momentum of the narrative comes almost to a halt under the detail proliferation, even as the reality effect coheres because of the superfluity of detail. As in White, the accumulative pleasure at work here—and the lack of winnowing details into categories of significance and insignificance—makes the end seem insignificant, and the long middle everything.

Coda: Towards an Understanding of Length in the Nineteenth-Century Novel

The bounded ecologies of White and Mitford demonstrate how we get from naturalist description informed by natural theology to a secular novelistic tradition, and point us towards a large claim: the ethical justification for and practice of description in the nineteenth-century British novel (especially the novel of everyday life, where the quotidian is given its fullest narrative play) derives at least in part from the importance placed on quotidian observation by natural theological discourses. The sort of "accumulative pleasure," thus, that we derive from reading the dilated middle of the nineteenth-century novel might be founded upon what amounts to a religio-ethical practice of observation. This is not to deny the novel's secular vocation. Let us think instead how the formal mechanics of description in narrative may have a theological basis—that the religio-ethical imperative of natural theology is preserved in realism, and that it may no longer be tenable to describe the British novel as purely secular. In so doing I believe that we gain the following: a cogent explanation of why many nineteenth-century narratives linger in the humblest of details and elaborate *ad infinitum* on their subjects. Length ceases to be a simple fact of the genre, but is rather a reflection of a sensibility and even a religiously sanctioned ethics: to observe, to describe, to elaborate or dilate is to 1) be reverent, and to 2) yield truths inaccessible to wider gazes. The realist mode of the nineteenth-century British novel preserves the religio-ethical imperative of natural theology by giving the quotidian detail (as a building block of length) a frankly literary and secular home. To what ends? Provisionally, the seriousness of purpose and loving lingering that we see in narrative descriptions such as George Eliot's *Adam Bede* or Elizabeth Gaskell's *Mary Barton* or *Sylvia's Lovers* works—or even Trollope's Barsetshire series with its elaborated social localisms—might be better understood if we allowed that description may be historically conditioned.

The risk the nineteenth-century novel would take as it expanded to ever greater lengths—as it capitulated, as it were, to the pleasures of accumulation and the instantiation of reality—was the risk of bogging down in the middle, of stilling the narrative's forward momentum: as the headlong thrust towards closure is impeded, the length of the narrative balloons and the experience of reading it becomes ever more protracted. Although space here does not permit me to unpack this claim in additional recourse to examples from nineteenth-century novels, one need only think of the example of Trollope's series fiction (and especially the Barsetshire series, with its dedication, à la White, to an intense locality) to begin to realize the implications: length is a by-product of the pleasures of accumulation, which were first learned in the positively inflected lingering in protracted description and everydayness of native natural history. Trollope's series fiction seen in this light teaches us that the narrative motor is not the basis of all reading pleasure—indeed we need not see length and the lack of foreseeable closure as an impediment to narrative pleasure, but instead we need to reconceive of it as the pleasure of pause over plot.

A desire based on pause is a celebration of length, one that owes something to genres where dilatoriness is indigenous: to the narrative natural history of White, and Mitford's paranaturalist prose. The formal descriptive practices of White and Mitford were justified by natural theology and enabled by a bounded perspective; it is from these native natural histories that I believe the impetus and ethical justification for dilated descriptions (the building block of length) ensued. Although neither generates much forward narrative momentum, they do not suffer for their dilatoriness; both were critically admired and repeatedly reprinted throughout the nineteenth century. It is telling that it is only the length of both narratives that proves to be a problem: in most nineteenth- and twentieth-century editions of *The Natural History and Antiquities of Selborne* the antiquities section is dropped, and *Our Village* was quickly edited and anthologized in later volumes into much shorter versions. In these expurgations one might find a caveat—untaken, one might add—for the nineteenth-century British novel: the dilatoriness of individual descriptions may be admired, but the accumulation of them over the vast expanse of pages may prove more troubling. In the meantime, for those of us who are so inclined, we linger in the pause begotten by description.

Notes

1. Portions of this essay originally appeared in "Stillness: Alternative Temporalities in Nineteenth-Century Narrative" (*English Language Notes* 46, no. 1 [Spring/Summer 2008]. Copyright the Regents of the University of Colorado. All rights reserved. Used by permission) and in "Natural History and the Novel: Dilatoriness and Length and the Nineteenth-Century Novel of Everyday Life," *Novel: A Forum on Fiction* 42, no. 3 (2009): 460–66.

2. *The Letters of Mary Russell Mitford*, ed. R. Brimley Johnson (New York: The Dial Press, 1977), 129. Letter dated May 13, 1815.

3. Jane Austen, *Emma*, The Oxford Illustrated Jane Austen (Oxford and New York: Oxford University Press, 1988), 233.

4. See John H. Brooke and R. Hooykaas, *New Interactions between Theology and Natural Science: Natural Theology in Britain from Boyle to Paley* (Milton Keynes: Open University, 1974); John H. Brooke and Geoffrey Cantor, *Reconstructing Nature: The Engagement of Science and Religion* (Edinburgh: T&T Clark, 1998); and *Science and Religion: Some Historical Perspectives* (Cambridge: Cambridge University Press, 1991).

5. The larger implications of such a claim, which are beyond the reach of this forum, are that it may no longer be tenable to describe the British novel as purely secular. That our general consensus that the novel is wholly secular (true to a point, particularly thematically) should perhaps be reconsidered, especially in light of the formal mechanics of description in which theological energies may have found a home.

6. Seen from the vantage point of the present day, the most striking similarity of canonical theories of narrative and the novel, be they structuralist, psychoanalytic, or Marxist, is their reliance upon a language of "desire," which in each case is understood as desire for conclusion: see Peter Brooks, *Reading for the Plot: Design and Intention in Narrative* (Cambridge, MA, and London: Harvard University Press, 1984); Roland Barthes, *S/Z*, trans. Richard Miller (New York: Hill and Wang, 1974); René Girard, *Deceit, Desire, and the Novel* (Baltimore: Johns Hopkins University Press, 1966); Fredric Jameson, *The Political Unconscious: Narrative as a Socially Symbolic Act* (Ithaca: Cornell University Press, 1981). Whether novelistic desire is essentially more akin to female than to male pleasure is a point worth considering but beyond the scope of this article. See Susan Winnett, "Coming Unstrung: Women, Men, Narrative, and Principles of Pleasure," *PMLA* 105, no. 3 (May 1990): 505–18.

7. Theorists of the novel generally ignore description, but Genette does refer to it during his analysis of duration in narrative. See Gerard Genette, *Narrative Discourse: An Essay in Method*, trans. Jane Lewin (Ithaca: Cornell University Press, 1983).

8. Catherine Gallagher, "Formalism and Time," *Modern Language Quarterly* 61, no. 1 (March 2000): 229.

9. See Mikhail Bakhtin, "Forms of Time and of the Chronotope in the Novel: Notes

toward a Historical Poetics," in *The Dialogic Imagination,* trans. Caryl Emerson and Michael Holquist (Austin: University of Texas Press, 1981), 84–258.

10. The persistence of multiple natural theologies occurred despite the increasing estrangement of those ideas from the newly emerging professional science, and despite the philosophical inroads of the philosophical discourse of Kant and Hume. This is also not to bypass Romantic poetry, especially Wordsworth's near pantheistic reverence for nature, but rather to understand, rehearsing M. H. Abrams, Wordsworth's reverence for nature as a secularized version of a traditional theological concept. As Abrams classically argued, "characteristic concepts and patterns of romantic philosophy and literature are a displaced and reconstituted theology, or else a secularized form of devotional experience" (65). See: Alison Fyfe, *Science and Salvation: Evangelical Popular Science Publishing in Victorian Britain* (Chicago: University of Chicago Press, 2004); Jonathan Topham, "Beyond the Common Context: The Production and Reading of the Bridgewater Treatises," *Isis* 89 no. 2 (June 1998): 233–62; M. H. Abrams, *Natural Supernaturalism: Tradition and Revolution in Romantic Literature* (New York: Norton, 1971), 65.

11. John Ray, *The Wisdom of God Manifested in the Creation* (Glasgow: William Duncan Junior, 1750).

12. D. A. Miller, *Narrative and Its Discontents: Problems of Closure in the Traditional Novel* (Princeton: Princeton University Press, 1981), 19.

13. See Lisbet Rausing, "Underwriting the Oeconomy: Linnaeus on Nature and Mind," *History of Political Economy,* Annual Supplement to Volume 35 (2003): 173–303.

14. Peter J. Bowler, *The Eclipse of Darwinism: Anti-Darwinian Evolution Theories in the Decades around 1900* (Baltimore: Johns Hopkins University Press, 1983); Bernard Lightman, *The Origins of Agnosticism: Victorian Unbelief and the Limits of Knowledge* (Baltimore: Johns Hopkins University Press, 1987); Frank M. Turner, *Contesting Cultural Authority: Essays in Victorian Intellectual Life* (Cambridge: Cambridge University Press, 1993).

15. See Bernard Lightman, "'The Voices of Nature': Popularizing Victorian Science," in *Victorian Science in Context,* ed. Bernard Lightman (Chicago: University of Chicago Press, 1997), 187–211.

16. Turner, "Secularization," 101.

17. See, most influentially, Susan Cannon, *Science in Culture: The Early Victorian Period* (New York: Science History Publications, 1978).

18. Colin Jager, "*Mansfield Park* and the End of Natural Theology," *Modern Language Quarterly* 63, no. 1 (March 2002): 31–63.

19. David Elliston Allen, *The Naturalist in Britain: A Social History,* 2nd ed. (Princeton: Princeton University Press, 1994), 44.

20. Gilbert White, *The Natural History of Selborne* (Oxford: Oxford University Press, 1993), 240. Hereafter cited parenthetically.

21. Stuart Peterfreund goes considerably further by suggesting that White is not only writing in the long religious tradition of natural theology, but is (more specifically) writing providentially. Peterfreund's argument is that the combination of severe weather White records and the political upheavals in France and America contribute to a catastrophic narrative, one in which White becomes to believe that the "last days" are upon them. Lucy Maddox, in contrast, argues that White was writing knowingly to an audience that shared his ideology, specifically about revolutionary sentiment; in this way, White, according to Maddox, is a quieter expositor of conservative values than Burke, but like him equally concerned with political disruption. Stuart Peterfreund, "'Great Frosts and . . . Some Very Hot Summers': Strange Weather, the Last Letters, and the Last Days in Gilbert White's *The Natural History of Selborne,*" in

Romantic Science: The Literary Forms of Natural History, ed. Noah Heringman (Albany: SUNY Press, 2003), 85–108; Lucy Maddox, "Gilbert White and the Politics of Natural History," *Eighteenth-Century Life* 10, no. 2 (May 1986): 45–57.

22. Inspired by the example of the natural calendar that Benjamin Stillingfleet introduced in 1762—a record of the year's natural occurrences, seasonal changes, planting and harvesting—White began keeping detailed records of his local world. In 1768, the same year that Joseph Banks was to begin his circumnavigation of the globe, White went to work in earnest, adapting the design of Daines Barrington's 1767 *The Naturalist's Journal* to his own purposes: on January 1 he made his initial record, a habit that he continued for some twenty-five years and which did not cease until ten days before his death; the final record is June 15, 1793. See Gilbert White, *The Naturalist's Calendar; with observations in various branches of natural history* (London: B. & J. White, 1795).

23. Alan Bewell, "Romanticism and Colonial Natural History," *Studies in Romanticism* 43, no. 1 (2004): 5–34.

24. It would be a mistake to ascribe to White the status of a naïve and isolated localist, for he corresponded with a number of prominent naturalists; used the then current Linnaean taxonomy; and, through his brother Benjamin White (a prominent publisher of natural history in London), was part of what Tobias Menely has called "his period's cosmopolitan natural history." See Tobias Menely, "Traveling in Place: Gilbert White's Cosmopolitan Parochialism," *Eighteenth-Century Life* 28, no. 3 (Fall 2004): 48. For Benjamin White's natural history publishing concern, see Elizabeth Heckendorn Cook, *Selborne's Cultural Landscapes: An Exhibition* (Stanford: Stanford University Libraries, 1989). The bookshop and publishing concern was a gathering point for important naturalists, including White's correspondents Pennant and Barrington; White is said to have met them here in his annual visit to London.

25. See, for instance, Mary Louise Pratt, *Imperial Eyes: Travel Writing and Transculturation* (London and New York: Routledge, 1992); Tim Fulford, Peter Kitson, and Debbie Lee, *Bodies of Knowledge: Romanticism, Science, and Empire* (Cambridge: Cambridge University Press, 2004).

26. See Barthes, "The Reality Effect," in *The Rustle of Language*, trans. Richard Howard (Berkeley: University of California Press, 1986), 141.

27. This is a subject to which he alludes in *Selborne* by praising fellow naturalist Giovanni Scopoli, and asserting (in reference to Scopoli's 1769 *Annus I Historico-Naturalis*) that "men that undertake only one district are much more likely to advance natural knowledge than those that grasp at more than they can possibly be acquainted with: every kingdom, every province, should have its own monographer"(115). According to the White scholar and biographer Paul Foster, Giovanni Scopoli was a doctor and naturalist who wrote the 1769 volume *Annus I Historico-Naturalis* that White is alluding to in letters 6 and 7 of "Letters to Barrington." Scopoli was the first to write a natural history of what White calls "Carniola," which is now part of western Slovenia. As Foster writes, Scopoli "was valued by White as a monographer, as someone who restricted his observations to a limited field in an age which, generally, attempted universal natural histories." See "Biographical Notes," in *The Natural History of Selborne*, ed. Paul Foster (Oxford and New York: Oxford University Press, 1993), 300.

28. Jager, "Mansfield Park," 32.

29. The first part of *The Natural History of Selborne* consists of "Letters to Pennant," and the second consists of "Letters to Barrington." The letters do not always proceed chronologically—the first letter in the Barrington section is from June 30, 1768, and the last letter in the preceding Pennant section is from November 30, 1780—and some are not given dates at all.

30. As with many general monikers, the title ("founding father of ecology") is shared by many. Although some historians trace the emergence of modern ecological thought to Aristotle and Theophrastus, others tend to locate the emergence of an ecological viewpoint in the eighteenth century, and single out Gilbert White and Alexander von Humboldt, who first showed the relation between observed plant species and climate (or vegetation "zones"), for the honor. Others cast White within a broader triad: "some historians have dubbed Linnaeus the father of ecology, together with English naturalist parsons such as John Ray (1628–1705) and Gilbert White (1720–93)." See Rausing, "Underwriting the Oeconomy," 173.

31. Peterfreund, "Great Frosts," 85.

32. Elizabeth Gaskell, *Sylvia's Lovers* (Oxford: Oxford World's Classics, 2008), 34.

33. Elizabeth Gaskell, *Wives and Daughters* (Oxford: Oxford World's Classics, 2009), 384.

34. Mary Russell Mitford, *Our Village*, vol. 1 (London: G. and W. B. Whittaker, 1824), 1–2. Hereafter cited by volume and page number within the text; the dates for subsequent volumes are as follows: volume 2 (1826), volume 3 (1828), volume 4 (1830), volume 5 (1832).

35. Martha Adams Bohrer refers to Gilbert White's *The Natural History of Selborne* as a "tale of locale," and connects it interestingly to Maria Edgeworth's *Castle Rackrent*. Bohrer is interested in reviving what she sees as a genre we have lost sight of, the tale of locale, and its influence on the Victorian novel, and in this way we share a common interest in White and his scientific context, as well as the relation between empirical observation and novelistic representation. Unlike Bohrer, I am not so much tracing a literary history back to a neglected Romantic genre as assessing the formal features of description and length by looking at the progenitive features of natural theology. See Martha Adams Bohrer, "Tales of Locale: *The Natural History of Selborne* and *Castle Rackrent*," *Modern Philology* 100, no. 3 (February 2003): 393–416.

36. The *Oxford English Dictionary* gives the first usage for habitat as a 1762 natural history (William Hudson's *Flora Anglica*); the more general usage of habitat as meaning a dwelling place or habitation did not evolve until the mid-nineteenth century.

37. Fyfe, *Science and Salvation: Evangelical Popular Science Publishing in Victorian Britain*..

38. Volume 1 (1824) has 292 pages, of which 81 pages (or 28 percent) are devoted to subjects of interest to the naturalist and paranaturalist description. Volume 2 (1826) has 311 pages, of which 76 pages (or 24 percent) are naturalist description. Volume 3 (1828) has 315 pages, of which 73 pages (or 23 percent) are naturalist in spirit and description. Volume 4 (1830) has 345 pages, with 58 pages (17 percent) naturalist-oriented pages. Volume 5 (1832) has 362 pages, of which 42 pages (or 12 percent) could be described as naturalist. Overall, the percentage of pages in Mitford's narrative that directly address scenes and objects from nature is as much as 20 percent.

39. The best recent scholarship on Mitford has engaged the complex political ramifications of her sketches, while one recent study persuasively highlights the influence of Mitford's sketches on the formal contours of the Victorian novel: Amanpal Garcha, *From Sketch to Novel: The Development of Victorian Fiction* (Cambridge: Cambridge University Press, 2009). See, in particular, Deidre Lynch, "Homes and Haunts: Austen's and Mitford's English Idylls," *PMLA* 115, no. 5 (October 2000): 1103–8; Franco Moretti, *Graphs, Maps, Trees: Abstract Models for a Literary Theory* (London: Verso, 2005); and Elizabeth K. Helsinger, *Rural Scenes and National Representation: Britain, 1815–1850* (Princeton: Princeton University Press, 1997). See also Roger Sales, *English Literature in History 1780–1830: Pastoral and Politics* (London: Hutchinson, 1983); Anne D. Wallace, *Walking, Literature, and English Culture: The Origins and Uses of Peripatetic in the Nineteenth Century* (Oxford: Clarendon, 1993); and Shelagh Hunter, *Victorian Idyllic Fiction: Pastoral Strategies* (London: Macmillan, 1984).

40. Moretti, *Graphs, Maps, Trees*, 39–42.

41. The work that the historian of science Anne Secord has done is germane here; her remarkable work on artisan botany uncovers an alternative site for science as well as a previously unacknowledged set of participants. Secord reevaluates the botany as practiced by a set of early-nineteenth-century Lancashire artisans, granting to their work an acknowledgment of its scientific contribution that internalist histories of science had neglected. See Anne Secord, "Science in the Pub: Artisan Botanists in Early 19th-Century Lancashire," *History of Science* 32 (1994): 269–315. It is not my goal to have Mitford reassigned, as it were, to the category of naturalist, but rather to suggest that the arena of observational science was broader than we have imagined, and that the work of carefully observing and describing nature was not restricted to institutionally affirmed voices. In understanding Mitford's marginal position within a broader discourse of science we might better contextualize her within other (including aesthetic and political) discourses of nature.

42. Roger Cooter and Stephen Pumfrey, "Separate Spheres and Public Places: Reflections on the History of Science Popularization in Popular Culture," *History of Science* 32 (1994): 254.

43. White draws distinctions between those who bring him observations and his own, more educated eye: "my Sussex friend, a man of observation and good sense, but no naturalist, to whom I applied on account of the stone-curlew, *oedicnemus,* sends the following account" (77). However, this is not mere snobbery on White's part; he quotes his Sussex friend's account in full, taking care to put the prose in quote marks, which gestures to White's respect for the amateur observer but also to his own strictness about the difference between first-hand observation and second-hand information. White, that is, seems to value most the reliability of first-hand observation, and though he distinguishes "a man of observation and good sense" from a "naturalist," he depends upon the former. Mitford too makes such discriminations, invoking with more authority published naturalists, but also quoting as well acquaintances, including her godfather, who "dabbled in natural history" and had a home museum (2. 256); in a comic sketch in the first volume titled "A Village Beau," she catches her servant Harriet being courted by a Joel Brent, whose "birdcall" summons makes her father, a "dabbler in natural history" with an "ornithological iear," almost record in agreement "with Mr. White, of Selborne . . . an original observation, in the Naturalist's Calendar." The humor of this original observation—a skylark singing in Berkshire in December—is based in a naturalist's knowingness, and is typical of Mitford.

44. She also calls her father hunting for fossils at the seashore a "dabbler in science," the most modest of accolades that she nevertheless does not bestow on herself: "now for a moment losing sight of the dear papa, and now rejoining him with some delicate shell, or brightly coloured sea-weed, or imperfect *cornua ammonis,* inquiring into the success of his graver labours" (5. 337).

45. See in particular Helsinger, *Rural Scenes and National Representation.* Helsinger's politically suspicious mode of reading Mitford has been influential, but I would suggest that in folding the paranaturalist description into the whole, it mischaracterizes the impact—literary, ethical, and political—of some of Mitford's descriptive work.

46. Helsinger acknowledges that Mitford's "resolute commitment to literal, particularized description does . . . offer a kind of protection to her subjects from the uses to which generalizing or symbolizing writers like Cobbett or Wordsworth might put them." Helsinger does say that "flowers, places, and people are described with a detailed specificity that insists on the importance of the unique individual" [and] "in this sense, . . . can be said to shield her subjects from some of the consequences of the dominant class gaze." However, Helsinger does not consider what the impetus for these details might be—as I claim, the regime of

natural theology—and returns instead to a posture of suspicion: "Yet her immersion in detail also helps maintain the illusion that the rural scene exists apart from history, as the stage for a private quest for identity and security." See Helsinger, *Rural Scenes*, 131–32.

47. Moretti, *Graphs, Maps, Trees*, 38–39.

48. Allen, *Naturalist in Britain*, 84–85.

49. See, for instance, Mary Poovey's intriguing claim that the working procedures of contemporary critical work are geared toward lyric poetry rather than narrative, in "The Model System of Contemporary Literary Criticism," *Critical Inquiry* 27 (Spring 2001): 438.

EIGHT

An Anatomy of Suspense

The Pleasurable, Critical, Ethical, Erotic Middle of
The Woman in White

CAROLINE LEVINE

When I was a teenager, I found a copy of *Anna Karenina* on the library shelves. I had never read Tolstoy before, and for the first few chapters I was riveted. First came the tension between Oblonsky's careless philandering and Levin's passionate intensity. And then, even more thrilling, came that anxious, restless moment when Vronsky and Anna first meet at the train station. But just as the erotic tensions began to mount, an editorial footnote intruded. Annoyed at the interruption, I glanced down at the bottom of the page, expecting the editor to offer some scrap of historical detail. But information about nineteenth-century Russia was not, apparently, this editor's concern. Instead, the note went out of its way to inform readers that the scene at the train station foreshadowed Anna's eventual suicide. An interpretive tidbit, a matter of purely literary interest—set there, perhaps, to enhance an appreciation of the careful construction of the novel as a whole. But this footnote transformed my reading experience. Suddenly my keen interest in the tensions of the narrative collapsed. I tried to ignore the knowledge of the future, to forget it, to reinvigorate my own deflated curiosity. But once I was aware of what was to come, I found myself gloomily plodding through the next seven hundred pages, waiting to meet the inevitably dismal end.

Years later, I was startled to discover that the footnotes to the Penguin edition of *Jane Eyre* also gave away the mystery, referring explicitly to Bertha

Mason well before the narrator was ready to reveal her.[1] And here the editorial crime seemed even more shocking than in the case of Tolstoy, since *Jane Eyre* is so meticulously structured around its careful withholdings. Grace Poole is surely the one of the first and most effective red herrings in the world of fiction, and as my students can attest, the mysterious laughter in the attic still keeps first-time readers guessing until the madwoman is revealed. Why is it, then, that critics and editors have read these texts as if we knew it all before we began—as if the novel's mysterious middle had no interest, no content, no value? And what does it say about us that we see fit to thwart the thrills of first reading, to deny some of the pleasures of suspenseful narrative?

Of course, pleasurable reading has long been dismissed and condemned by critics who span the whole political spectrum—from followers of Matthew Arnold concerned about philistines overtaking a national culture to Marxists dismayed by the powerful network of capitalist interests that strive tirelessly to keep the masses obedient by lulling them with entertaining deceptions that fill every hour not taken up by deadening and dehumanizing labor.[2] Countless critics have claimed that suspense plots encourage a passive readership: the "readerly" text is understood to raise doubts and anxieties only in order to close them down by offering us the pleasure of reassuring endings that reaffirm the status quo—a happy marriage, a successful career, a captured criminal.[3] Indeed, it is precisely pleasures of popular culture that are the real mechanism of oppression, according to theorists of the Frankfurt School, because they distract us from any possibility of resistance. As Adorno and Horkheimer write: "To be pleased means to say Yes."[4]

It is my own hypothesis that to be pleased does not always mean to say Yes at all. In fact, when it comes to the fiction of the Victorian period, to be pleased sometimes means to say No, and more often it means to say Maybe or Maybe Not. I suggest that the suspense of the middle offers a curiously composite kind of pleasure that manages to bring together the satisfactions of a mass readership with a set of probing values more akin to a critical consciousness than to a complacent passivity.[5] Here I offer a reading of Wilkie Collins's *The Woman in White* (1860) to make my case, though I want to suggest, too, that it is one particularly self-conscious and brilliant instance among many of Victorian narrative middles that are more inclined to invite an active, engaged, critical thinking than a helpless, thoughtless submission.

Defining Suspense

Suspense has often been associated with specific genres—thrillers, mystery and detection, espionage, even romance—and one might make the case that it is one of the most common hallmarks of "genre fiction" in general. Some critics have distinguished among genres, however, arguing that suspense is a feature of thrillers but not of detective fiction.[6] Others have suggested that suspense is an aspect of all narrative and thus transcends genre distinctions.[7] I suggest starting instead from the observation that a vast range of nineteenth-century novelists at some point employed techniques of suspense, whether their narratives were "high" or "low," plausible or sensational, published in cheap weekly parts or in expensive volumes.[8] Thus suspense emerges as neither an aspect of particular generic traditions nor as the general condition of narratability itself, but as a specific technical device or strategy that can be more closely associated with some particular historical contexts than with others.

To be sure, suspense has sometimes been defined not by its generic associations but by its effects on readers: it succeeds when it produces "a strong sense of uncertainty . . . about how some present situation will resolve itself [or] what will happen next."[9] Defined in this way, suspense is an experience that varies among audiences—some readers do not feel it, for example, because they already know the outcome, or feel certain that they can predict the ending because they recognize the conventions of the genre. Such variation among reader responses suggests that audiences themselves participate in the production of suspense. But suspense is not *only* a readerly effect. The kind of pleasurable readerly anxiety that we call suspense happens as the consequence of a particular formal strategy. Hans J. Wulff argues that suspenseful narrative produces cues—what he calls *cataphors*—that are signals of some event or revelation to come later in the narrative.[10] The text might indicate that we are missing a piece of information—a secret, a mystery—or it might deliberately prolong a temporal process, keeping back a knowledge of the outcome—a chase, a threat, a flirtation. In either case, the possibility of suspenseful uncertainty emerges when the text clearly signals that it is holding something back. Thus the suspenseful text flaunts the fact that it is withholding information: it hints and then halts, begins to tell and then checks itself, flirts, teases, and insinuates. This kind of narrative captivates the reader, as one critic for the *Times* put it in 1860, by "letting out a little bit of information here and a little bit farther on, continually making us feel our ignorance."[11]

I have argued elsewhere that nineteenth-century scientists and philosophers of science frequently used the term "suspense" to describe what they saw as a proper epistemological relationship between mind and world.[12] Genuine knowledge was not immediate, since appearances could always deceive. Victorian thinkers therefore argued that it was crucial to hypothesize about the world and then to put these guesses to the test: a good scientist, they suggested, rigorously examines even those opinions that seem most obvious and most true, checking all speculations against the evidence offered up by the world.

Thus the delays of suspense emerged as essential to the task of gathering knowledge. As philosopher Stanley Jevons put it, "The successful investigator must have . . . clear notions of the result he expects and confidence in the truth of his theories, and yet he must have that candour and flexibility of mind which enable him to expect unfavourable results and abandon mistaken views."[13] The scientist must wait—suspended, flexible, open—to see whether or not the world will match the theory. And so we find Michael Faraday, the most famous Victorian experimenter, torn by doubts, writing of his determination to "hold [his] judgment in suspense."[14] And John Tyndall insists that whenever the data is missing, "the judgment ought to remain in suspense."[15] Surprisingly, then, it is the pause—the doubtful, hopeful middle of the process—that lends the scientific method its legitimacy.

I have argued that it is in this intellectual context that Victorian novelists took up the epistemological seriousness of the suspended middle, and disseminated it widely as a way to approach conventional hypotheses and orthodoxies. They made it clear that we cannot simply take appearances, authorities, virtuous hopes, or even generic conventions on faith; the withholdings that generate suspense compel us to recognize that we do not know, that we can only guess, and so must subject even our deepest and most longstanding beliefs to the rigorous test of skepticism.

If suspense had a cognitive seriousness to it, however, it was not *only* a serious epistemological venture. Here I rely on Wilkie Collins to theorize the many affects of suspense, including hope, desire, skepticism, distrust, suspicion, anxiety, longing, superstition, dread, uneasiness, tension, prediction, calculation, speculation, curiosity, and conjecture. Not only a matter of getting at the truth, suspense emerges in *The Woman in White* as ethical *and* erotic too—joining skeptical inquiry to the rigorous demands of conscience and the suggestive allure of seduction. If this seems like an impossibly incongruous combination, it is Collins's genius to show us how they work together. *The Woman in White*, that is, produces a richly detailed anatomy of suspense.

Collins withholds many secrets from us. In fact, the list is so long that it defies a full account: from the "something missing" in Laura Fairlie's face to Count Fosco's sinister plans, from "the Secret" kept by Sir Percival Glyde to Marian's sudden disappearance from Blackwater Park. The narrative also frequently keeps us suspended in time, as Marian waits for letters that may have been intercepted and as Laura waits for Anne Catherick, as Marian risks her life to eavesdrop on the Count and Sir Percival and as Walter tries to outpace Sir Percival on the trail of his forgery. Alfred Hitchcock, famously the "master of suspense" in film, insists that suspense works only when the audience is let in on a secret that is kept from the characters. "If the audience . . . have been told all the secrets that the characters do not know, they'll work like the devil for you because they know what fate is facing the poor actors. That is what is known as 'playing God.' That is suspense."[16] But the secrets that Collins withholds from Walter, Marian, and Laura are precisely the ones that he withholds from us, and there is no indication that this fact renders the text less suspenseful. Indeed, although contemporary critics typically condemned Collins for his "mechanical" obsession with plots and puzzles, they were almost universal in their praise for his skill at keeping readers fascinated: this novel "rouses your curiosity, it thrills your nerves," wrote the *Critic;* and the *Guardian* speculated that readers had "waited for every chapter with an intenser interest than has, perhaps, ever before given to periodical fiction."[17]

Keeping secrets from both readers and characters alike, Collins succeeded in producing a generalized experience of suspense both on and off the page. No one, except Mrs. Catherick and Sir Percival Glyde, knows that the Baronet has fraudulently claimed a legitimate identity until Walter discovers the truth. Even Count Fosco is kept in the dark. No one—character or reader—knows for sure from the outset whether Marian will be caught on the balcony, Laura restored to health and identity, Sir Percival's secret revealed, or Count Fosco defeated. In response to the wealth of information that is kept back, Collins's characters generate a whole spectrum of reactions, from a desperate desire to know the truth to complete indifference. And by making suspense not only an experience *of* the text but an experience *within* the text, Collins allows suspense to become the content as well as form of his narrative. That is to say, the characters in *The Woman in White* model a range of reactions to the very mysteries that also form the pleasurable middle of the narrative for the reader, and so invite us to reflect on what the suspense does, why it matters, and how one might best respond to the mysteries of the world.

Scientific Epistemology, Madness, and Desire

Walter and Marian, our two main detectives in the text, show how the experience of suspense prompts a desire for knowledge. They then model a set of methods for acquiring that hidden knowledge. The first, and most pervasive, has everything in common with science, as Walter and Marian actively produce hypotheses in response to the emergence of a mystery. When we first meet the mysterious Woman in White and overhear the men who are in hot pursuit of her, Walter offers competing guesses and speculations: "What had I done? Assisted the victim of the most horrible of all false imprisonments to escape; or cast loose on the wide world of London an unfortunate creature, whose actions it was my duty, and every man's duty, mercifully to control? I turned sick at heart when the question occurred to me" (55). Prevented from answering this question because he is in possession of no further knowledge than we are, Walter generates an insistent string of questions: "Had the forlorn creature come to any harm? . . . Where had she stopped the cab? What had become of her now? Had she been traced and captured by the men in the chaise?" (56). Walter's partial knowledge, here, generates an almost obsessive desire to know more, but it also prompts him to articulate a set of possible explanations for the missing truth.

Later, when they are working together, Walter and Marian make their guesses in concert and try to reason them through together. "'That is not an illiterate letter,'" says Marian in response to the anonymous missive warning Laura against marrying Sir Percival Glyde:

> "and at the same time, it is surely too incoherent to be the letter of an educated person in the higher ranks of life. The reference to the bridal dress and veil, and some other little expressions, seem to point to it as the production of some woman. What do you think, Mr. Hartright?"
>
> "I think so too. It seems to me to be not only the letter of a woman, but of a woman whose mind must be—"
>
> "Deranged?" suggested Miss Halcombe. "I thought so too." (104)

Conferring and converging, Walter and Marian form a community of readers who, when confronted with a secret, construct hypotheses which they try to "reconcile with reasonable probability" (447). They then wait for answers, and it turns out, in the end, that these two are more often right than wrong.

Suspense fiction seems entirely in harmony with scientific knowledge here—involving the recognition of one's ignorance, the making of reasonable guesses, and then a willingness to pause for the truth to emerge. And yet, Walter's responses to secrets in the text sometimes seem to have more in common with madness than with reason. He admits to "inexplicable," "unreasonable," and "unaccountable perversity" in his reluctance to go to Limmeridge House for the first time (43–45). On the night when he rescues Anne from her pursuers, his "disturbed state of . . . mind" is what produces his insistent questions about her; and much later, he confesses that his "old superstition" about the Woman in White's importance still "clings" to him, well after her death (471). Similarly, Marian cannot account for her persistent hesitation about Sir Percival's proposal. Unable to provide evidence, she claims to have been the victim of "a fancy": "Don't attach any weight to my hesitation," she says to Mr. Gilmore, the family lawyer, "I can give no better reason for it than that I have been over-anxious about Laura lately" (158–59). Unreasonable though the presumption is, Marian is vindicated quite soon after. Similarly, Walter wonders if his early forebodings about Sir Percival Glyde are downright crazy, though he will soon be proved right:

> Judging by the ordinary rules of evidence, I had not the shadow of a reason, thus far, for connecting Sir Percival Glyde with the suspicious words of inquiry that had been spoken to me by the woman in white. And yet, I did connect him with them. Was it because he had now become associated in my mind with Miss Fairlie, Miss Fairlie being, in her turn, associated with Anne Catherick, since the night when I had discovered the ominous likeness between them? Had the events of the morning so unnerved me already that I was at the mercy of any delusion which common chances and common coincidences might suggest to my imagination? (101)

Caught up in his own metonymic logic, Walter's guesses here are informed by a complex of entirely unreasonable factors: his desire for Laura, a strange coincidence, and his own "unnerved" temper. Walter's guesses and Marian's hesitations suddenly look less like scientific rationality than like desperate longings, mad imaginings, and sheer superstition.

Intriguingly, this tendency to madness makes Marian and Walter no less successful in solving mysteries. And indeed, according to Victorian philosophers of science, the act of hypothesizing was a little more like madness than one might expect. "The first impulses of the human mind, even when it makes experience its starting point, are fallacious and delusive," wrote Cambridge scientist and theologian William Whewell in 1857, but, he added, empirical knowledge is not possible without the impulses of the mind to direct us to possible truths, and so "the questioning temper, the busy suggestive mind is needed at every step."[18] Or, as Stanley Jevons put it, "there is no hypothesis so improbable or apparently inconceivable that it may not be rendered probable, or even approximately certain, by a sufficient number of concordances."[19] *In the moment of the hypothesis*, then, scientific knowledge depends as much on wild intuition and speculation as it does on reason. In Collins's novel as in Victorian scientific theory, the protagonists' guesswork is sometimes undisciplined, wild, and intuitive, but that does not make it any less productive. Curiously, scientific hypotheses and the speculations of sensation fiction share a certain unreason that is ultimately necessary to the accumulation of knowledge.

When it offers us mysteries, then, *The Woman in White* suggests a range of cognitive responses to the recognition of a secret, all of them productive:

hypotheses, conjectures, and speculations; superstitions, hunches, and desires. And Collins suggests, too, that epistemological pursuits may be fruitfully bound up with other powerful affective experiences, including desire. Marian is "aflame with curiosity" at the same time that she is driven by her wishes and anxieties for her sister. Walter is eager to guess Sir Percival's secret in part so that he can restore his beloved to her rightful social place, and he speculates that Sir Percival is bound up with the woman in white because he wants to take Laura for himself. There is no strict division between intellectual guesswork and passionate feeling. Indeed, I would argue that it is part of the power of Victorian suspense—both scientific and fictional—that it joins the rigorous demands of cognition to the intensity of longing. Without powerful desires, neither scientists nor readers would pursue the truth.[20] And so, in keeping with a certain unreason at the heart of Victorian experimental science, the text of *The Woman in White* makes evident that fastening thought to desire may be the very most productive response to suspenseful delays and withholdings. Walter and Marian model an active, speculative, desiring middle, where the anxious provocations of suspense teach us to question, guess, and speculate in our passionate pursuit of the truth.

Surprise and Convention

And yet, sometimes, the truth, when it does come out, is so surprising that it defeats all conjecture, both reasonable and unreasonable. Walter's pursuit of Sir Percival leads him to the truth, but once he finds it, he confesses that the solution "had never once occurred to my mind." Walter confesses to having made various guesses—"At one time I thought he might be Anne Catherick's father—at another time I thought he might have been Anne Catherick's husband," but in this case, he says, the truth "had been, from first to last, beyond the wildest reach of my imagination" (529–30). This is our first explicit inkling of Walter's earlier guesses about Sir Percival's secrets—both having to do with sexual indiscretions—and they are put to rest by a truth that surprises him into the recognition of a possibility too wild even for his imagination. His first conjectures have been conventional—reflecting bourgeois assumptions about the immoral life of aristocrats—but the truth has defied convention. Suspense has prepared us for the revelation of a secret—but not for the revelation of *this* secret. Or to put this another way, sometimes the solution to the mystery is so unexpected that it defies speculation and catches us entirely by surprise.[21]

Collins suggests, then, that although we may read on in the expectation of a resolution of some kind, the particular content of the narrative's resolutions might turn out to be probable or improbable, wholly conventional or entirely unexpected. Crucially, there would be no experience of radical uncertainty—no suspense at all—without a real recognition that events might actually turn out in a range of ways, including the possibility that the solution will be something that we have not even predicted. Walter therefore models for us the genuine *openness* of suspenseful outcomes: he has made some guesses about Sir Percival's secret, but all he has really known is that he does not know. Similarly, we readers might be absorbed in speculating about the future, in guessing the story's outcomes, but the solutions might well defeat our best hunches. Thus suspense teaches us, paradoxically enough, *to be ready to be surprised.*

If suspenseful withholdings train us to expect the unexpected, they have the potential to wreak havoc on the authority of convention. Marian tells Walter early on that "not a whisper" of suspicion attaches to Sir Percival Glyde, and she offers the following evidence: "He has fought successfully two contested elections, and has come out of the ordeal unscathed. A man who can do that, in England, is a man whose character is established" (107). But Sir Percival's character is precisely what is *not* established, and as the text proceeds to unravel that character, bit by bit, the conventional wisdom Marian trusts to here—that anyone who has won contested elections must have gone through the wringer—looks increasingly untrustworthy. Of course, Collins is having some fun here at the expense of the electoral process, but the lesson is a serious one: the suspenseful pause of the middle throws conventional wisdom into question.

Perhaps any convention can be turned, in the space of the middle, into a hypothesis to be questioned and tested. From Marian to Mr. Gilmore, a range of characters judge Sir Percival on the basis of his appearance, and find him perfectly satisfactory: regular features, a graceful manner, "bright brown eyes" and "ready, pliant conversational powers" (210) suggest that he is a perfect model of gentlemanliness. And yet, the fact that he is clearly withholding something—that he generates suspense—immediately suggests that appearances of gentlemanliness may deceive and conventional judgments about class fail in the face of the hidden truth. As it turns out, of course, the looks and manner of a gentleman prove nothing, and we are right to be wary of the most persuasive appearances of aristocratic bearing. By keeping us in suspense, the novel repeatedly hints that it might or might not end the way convention would have it. To put this another way, the flagrant withholding strategies of the narrative turn Marian's assertion of an established consensus into a guess, a hypothesis, such that it can no longer be taken on faith, and must be subjected to the test of experience like the wildest of speculations. And indeed, however the novel of suspense ends, it typically spends the middle encouraging readers to transform their faith in tradition and authority into curiosity, speculation, suspicion—that is, into political and social skepticism.

Some recent readers have claimed that there are no genuine surprises in a text such as this one.[22] The conventions of the genre promise a "happy" bourgeois ending, and we might presume that we all know, on some level, that Walter and Laura will be rewarded, the Count and Sir Percival bested. Setting aside for the moment the fact that the genre was itself new in 1860—and its conventions clearly up in the air—I want to suggest that Wilkie Collins actually stages the question of ideological assurance and skepticism within the text. That is, he offers us characters who think they know it all from the beginning—that there are no mysteries that can be kept from them.

For example, Mr. Gilmore has been playing a game of écarté with Marian when Laura uncharacteristically strikes a false note on the piano, and Marian hastily gives up the game. Walter, Marian, and the reader know that Marian is concerned about Laura, who, in turn, is disturbed by Walter's imminent departure and her own impending engagement to another man, but Mr. Gilmore interprets Marian's "abrupt change in the card-table arrangements to a lady's inability to play the losing game" (146). In a novel that throws gender orthodoxies routinely into question, Mr. Gilmore trusts to conventional ideas about women that in this instance we know to be wrong. And he is one of the characters in the text who is typically untroubled by questions and anxieties, proudly conservative in his political and social attitudes. Indeed, he is determined to "promote the interests of Sir Percival Glyde," "a gentleman, every inch of him" (169).[23]

Contemporary critics who dismiss suspenseful narratives as necessarily conservative are, perhaps surprisingly, a little like the staid Mr. Gilmore. We refuse to unsettle our presumptions and thereby miss the surprising truths that are right under our noses. For example, when we knowing critics presume that we know how a novel such as this one must end—especially if we have read it before— we put ourselves beyond the reach of both surprise and suspense. But I want to suggest that the doubts disseminated by suspense might work to throw even our own views about novelistic ideology into doubt. Let us take a famous example from *The Woman in White*. Marian and Laura are shocked by Count Fosco's assertion that crimes committed by wise murderers usually go undetected, but we may think that we know—given the conventions of the Victorian novel—that he will not be able to get away with his misdeeds. Laura protests on the basis of the moral precepts she has been taught: "I have always heard that truly wise men are truly good men, and have a horror of crime" (254). And it is true that Laura will be proved right in her own particular case. But the ending, it seems to me, matters much less than we might think.

Consider Count Fosco's account of endings in terms of statistical probabilities:

> "Crimes cause their own detection, do they? And murder will out (another epigram), will it? Ask coroners who sit at inquests in large towns if that is true, Lady Glyde. Ask secretaries of life-assurance companies if that is true, Miss Halcombe. Read your own public journals. In the few cases that get into the newspapers, are there not instances of slain bodies found, and no murderers ever discovered? Multiply the cases that are reported by the cases that are *not* reported, and the bodies that are found by the bodies that are *not* found, and what conclusion do you come to? This. That there are foolish criminals who are discovered, and wise criminals who escape. . . . When the criminal is a brutal, ignorant fool, the police in nine cases out of ten win. When the criminal is a resolute, educated, highly-intelligent man, the police in nine cases out of ten lose. If the police win, you generally hear all about it. If the police lose, you generally hear nothing." (255–56)

Count Fosco's probabilistic reasoning generates a chain of striking effects. First, he produces a set of generalizations to counter Laura's and thus sets up two ways of thinking about the world: one moral, the other empirical. And he appeals to readers to cast off moralizing orthodoxies in favor of an empirical model that might, if we allowed it to, throw any entrenched moral precepts into doubt. Second, in depending on an empirical model general enough to reach beyond the boundaries of this particular text, the Count implies that the clever criminal's ultimate escape is always entirely plausible, even when it does not come to pass in some particular case. On the one hand, this gesture clearly invites us to imagine that it is perfectly possible that he might himself escape, thereby generating a suspense that will haunt the novel right up to the spectacle of his dead body at the morgue; but it is also important to note that this suspense may actually operate beyond the limits of this plot, since even when it kills the Count, the novel's appeal to statistics compels us to recognize that other clever criminals may yet escape, in other fictions and, more frighteningly, in our own world. Finally, the Count's argument suggests that the novel is more beholden to probability than to morality as the test of truth, and this has both narrative and political consequences, since the question of probability necessarily entails a skepticism about *any* single ending. That is, even when the narrative reaffirms conventional morality in the end, the Count's whole mode of probabilistic reasoning suggests that it is only one ending among many—that it just happens to be the tenth case out of ten, in which the wise criminal loses, rather than the only natural and inevitable ending that fits the evidence of the text.

We might object here, of course, like Laura and Marian, that the Count's amoral mode of reasoning is simply the wrong way to live in the world, and that the novel puts his way of thinking to rest along with his dead body. But the novel's own use of suspense brings it significantly closer to Count Fosco's empiricism than to Laura's moralistic copy-books. Indeed, we could read Count Fosco's arguments as brilliant defamiliarizations of the suspense of the middle: I have suggested that suspense works by keeping us in doubt about how things will turn out, and so it always depends on our sense that there is more than one plausible outcome to the narrative. But here the novel specifically sets the doubts of suspense against the assurances of convention to suggest that suspense invites not only a generalized skepticism but a certain kind of probabilistic reasoning. When we feel the doubts and anxieties of information withheld, we may know that some outcomes are highly probable, but we must also face the fact that more exceptional eventualities also have a chance—however slim—of prevailing in any particular case. In the moment of suspense, when the question is still up in the air, we must linger in the recognition of our own ignorance. And even after the fact—even after we have found out the ending for sure—probabilistic reasoning implies that this particular conclusion was not the only natural and necessary one: perhaps this was just the tenth case out of ten. And so suspense, whether it reaffirms or upends conventional wisdom in the end, teaches us along the way that even the most likely, most predictable outcomes always compete with more startling, more improbable ones. And they do so both within the text and without, where the evidence of the social world, judged on empirical grounds, is also busily upsetting traditional moral expectations. Paradoxically, then, we might say that sensation fiction is at its most realistic when it produces its most startling coincidences and strange, unconventional conclusions.

If critics assume from the outset that suspenseful fictions only generate anxiety for naïve readers, and that that anxiety is only there to be put to rest with ideologically reassuring closures, we prevent ourselves from noticing the radical work of Victorian suspense. By refusing the serenity of untroubled orthodoxy *and* any settled sense of necessity or inevitability, Collins hints that suspenseful withholdings always and necessarily call the likelihood of conventional happy endings into question.

Ethics

When Hitchcock argued that readers' consciousness must be set in contrast to characters' ignorance, he presumed that our helplessness in the face of our knowledge was what generated the intensity of suspense. But Collins made quite sure that the characters who were most sympathetic would be those who most closely shared the readerly experience of suspense. Think of Marian, combing the evidence for clues; or Walter in hot pursuit of Sir Percival's secret. But perhaps no novelist has to work to make suspense a sympathetic enterprise: perhaps the characters who throw themselves eagerly into the doubting, questioning experience of suspense are just the ones we readers tend to like the best.

Many scholars have recorded the remarkable fact that numerous readers wrote to Collins to ask for Marian's real name so that they could propose marriage, and critics of *The Woman in White* have certainly noted that the childlike, trusting Laura seems much the less appealing character than her sister. It is my contention that it is in part their affective responses to suspenseful withholdings that makes the difference. Marian warns Walter not to speak of the mystery of Anne Catherick to Frederick Fairlie or to Laura:

> "They are both of them, I am certain, quite as ignorant of who the woman is, and of what her past history in connection with us can be, as I am myself. But they are also, in widely different ways, rather nervous and sensitive; and you would only fidget one and alarm the other to no purpose. As for myself, I am all aflame with curiosity." (63)

Marian is right that her sister is given to alarm. Laura pleads to be put out of "the misery of suspense," and then again, a couple of pages later, to end the "dreadful suspense" of not knowing (407, 409). Early on, Walter suggests that she is incapable of serious doubt. When he asks her why he should not pay her compliments, she says, "Because I shall believe all you say to me" (78). "In those few words," Walter explains, "she unconsciously gave me the key to her whole character: to that generous trust of others which, in her nature, grew innocently out of the sense of her own truth" (78). What Walter here calls innocence and generous trust we might rather call downright foolishness. Laura trusts her father's choice of husband for her, she says, "because I had always found him the truest of all advisors, the best and fondest of all protectors and friends. . . . I believe at this moment, as truly as I have ever believed, that he knew what was best, and that his hopes and wishes should be my hopes and wishes too" (190). Simply believing that her father "knew what was best," she submits to his wishes without question. And yet we later learn from Marian that this same father had been "the spoilt darling of society, especially of the women—an easy, light, affectionate man, generous to a fault—constitutionally lax in his principles, and notoriously thoughtless of moral obligations where women were concerned" (574). Marian's description of Philip Fairlie functions for Walter as evidence that he must have been capable of fathering an illegitimate child with the unappealing Mrs. Catherick, but Laura never hears or entertains a doubt about her father's integrity. The "key" to Laura's "whole character," then, is her credulity, her trusting refusal to ask questions.

If Marian's flaming curiosity forms part of her appeal, the Fairlies as a clan are singularly unappealing as characters. Thoughtless when it comes to his daughter, clearly, Philip Fairlie shares with the other members of his generation—his brother Frederick and his sister, the sinister Countess Fosco—an almost criminal neglect of Laura's interests. If the novel's four Fairlies lack a strong family resemblance in most respects, they do have one thing in common: they all share an antipathy to the questioning attitude provoked by suspense. And what I want to suggest is that it is this very lack that makes all four characters unsympathetic. Because suspense, Collins implies, is not only an epistemologically and politically unsettling posture; it is also a deeply ethical one.

It is an understatement to say that Frederick Fairlie has exceptionally little curiosity about others. His refusal to take any interest in the details of Laura's marriage settlement are an obvious indication of his indifference, since even the placid Mr. Gilmore is intrigued and disturbed by Sir Percival's unreasonable demands on Laura's estate and warns Mr. Fairlie of the danger to his niece in no uncertain terms (183). Mr. Fairlie shares the attitude of hard indifference with another of the novel's least attractive characters: Mrs. Catherick. The latter tells Walter: "You are interested in my affairs. I am not interested in yours" (506). And these are the characters who take least responsibility for the welfare of those under their guardianship. All of this is clear enough, but what is important, I think, for the novel of suspense, is that care for others—ethics—requires a willingness to consider the ways that events will play out in the future. When Laura seeks refuge with her uncle, he says, "I am not answerable for a deplorable calamity, which it was quite impossible to foresee" (378). He is entirely wrong, of course: not only could he have predicted the trouble, he was in fact explicitly *warned* that it might follow. Thus his refusal to make conjectures about the future is not only a failure to be curious, it is a failure to recognize his own participation in Laura's fate. It is the consummate failure of guardianship.

Suspense, in this context, takes on an altogether new dimension. We have seen that suspenseful reading entails a willingness to hold one's judgment in doubt as events unfold, but here it has a more affirmative side too: the reader who approaches the world in suspense is one who not only waits but also *looks forward,* one who cares about and anticipates the future; this is the reader who might know that she does not know the future but nonetheless tries to predict the ways that events will unfold. Or, to put this another way: a speculation about outcomes is a hallmark of the middle of suspenseful plots, but it is just as much a hallmark of the subject who wants to take responsibility for a foreseeable succession of events.

It is no surprise, then, that one of Marian's distinctive characteristics is her interest in looking forward. It is certainly one of the most important elements of Count Fosco's admiration for her: "'Can you look at Miss Halcombe and not see that she has the foresight and resolution of a man? With that woman for my friend I would snap these fingers of mine at the world'" (346). Foresight does not mean perfect foreknowledge, since for much of the narrative Marian is as ignorant as we are of the secrets of the text. But care for others, in this novel, does mean a vigilant attempt to avert the dangers that might be waiting for them. Marian thus tries to anticipate, "calculate," and prevent all risks to Laura (323). Intent on foreseeing the future as well as she can, she joins her fiery curiosity with a ferocious care for her half-sister's fate in a way that sets up a marked contrast to Countess Fosco's icy composure and indifference, Mr. Fairlie's refusal to take responsibility, and Laura's own naïve credulity. Unlike the impassive Fairlies, then, Marian's flaming inquisitiveness, coupled with her care for the welfare of those she guards, makes her an ideal ethico-suspenseful subject—and the novel's most attractive character.

Erotics

If suspense teaches us to pause and doubt our best guesses, to overturn our deepest convictions, and to try to take responsibility for the future, it begins to sound like something of a dour enterprise. But we began with the critical consensus that suspense is so closely associated with *pleasure* that it must serve the crassest market-driven interests. So what, precisely, is the pleasure that the suspense of the middle affords its readers? How does it hold us in its grip, keep us on the edge of our seats, refuse to let us sleep—while at the same time teaching us the most serious of epistemological, political, and ethical lessons?

At various points in *The Woman in White*, Collins suggests that the curiosity incited by suspenseful narratives might provoke the same pleasurable feeling as an erotic pursuit, a seduction. Mrs. Catherick puts curiosity and sexual seduction together after she hears of Sir Percival Glyde's death and writes to Walter to thank him:

"How can I pay my debt? If I was a young woman still I might say, 'Come, put your arm around my waist and kiss me, if you like.' I should have been fond enough of you even to go to that length, and you would have accepted my invitation—you would, sir, twenty years ago! But I am an old woman now. Well! I can satisfy your curiosity." (548)

In place of sexual gratification, Mrs. Catherick offers the satisfaction of Walter's interest in her part of the mystery—and ours. It is not hard to see how the erotic and the epistemological might substitute for one another, narratively speaking: the slow unfolding of a mystery, as the text hints at what is to come only to hold back the full disclosure, suggests the same pattern as a seductive striptease.[24]

Lisa Sternlieb points out that there is actually a literal striptease in the novel. Surprisingly, perhaps, this seductive display is not the work of one of the morally suspicious characters in the novel. It is Marian who strips for Walter. In a canny close reading of the text, Sternlieb points out that "neither the reader nor Hartright has access to Marian's diary," since we are told that Marian prefers to read the relevant sections aloud to Walter rather than allowing him to read the primary documents himself. As a result, Marian's "diary," spoken in the intimacy of "three late-night tête-à-têtes," as the childlike Laura sleeps nearby, can be read as a seduction of Walter.[25] For Sternlieb, the culmination comes in "Marian's greatest scene," her risky eavesdropping on the Count and Sir Percival from the balcony, which many critics have read as her attempt to masculinize herself. But Sternlieb notes that the scene "begins by Marian taking off her silk gown and next removing the white and cumbersome parts of her underclothing," in order, perhaps, "to draw Walter into the scene and excite his curiosity about how she has undressed in order to go to work."[26] He does tell us that she intends to be her own editor: "There were passages in the diary relating to myself which she thought it best that I should not see" (456), he says, tantalizing us with the suggestion that Marian has secrets about her responses to Walter that we—and he—*never* hear. But if Marian can be read as calculating and purposeful when it comes to what she tells and what she withholds, we might expect, in the interests of ordinary Victorian propriety, that she certainly *ought* to have excised the details of her undressing. And yet Collins has his heroine deliberately decide to keep her striptease in. Marian, then, brings together not only her own curiosity, her speculative attention, and her ethical care for the future, but also a crafty sense of the erotic pleasure of the chase, the seduction, the slow undressing that is like the unfolding of a narrative mystery.

That readers were so taken with Marian that they longed to propose to her suggests that Collins succeeded in enchaining their interests not only in her story, but in her person, and perhaps specifically in her body.[27] Collins's famous introduction of Marian as a character is itself remarkably like a striptease. Walter draws out his narration of their first encounter, beginning with a slow description of her appearance from the back:

> The instant my eyes rested on her, I was struck by the rare beauty of her form, and by the unaffected grace of her attitude. Her figure was tall, yet not too tall; comely and well-developed, yet not fat; her head set on her shoulders with an easy, pliant firmness; her waist, perfection in the eyes of a man, for it occupied its natural place, it filled out its natural circle, it was visibly and delightfully undeformed by stays. She had not heard my entrance into the room; and I allowed myself the luxury of admiring her for a few moments, before I moved one of the chairs near me, as the least embarrassing means of attracting her attention. She turned towards me immediately. The easy elegance of every movement of her limbs and body as soon as she began to advance from the far end of the room, set me in a flutter of expectation to see her face clearly. She left the window—and I said to myself, The lady is dark. She moved forward a few steps—and I said to myself, The lady is young. She approached nearer—and I said to myself (with a sense of surprise which words fail me to express), The lady is ugly! (58)

The beginning of this description presumably sets the reader up to expect that Marian will be the object of Walter's love. The narrative introduces a tall, graceful, and provocatively pliant feminine body—and even suggests a look under her clothing: Walter sees her sexy curves "undeformed by stays." His own feelings might best be described as suspense. In a "flutter of expectation," he longs to see her face. But then, in order to produce the same sensations in the reader, Walter generates suspense for *us:* he deliberately prolongs his description, adding to it only slowly, so that we become aware that we are waiting for something that is temporarily withheld. And of course, it turns out that we ought to be ready to be surprised. The truth, when it emerges, unsettles not only novelistic conventions but epistemological ones. As Walter puts it: "Never was the old conventional maxim, that Nature cannot err, more flatly contradicted" (58). The suspense of Marian's unveiling, then, overturns not only our expectation that we are about to meet the marriageable heroine, but a long philosophical tradition that puts its faith in nature's harmonious and perfect design. Indeed, by invoking an ill-designed nature, Collins seems just a little bit willing to cast some doubts on God himself.

In this startling early scene, then, the novelist brings together the many strands of suspense which he will weave through *The Woman in White*. He inserts an unmistakable withholding, so that we must become aware of our ignorance. He sets up conventional expectations, but then suspends them, only to spring a surprising—but entirely plausible—outcome on us. That outcome unsettles convention and thus teaches us to be on our guard for the further disturbances suspense can offer. By having us repeat Walter's experience of suspense, Collins also invites us to share the experiences of those characters who desire, predict, and hypothesize. And finally, he takes the doubting, speculative, hopeful, politically unsettling, ethical, and sympathetic experience of suspense and binds it tightly to the slow and delicious pleasures of sexual seduction.

Notes

1. A footnote to chapter twelve, for example, reads: "*Grace Poole's laugh:* It is often observed that this renewed allusion to the imprisoned Bertha comes immediately after a protest against the 'rigid . . . restraint,' 'stagnation,' etc. of ordinary women." Charlotte Brontë, *Jane Eyre*, ed. Michael Mason (Harmondsworth: Penguin, 1996), 513.

2. Arnold, though he enjoyed reading novels, wrote contemptuously of them in general, calling them "the least profitable sort of books" and claiming that "Of the contemporary rubbish which is shot so plentifully all round us, we can, indeed, hardly read too little." See *The Complete Prose Works of Matthew Arnold IX*, ed. R. H. Super (Ann Arbor: University of Michigan Press, 1973), 125–26, 273–74; and Christopher Ricks, "Matthew Arnold and the Novel," *Salmagundi* 132 (2001): 76–95. Douglas Kellner writes critically of the Frankfurt School's tendency to dismiss all consumer pleasures: "On this view *all* commodities are *uniformly* seductive instruments of capitalist manipulation, which engineer homogeneous false needs and consciousness. . . . Commodity fetishism and false needs, then, supposedly enchain willing consumers into the institutions, practices and values of consumer capitalism." *Jean Baudrillard: From Marxism to Postmodernism and Beyond* (Cambridge: Polity Press), 158–59. Emphasis in original.

3. In *S/Z* and *The Pleasure of the Text*, Barthes argues that the "readerly text" provides ideological comforts, offering an "organized set of stoppages" en route to conclusions that provide resolutions to social contradictions. Suspenseful strategies organize "the text that comes from culture and does not break with it"; they are "linked to a *comfortable* practice of reading." Barthes, *S/Z*, trans. Richard Miller (New York: Hill and Wang, 1974), 76; *Pleasure of the Text*, trans. Richard Miller (New York: Hill and Wange, 1975), 14. Foucauldian critics, too, have come to similar conclusions. In Ronald R. Thomas's account of detective fiction, for example, "detective stories help to provide reassurances . . . by continually reinventing fictions of national and individual identity to respond to rather specific historical anxieties" (6). *Detective Fiction and the Rise of Forensic Science* (Cambridge and New York: Cambridge University Press, 2001).

4. Theodor Adorno and Max Horkheimer, "The Culture Industry: Enlightenment as Mass Deception," in *Dialectic of Enlightenment* (London: Verso, 1979), 120–67; 144.

5. Eve Kosofsky Sedgwick has made the case that literary and cultural studies have been driven by a "paranoid imperative," "mainly organized around anticipating, identifying, and

warding off the negative affect of humiliation." The consequences of this paranoid style of reading, she argues, are that "reparative" readings have become "inadmissible" because they "are about pleasure ('merely aesthetic') and because they are frankly ameliorative ('merely reformist')." She claims that it is time for a recuperation of reading for pleasure within academia. What is odd about suspense, I would argue, is that it is *both* paranoid *and* reparatively pleasurable. See Sedgwick's "Paranoid Reading and Reparative Reading, or You're So Paranoid You Probably Think this Introduction Is About You," in *Novel Gazing: Queer Readings in Fiction* (Durham and London: Duke University Press, 1997), 1–37; 23–24, 22.

6. Deborah Knight and George McKnight, "Suspense and Its Master," *Hitchcock: Centenary Essays,* ed. Richard Allen and Sam Gonzales (London: British Film Institute Publications, 1999), 108.

7. See, for example, the idea of "narratability" in D. A. Miller, *Narrative and Its Discontents: Problems of Closure in the Traditional Novel* (Princeton: Princeton University Press, 1981).

8. Elizabeth Deeds Ermarth writes that the codes of suspense are "evident in almost all Victorian novels . . . from the superlative achievements of Charles Dickens and George Eliot to the lesser ones of Charles Reade, Wilkie Collins, and Conan Doyle." *English Novel in History* (London and New York: Routledge, 1996), 2.

9. Knight and McKnight, "Suspense and Its Master," 108.

10. Hans J. Wulff, "Suspense and the Influence of Cataphora on Viewers' Expectations," in *Suspense: Conceptualizations, Theoretical Analyses, and Empirical Explorations,* ed. Peter Vorderer, Hans Jürgen Wulff, and Mike Friedrichsen (Mahwah, NJ: Lawrence Erlbaum, 1996), 1–17.

11. Unsigned review, "*The Woman in White,*" *The Times,* October 30, 1860, 6.

12. Caroline Levine, *The Serious Pleasures of Suspense: Victorian Realism and Narrative Doubt* (Charlottesville and London: University of Virginia Press, 2003).

13. W. Stanley Jevons, *The Principles of Science: A Treatise on Logic and Scientific Method* (1873; London and New York: Macmillan, 1877), 404.

14. Quoted in Stanley Jevons, *The Principles of Science,* 591.

15. Quoted in Clyde de L. Ryals, *A World of Possibilities: Romantic Irony in Victorian Literature* (Columbus: The Ohio State University Press, 1990), 2–3.

16. Alfred Hitchcock and Stanley Gottlieb, *Hitchcock on Hitchcock* (Berkeley, Los Angeles, and London: University of California Press, 1997), 113. Deborah Knight and George McKnight observe that suspense is "not, in fact, an experience available for God," and so they gloss Hitchcock's claim this way: "The sort of relationship suspense requires is one in which spectators observe the fictional events from a position not identical to that of any of the characters" ("Suspense and Its Master," 109).

17. Unsigned review, *Critic,* August 25, 1860, 233–34; unsigned review, *Guardian,* August 19, 1860, 780–81.

18. [William Whewell], "Spedding's Complete Edition of the Works of Bacon," *Edinburgh Review* 106 (October 1857): 289–322; 303–4, 314.

19. Jevons, *Principles of Science,* 514.

20. See Levine, *Serious Pleasures.*

21. Since Alfred Hitchcock, narrative theorists have been inclined to distinguish between surprise and suspense. Surprises, Hitchcock maintained, hit us as if from out of the blue, without augury or premonition, whereas suspense happens when we know that something is going to happen. "Terror is induced by surprise," he argued, "suspense, by forewarning." François Truffaut, *Hitchcock,* trans. Helen G. Scott (New York: Simon and Schuster, 1983), 73. Meir Sternberg, similarly, distinguishes between suspense, "hinging on the reader's early awareness

of informational gaps," and surprise, "hinging on a more or less imperceptible suppression of temporally anterior material and then a sudden retrospective illumination of what has gone before." Sternberg is particularly interested in the ways that surprise and suspense have a different relationship to temporal ordering: suspense early on suggests withheld knowledge that then emerges later; surprise emerges suddenly, and throws light on an earlier moment. But Sternberg also makes clear that some narratives, including Jane Austen's *Emma,* combine suspense with surprise, as I would argue Collins does. See Sternberg's *Expositional Modes and Temporal Ordering in Fiction* (Bloomington: Indiana University Press, 1993), 157.

22. D. A. Miller, *The Novel and the Police* (Berkeley: University of California Press, 1988).

23. When Frederick Fairlie accuses him of holding radical sentiments, he protests: "A Radical!!! I could put up with a good deal of provocation, but, after holding the soundest Conservative principles all my life, I could *not* put up with being called a Radical. My blood boiled at it—I started out of my chair—I was speechless with indignation" (182). The irony is that Gilmore has been pleading with Fairlie on relatively radical grounds: against his better judgment, he has begun to suspect the gentlemanly Sir Percival, whom he has claimed to trust on the grounds of his aristocratic mien, and he has begun to believe the strangely hesitant Marian and the despairing Laura, whom he has wanted to dismiss on the grounds of their flighty femininity. The solid foundations of class and gender distinction have started to look remarkably unstable.

24. In *The Pleasure of the Text,* Barthes carefully distinguished his "pleasure of the text" from "the pleasure of the corporeal striptease or of narrative suspense" (10). But it is also true that by setting these lesser pleasures apart from the one he was most interested in, he also brought them together.

25. Lisa Sternlieb, *The Female Narrator in the British Novel: Hidden Agendas* (Houndmills and New York: Palgrave, 2000), 58.

26. Sternlieb, *The Female Narrator,* 68.

27. As Collins wrote in the preface to the French edition: "*Miss Halcombe, en particulier, fut tellement prise en faveur qu'on me mit en demeure,—ceci plus d'une fois,—de déclarer si ce caractère était peint d'après nature; le cas échéant, on voulait savoir si le modèle vivant d'après lequel j'avais travaillé, consentirait à écouter les sollicitations de différents célibataires qui, parfaitement convaincus d'avoir en elle une femme excellente, se proposaient de lui demander sa main!*" Preface to *La femme en blanc* (1861), trans. Emile Forgues (Paris: Hetzel, 1861), iv–v. "Miss Halcombe, in particular, was so well-liked that people forced me—more than once—to tell them if this character was painted from nature; they wanted to know if the living model would agree to hear the appeals of various single men who were so completely convinced of her excellence as a woman that they wanted to ask her for her hand!" (my translation).

NINE

The Latent Middle in Morris's *News from Nowhere*

MARIO ORTIZ-ROBLES

Unlike the classic utopias of the early modern period, the utopian narratives that flourished in late-Victorian England involve time travel rather than journeys through space. The narrative model inaugurated by More's *Utopia*—a traveler who discovers a previously unknown society that is both prosperous and peaceful and which comes to represent the ideal of social organization—gives way in the last three decades of the nineteenth century to a different form of narrative: the voyage now occurs through time and the "no place" visited is familiar, a "here" now transformed into an idealized version of itself. In these novels, time travel usually occurs in the direction of the future, but the future is curiously historical, riddled with the presence of enigmatic relics from an undetermined past, such as the White Sphinx in H. G. Wells's *The Time Machine* (1895), or marked in its representation of everyday life as a return to a simpler, pre-industrial way of life, as in the medieval pastoralism of William Morris's *News from Nowhere* (1890). At once future-oriented and thoroughly historical, nineteenth-century utopian fiction can thus be said to occur in a fictional "no time" in which the "now" of traditional realist representation becomes unmoored from its programmatic presentism.

This state of affairs results in a curious narrative paradox. On the one hand, the middle of the narrative is suspended between a fully realized future (utopia proper) and a doomed or unpromising present for which the future seems to exist beyond its own capacity to think or imagine it; that is, there is no middle. On the other, the structural suspension of the middle accounts for a characteristic feature of the genre: long expository passages that describe the functioning of the new or evolved society and provide, in retrospect, a historical account of how it came to pass; that is, there is nothing but middle. The suspension of the middle could lead us into a world of pure fantasy in which time would cease to be relational and the temporal division into past, present, and future would no longer obtain. Or indeed it could lead us to its obverse: a thickly described preterite governed by the sequential, expository logic of historical writing in which the past is ever expandable *as* past. Yet, in the case of late-Victorian utopian fiction (LVU), the latency of the middle gives rise to formal patterns and rhetorical effects that lend the genre a promissory quality we tend to associate less with fiction than with political discourse and which had up to this point been all but absent in post-Romantic literature.

From the perspective of literary form, the latency of the middle accounts for the peculiar amorphousness of the genre. To begin with, LVU consists of a travel narrative in which traveling does not organize the story. Unlike works belonging to the Bakhtinian chronotope of the road (Chaucer's *Canterbury Tales,* Cervantes' *Don Quijote,* Smollett's *Humphry Clinker,* all belong to this series), LVU takes for granted the displacement of the protagonist and uses his destination, rather than the incidents experienced along the way, as the narrative node of the story. This is true of classic utopian narratives, but, as Swift's *Gulliver's Travels* so amply illustrates, traveling remains the guiding structural conceit making possible the protagonist's chance encounters with previously unknown societies. The time of time travel in LVU is itself compressed or entirely elided in a before-and-after structure more reminiscent of dream or dreamlike states than of physical displacements. The plot of LVU, moreover, generates no suspense since it is unmotivated, at least internally, by desire.[1] Insofar as it is perceived to have already been fulfilled in the event of utopia proper (the happy ending to end all happy endings), desire is replaced for the protagonist by a sense of enchantment or wonderment that raises expectations about his own society but is experienced as a plentitude arrived at rather than pursued. If LVU lacks the disorienting anxiety and tingling sensations created by suspense when it occurs in a story whose ending is unknown, it also exists in a permanent state of suspension in which no doubt, no enigma, no mystery remains to be solved in a utopian space that, by definition, need not, or need no longer, look forward to a better future. The character system, too, is curiously barren in LVU given that the time traveler always travels alone and neither acts nor is acted upon by those he encounters. The characters he does encounter, moreover, are representative by design and tell us more about their society than about themselves as individuals. Indeed, as a passive witness to a new way of life that he strives to describe but in which he cannot readily participate, the time traveler in LVU engages in none of the transformative logic on which the biographical narratives so common to the nineteenth century are premised and which the *Bildungsroman* so aptly illustrates. The travel narrative in LVU treats or exposes the transformation of place rather than of character, of the collective rather than of the individual, and therefore does not follow realism's traditional narrative logic of development in which the life of a youthful protagonist comes into focus only from the retrospective perspective of his or her mortality.[2] The juxtaposition of two distinct time periods elides the process whereby "this" became "that" and "then" becomes "now." In LVU, the destination of the time traveler, even though it is portrayed as a radically transformed version of the origin, is presented as a *fait accompli* rather than as the result of an ongoing process. The narrative form of LVU, in short, is defined by static states rather than by the events that would bring them about.[3]

On a rhetorical level, however, the same narrative reserve that undermines the architecture of the story becomes the condition of possibility of a properly utopian vision insofar as it creates a semantic vacuum that invites speculation on what should come to fill it. In an absent or suspended middle, form is divorced from its putative content, with the result that the unpromising present can no longer appeal to its narrative representation as a means of legitimating it (as in traditional realism) and the future presents itself only as pure or empty form, an abstract construct that is yet to be invested with referential attributes: objects, affect, identifications, institutions, expressiveness, and so forth. Indeed, the hard tendency toward referential density of what Fredric Jameson has usefully called "ontological realism" is suspended in LVU or, better, displaced proleptically as something to be retrofitted into the real of a possible present.[4] To the extent that the absence of form is also a demand for form, the reticence of the middle thus becomes a precondition for reimagining society as something completely new, as something yet to be formed. Time travel situates utopia in the realm of the formally plausible since, by occupying the same geographical space—London in 1890 versus London in 2101, say— it calls for new content, which can only be constructed by evaluating existing social conditions and assessing historical alternatives. LVU can thus be said to gather in its narrative momentum the rhetorical conditions of possibility of the promise: the making of the promise and its fulfillment are separated by a time lag or period of latency during which nothing pertaining to the force of the promise made in fact happens. Similarly, narrative action in LVU is suspended between the present and a future to which it is connected only by virtue of its spatial continuity, a tenuous metonymic traversing the otherwise empty time lapse that separates two disparate moments of a historically sedimented geographical place. The narrative's discursive energies are thus directed towards shaping an image of the future as a reality far removed from an already inhabited present. The promise, a performative speech act that spans the middle, is ever open in LVU since the promise made by the imaginative representation of utopia is yet to be fulfilled from the perspective of the present, a fulfillment nevertheless towards which it makes us aspire by deliberately avoiding the false promise of narrative development. A pattern of expectation aptly captured in the title of William Morris's utopian novel: *News from Nowhere*.

That the future in LVU is as reassuringly uneventful as the narrative that shapes it—nothing actually *happens* in utopia—might well account for the genre's remarkable popularity.[5] Far from jeopardizing its success in the literary marketplace, LVU's unexceptional formal properties very possibly helped to guarantee it since the lack of narrative "middle" is also the absence or avoidance of historical change itself (understood as revolutionary violence). To travel into the future is to skip the time intervening between a present that needs to change and a future that represents an already changed reality but bears none of the marks of the transformative events that have led up to it. Edward Bellamy's *Looking Backward 2000–1887* (1888) is illustrative of such avoidance, proposing the peaceful transformation of nineteenth-century liberal capitalism into a popular twenty-first-century state monopoly that comes about "naturally" as industrial "evolution" leads to political consensus: "Public opinion had become fully ripe for [change], and the whole mass of the people was behind it."[6] LVU promises change, to be sure, but in the form of a future in which the sense of regularity in the everyday has been restored after the messy convulsions we tend to associate with revolutionary change have become a thing of the past or have been altogether avoided. Bourgeois terror of proletarianization is attenuated by staging change as rational choice, while change is itself assimilated into a structure of sameness more in keeping with an ethos of shared prosperity than with an ingrained belief in social equality. From the perspective of narrative dynamics, LVU thus makes a fitting end to a "serious century," to use Franco Moretti's suggestive diagnostic, in that it consists almost entirely of narrative "fillers" and points in the direction of an uneventful future filled with nothing but more "fillers."[7]

Expressed in this manner, the narrative paradox of LVU must be understood to provide imaginative solutions to the cultural anxieties and political aspirations of a society accustomed to a gradual pace of change that now found itself in the midst of transition. But the latency of the middle, as I shall argue in what follows, is more than the formal condition of possibility for imagining the future. The very shape of futurity is at stake in LVU, a genre that emerges at a historical crossroads in which the cultural assimilation of Marx and Darwin has radically transformed the subject's perception of time. The latency of the middle is thus the trace that makes visible the difference between the representation of time (narrative) and its allegorizations (mortality). I first trace a genealogy of late-Victorian notions of temporality, and, in the second part of the essay, I read Morris's *News from Nowhere* as an attempt to come to terms with this newfound sense of temporality by imagining the future as a belated recovery of the past. I end with a brief reflection on the "middleness" of LVU, which, like many of the other paraliterary genres that flourished in the last decades of the nineteenth century in England, belongs to what with hindsight can be described as a transitional narrative space that lies somewhere between a realism that is now perceived to be exhausted as a representational paradigm and the aesthetics of immanence we tend to associate with the as yet to be consecrated program of modernist representation.

The River of Time

Commentators of LVU have tended to focus on the economic and political conditions of England during the last three decades of the nineteenth century to account for its emergence. To be sure, the transformational events that gave this period an unmistakable sense of economic and social malaise[8]—the crisis of capitalism that came to be known as the Great Depression of 1873–96; the "scramble" for overseas territories on the part of Western European imperial powers; the political organization of the growing industrial labor force—gave imaginative writers the impetus to speculate on new forms of social organization. But, to the extent that capitalism, imperialism, and socialism were all international in scope, utopian speculation was now obliged to accommodate or be responsive to a new conception of the global. Indeed, the shift in fictional paradigms from a spatial to a temporal horizon of perfectibility at the turn of the nineteenth century corresponds at least in part to the considerable conceptual distance separating the early modern vision of the globe from its modern counterpart. The world from which early modern utopias emerged was still in the process of being charted and news of European explorations made the concept of utopia fathomable at its geographical limits. In contrast, the interconnectedness of the world at the end of the nineteenth century, achieved materially through an ever-expanding network of maritime routes, railroads, and telegraphic cables, had transformed a discourse of "discovery" into one of commerce and colonization.[9] What little of the globe remained unexplored and unmapped by Europeans at century's end had ceased to hold the promise of a heretofore undiscovered El Dorado, coming instead to be envisioned as an unfathomable Heart of Darkness where civilization, far from reaching perfection, would find its negative image. By the 1880s, the world, as Eric Hobsbawm succinctly puts it, "was now genuinely global."[10] Accordingly, the conception of an isolated utopia, indeed the conception of utopia as an island like the ones we find in More or in Francis Bacon's *New Atlantis* (1627), was no longer available as an imaginative possibility. When H. G. Wells calls for a planetary conception of utopia in *A Modern Utopia* (1905)—"No less than a planet will serve the purposes of a modern utopia"[11]—he is invoking the logic of interconnection that informed the different utopian visions that flourished during this period and for which his "World-State" serves as an appropriate speculative coda.

The globalization of the globe goes some way towards explaining why utopian thought at the end of the nineteenth century adopted a temporal narrative vehicle rather than a spatial one, but cannot fully account for the internal temporal dynamics of the genre. Why, for instance, should LVU be premised on a future vision of society that resembles the present only topographically, as in Edward Bellamy's *Looking Backward 2000–1887,* which takes place in a future Boston recognizable only by its harbor and the trace of the Charles? And what conditions the possibility of a narrative structure that deprives the middle of any recognizable semantic and cognitive referentiality? We must first briefly look at the cultural comprehension of time in late-nineteenth-century England in order to get a sense of how the Victorians might have understood time travel during a period in which time itself underwent a major conceptual realignment. Several political, technological, and social variables can be adduced to account for this realignment: the standardization of time with the adoption of Greenwich Mean Time in 1847 and its application in railway scheduling and maritime navigation; the acceleration of the pace of everyday life as urban living becomes the central cultural experience of the nation; the management of time in industrial production as a precursor to full-fledged Taylorism; the speeding-up of the means of communication with the reform of the General Post Office and the subsequent introduction of the Uniform Penny Post in 1840 and the GPO's monopolization of the telegraph after 1869; the implementation of political term limits as the pressures of democratization expand the electoral franchise and more and more citizens participate in a periodic ritual of cyclical political renewal; the future-oriented aspirations of a liberal culture geared towards progress, social mobility, and personal and professional improvement; the biopolitical recalibration of family size and generational turnover as birth-control practices, the prohibition of child labor, and improved rates of life expectancy bring the New Woman closer to the center of political and cultural life; the foreshortening of eternity and the foreclosure of the afterlife in an increasingly secular culture; serialization, mechanical reproduction, and iterative performative practices in the arts. The significance of each of these developments to a genealogical account of time in the late nineteenth century is considerable, but in order to understand the temporal horizon of LVU in particular we must consider two specific discursive formations whose influence among the imaginative writers who practiced it was determinant in bringing about their individual visions of utopia: Marxism and Darwinism.

It is in general well established that writers of LVU submitted the ideas of Marx and Darwin to the speculative pressure of social planning provided by More's narrative blueprint. The publication of Darwin's *The Descent of Man* in 1871 and the somewhat belated dissemination of *The Communist Manifesto* (1848) in English in the 1870s with a new preface by Marx and Engels coincided with the publication of Bulwer-Lytton's *The Coming Race* (1871) and Samuel Butler's *Erewhon* (1872), two of the texts most often cited in accounts of LVU for having been among the first to reinvent the utopian fictional paradigm in the nineteenth century.[12] The cultural assimilation of Marx and Darwin during the 1870s had in any case created the discursive conditions necessary for LVU to be intelligible both as a formal solution to contemporary social contradictions and, at the same time, as a generic logic in its own right given that both dialectical materialism and natural selection offered alternative narrative possibilities for imagining the world anew. Furthermore, the often explicit references to Marxian and Darwinian ideas that we find in LVU legitimated its utopian claims by providing an all-encompassing or indeed global theoretical framework for thinking about the future. Northrop Frye, in his analysis of utopia as a literary genre, remarks on its Marxian undergirding: "The nineteenth-century utopia had a close connection with the growth of socialist political thought and shared its tendency to think in global terms."[13] Socialism, as Engels conceived it, was "scientific" rather than "utopian," part of an all-encompassing historical process in which local, isolated manifestations of communal living, however perfect, could hamper or slow down the inevitable progress towards the global, properly scientific achievement of a classless society.[14] Darwin's theory of evolution was equally well suited to provide a conceptual framework for the global scope of the new utopian imagination in that natural selection is a law that is relevant to all living organisms and, whatever the merit of its social applications, still stands as an appealing mechanism for speculating on the malleability of human nature. A common *topos* of utopian fiction since More, the question of whether human nature is immutable or adaptable to political and moral exigencies becomes, after Darwin, a temporal rather than a categorical issue since change can now be understood to occur gradually and biologically, not abruptly and rationally. One must also include under this head Darwin's own story as a scientist who was uniquely positioned to formulate a theory of evolution after having traveled around the world aboard the *Beagle,* a story that had been popularized by the publication of his extraordinary travel journals in 1839. To the extent that his travel journals offer a description of the world as a vast laboratory, the cultural imaginary could hold Darwin's theory of evolution as a global phenomenon both by the manner in which it was formulated as well as by its promise of universal applicability. Little, however, has been made of the temporal implications of these theories to the conceptualization of time that informs LVU even as it is commonly acknowledged that many of its practitioners were keen readers of Marx and Darwin.

Of the two discursive formations, Marxism clearly offers the most immediately accessible temporal framework for utopian fiction, not least because it offers a theory of history that can be readily extrapolated into the future. If it is true, as Louis Althusser famously claimed, that Marx opened the "Continent of History" to scientific inquiry,[15] it is also true that historical materialism, the theory that he and Engels discovered in this continent, becomes the philosophical formalization of a complex recalibration of time. The first thing to point out in this regard is that in Marxism there is no historical time as such, only specific structures of historicity that are determined, in the last instance, by the different modes of production on which social formations are based. The Hegelian idea of history as a purposeful continuity of time subject to a sequence of presents is rejected in favor of a theory of history in which a number of different levels (economic, political, legal, ideological, etc.) coexist, each with its own historical structure, particular time, and mode of production. These levels are relatively autonomous, each following its own temporal rhythms (punctuated by development, revolutions, breaks, and so on) and articulated relative to the whole, a whole whose temporal structure cannot be read in the continuity of life or on the face of a clock, but must rather be constructed conceptually out of specific structures of production. Indeed, the history of society can be described as a discontinuous succession of modes of production. In *The Communist Manifesto,* in which we already find the mature formulation of their materialist conception of history, Marx and Engels describe historical change in these terms: "Does it require deep intuition to comprehend that man's ideas, views, and conceptions, in one word, man's consciousness, changes with every change in the conditions of his material existence, in his social relations and in his social life?"[16] Time, in this scheme, is multiplied, differentiated, complicated; in short, historicized.

Long-standing debates within Marxism on the question of whether historical materialism is teleological or not tend to obscure the degree to which it offers a law of historical development that transforms traditional conceptualizations of causality and temporal sequence. At any given historical conjuncture, several times or temporalities coexist, but we can talk of uneven development, backwardness, or the survival of archaic forms only as a differential articulation, not by reference to a particular temporal baseline against which to measure relative progress. Rather than a concatenation of events brought about by historical agents, history in Marx becomes a dialectical process propelled by class struggles based upon economic interest (upon "the antagonism of oppressing and oppressed classes," as the *Manifesto* puts it) whose internal contradictions will lead inexorably to the collapse of the dominant mode of production. In the case of the capitalist mode of production, the bourgeoisie unwittingly provides the proletariat with the very conditions for its own emancipation. "The advance of industry, whose involuntary promoter is the bourgeoisie, replaces the isolation of the labourers, due to competition, by their revolutionary combination, due to association. The development of modern industry, therefore, cuts from under its feet the very foundation on which the bourgeoisie produces and appropriates products. What the bourgeoisie therefore produces, above all, are its own grave diggers. Its fall and the victory of the proletariat are equally inevitable" (50). From the perspective of temporality, the point to be made is that historical materialism offers a vision of the future as an inevitable reality that now lies dormant or latent in the present conditions of existence. Internal contradictions doom the present configuration of society, but do not prescribe a particular future as such. Far from being a recipe for inaction, the inevitability of the triumph of the proletariat is conceived of as the result of political organization since the proletariat has first to be formed into a class. This is achieved by laying bare the secret of surplus value, the essential mechanism of capitalist exploitation.

With the formulation of historical materialism and the revelation of the character of surplus value, socialism became a science. In "Socialism: Utopian and Scientific," Engels elaborates upon this claim by sharpening the distinction, first made in *The Communist Manifesto,* between a reactive form of socialism that seeks a resolution to class antagonism through the creation of concrete utopian communities outside society and the properly scientific form of socialism that aligns itself with the working classes and participates in political and revolutionary action. The utopian systems developed by Saint-Simon, Fourier, and Owen were certainly founded in opposition to capitalism as living embodiments of the spirit of equality and cooperation, but, for Marx and Engels, they seemed both premature (the material conditions of possibility for the emancipation of the proletariat were not yet present in the early part of the nineteenth century) and counterproductive insofar as they sidestepped political action in favor of social experimentation. The ever-receding horizon of a classless society whose inevitability is scientifically ascertained by historical materialism trumps the actualization of discrete communities that discourage class identification. The point is not that utopia or utopian thought is to be rejected wholesale; rather, it is that concrete utopias make utopian thought seem all too possible. Though not commonly cited within Marxist circles, Derrida in this context offers a valuable insight:

> Although there is a critical potential in utopia which one should no doubt never completely renounce, above all when one can turn it into a motif of resistance against all alibis and all "realist" and "pragmatist" resignations, I still mistrust the word. In certain contexts, utopia, the word in any case, is all too easily associated with the dream, with *demobilisation,* with an impossibility that urges renouncement instead of action. The "impossible" of which I often speak is not the utopian, on the contrary it lends its own motion to desire, to action and to decision, it is the very figure of the real. It has duration, proximity, urgency.[17]

From this perspective, the constructedness and self-consciously fictive quality of utopian arrangements in LVU accords well with the open-endedness of scientific socialism in that its fantastic quality already places it beyond the realm of the possible and tends to postpone its concretization absolutely. Utopia is not to be thought of in teleological terms at all, but rather in terms of an unreachable ideal; utopia is not an end in itself but an imaginative means out of the present, a call for "permanent revolution" or, in Derrida's terms, for a "democracy to come."

There is a further temporal element in Marxist theory worth considering, for it offers a corrective to the seeming timelessness of utopia in LVU or, what amounts to the same thing, its seeming ahistoricity. In Althusser's classic formulation, the reproduction of the conditions of production is secured by ideology, which functions within ideological state apparatuses. Fictional utopias provide a limit case for the work of ideology insofar as the particular solutions they have brought to bear on the problem of reproduction—the abolition of property, the simplification of the means of production, the elimination of antagonistic classes, the invention or discovery of technologies that reduce or altogether do away with labor, and so forth—render ideology structurally inoperative, at least for as long as these solutions eliminate the need to interpellate individuals as subjects. Yet, the question of ideology remains relevant in these texts in that they commonly situate utopia in a timeless, ahistorical, static present that is all too reminiscent of the Marxist description of a naturalized ideological state. Ideology, as Althusser notes, is a concept and a category that has no history: "ideology in general has no history, not in a negative sense (its history is external to it), but in an absolutely positive sense."[18] As a point of comparison, consider that while ideology is hardly ever mentioned explicitly in LVU, it performs a key narrative function in dystopian fiction, acting as both the form and the content of the genre's critique of totalitarianism (think of doublespeak and Big Brother in George Orwell's *Nineteen Eighty-Four* [1949]). Indeed, the very absence of ideology in LVU may well have made the genre all the more appealing for a public living through a period of economic and political uncertainty. The absence of ideology in LVU's utopian arrangement, in any case, corresponds to the end-of-history moment it tends to occupy categorically, as though utopia's release from historical time were also an escape from ideology.[19]

Whether this is in itself an ideological effect of utopia (its irrelevance just another form of false consciousness) or a historical possibility in its own right matters less for our purposes than that its absence have some important narrative consequences in LVU. First, if the reproduction of the relations of production has been solved in utopia without recourse to ideology, this also means that there is no subject of ideology and thus no investment in individuality as a compensatory discursive site where the history of subjectification becomes naturalized. This may well account for the relative paucity of "interesting" characters in LVU, which as a genre tends to flatten individualities and do away with psychology altogether. What Fredric Jameson calls the "plebeianization" of the human landscape in utopia is in his view one of its greatest political strengths, signaling a form of desubjectification that eliminates "spiritual private property."[20] But the lack of character development tends also to attenuate narrative flow since the subject-centered realist protocols to which LVU is discursively indebted are premised on the expectation of personal transformation and psychological amplification. Second, the detailed description of the specific solutions each utopia brings to bear on the problem of production and the reproduction of its means often calls for lengthy digressions that, however vital to the content, contribute little to the interest of the plot *as* plot. In utopia, society is self-functioning and economic cycles are reduced to the ideologically neutral life cycles of the seasons. The reproduction of the means of production in this context becomes as predictable and as "natural" as biological reproduction.

Described in these terms, natural or naturalized cycles do not suggest themselves as the most absorbing of narrative patterns. The achievements of utopia as seen through the lens of the Marxian formulation of historical materialism and the theory of ideology that is derived from it result in a subdued sense of eventness in the development of utopian narrative and in an arrested or latent chronology that is made visible only in the retrospective account of its emergence. But nature reappears in LVU in a different register altogether, one that, while proper to the classical utopian genre, at least potentially offers a wider array of narrative possibilities when novelists begin to draw upon Darwin's theory of evolution: the recurring problem of "human nature." In its classical utopian articulation, the problem of human nature is categorical: if human nature is understood to be fixed and immutable, social equality can only be achieved either by repressing it (the elimination of private property in More's *Utopia,* for instance, curbs asocial human impulses such as greed, temptation, envy, etc.) or by enhancing it (the introduction and implementation of technological solutions to the perennial problem of labor in Bacon's *New Atlantis,* for instance, frees humans from unrewarding toil and increases the opportunities for sociability). After Darwin, however, human nature can be reimagined as an evolving adaptable feature (or, better, a conglomerate of evolving adaptable features) existing in a complex environment whose changing conditions will determine its most socially advantageous configuration. The question of whether this form of adaptation is Lamarckian rather than strictly Darwinian or turns out instead to be the by-product of a literary culture operating at some remove from biological determinisms matters less for our purposes than the fact that Victorians took seriously the prospect of an evolving human nature that, under the right circumstances, could overcome its social limitations. Indeed, by virtue of its generic disposition as speculative fiction, LVU makes visible the adaptability of evolutionary theory itself, giving imaginative flight to current ideas of social progress by reconceptualizing the trope of human nature as a variable, mutable, adjustable order subject to the vicissitudes of social competition within and across generations.

At the level of form, Darwin's theory of evolution offers a wealth of rhetorical possibilities for literary invention. The language of interconnection, kinship, and affinity, as the work of Gillian Beer has masterfully shown, provides a new figurative basis on which to plot human temporality.[21] George Eliot's "experiments of Time" in *Middlemarch,* to take one of Beer's examples, offers a view of human agency as an "incalculably diffusive" network of "unhistoric acts" that owes much of its poignancy to Darwin's description of natural selection as an imperceptible but nevertheless constantly operative mechanism of transformation that accounts for variation over time.[22] But the impact of Darwin's conceptualization of temporality on the construction of literary form goes beyond the structure of knowledge underpinning realist representation, however figurative. The fantastic or otherworldly character of LVU allows for a fuller expression of the narrative possibilities opened up by Darwinian evolution in that, unlike realism, it is not subject to the constraints of human mortality as the ultimate horizon of imaginative reason. While the temporal scope of realist fiction is biographical, generational, or even historical, LVU has no such limits as a narrative vehicle that, at least in theory, can transport us to a time beyond human history. Indeed, Darwin's theory of evolution vastly expands the scope of human temporality both by positing a distant common origin for life and by proposing a mechanism of evolution that is both purposeless and open-ended. In *The Structure of Scientific Revolutions,* Thomas Kuhn notes that it was the lack of a goal, rather than the notion of a common origin for the living, that made Darwin's theory a program hard to accept: "For many men the abolition of that teleological kind of evolution [the one espoused by Lamarck, Chambers, and Spencer] was the most significant and least palatable of Darwin's suggestions. The *Origin* recognized no goal set either by God or nature. Instead, natural selection, operating in the given environment and with the actual organisms presently at hand, was responsible for the gradual but steady emergence of more elaborate, further articulated, and vastly more specialized organisms."[23] The absence of a goal goes against the grain of utopian aspirations (utopia is traditionally conceived of as a goal to end all goals), but does not preclude the mechanism of evolution from being brought to bear on the social arena, since its gradualist sense of change accords well with certain views of social transformation. Indeed, in a society that had elected to transform its political institutions through reform rather than revolution, the precepts of Darwinian evolution could be easily transposed. Darwin's insistence on the slow processes whereby species adapt to their environments through natural selection provides a plausible, if often all too hastily assimilated, rationale for social evolution. Here is Darwin in *On the Origin of Species* (1859) on the temporal scale of evolution:

> It may be said that natural selection is daily and hourly scrutinising, throughout the world, every variation, even the slightest; rejecting that which is bad, preserving and adding up all that is good; silently and insensibly working, whenever and wherever opportunity offers, at the improvement of each organic being in relation to its organic and inorganic conditions of life. We see nothing of these slow changes in progress, until the hand of time has marked the long lapse of ages, and then so imperfect is our view into long past geological ages that we only see that the forms of life are now different from what they formerly were.[24]

In this striking description of evolution's time scale, the infinitesimal and the infinite coincide, simultaneously expanding the horizon of human history, which is now seen to be but a part of a much vaster natural history that remains inaccessible to human consciousness, and shrinking its domain insofar as human historical agency is in the last instance independent of the ongoing, "daily and hourly" operations of natural selection. Biological time is genetic and genealogical rather than temperamental and characterological, shifting emphasis away from the time scale of historical and fictional narrative in which human acts determine the conduct of life to a planetary time scale that dwarfs such acts. In addition, Darwin's theory posed distinct challenges to the prevailing conception of the nature of the event by reinvigorating the long-standing philosophical problem of chance versus design, mind versus matter, as the causal explanation of things in his formulation of variation as both useful and useless, improvement being relative only to the environmental conditions of an organism's existence. Moreover, random mutations, the events that natural selection "scrutinises," are invisible not only in the sense that the changes to which they give rise are slow; they are invisible insofar as they are manifested *as* variation after the fact, in the belated expression of offspring as a result of sexual selection. When it comes to species, change can indeed be described as "latent" since it is already contained within a generation that does not in itself express it as a general feature.[25] This time gap is perhaps more readily conceived when we consider change as originating in genetic variation, which, occurring constantly yet imperceptibly within a given species, becomes dramatically visible when members of the same species become separated geographically and new species are formed as each population adapts to its own environment. Darwin did not of course have any knowledge of genetics, but his observations led him to postulate that "natural selection will be enabled to act on and modify organic beings at any age, by the accumulation of profitable variations at that age, and by their inheritance at a corresponding age" (86). The time lapse between the event (random mutation) and its manifestation (variation)—what might be thought of as the rate of adaptation—varies widely among species and can often determine whether a species survives or becomes extinct. Insofar as human historical acts tend to be understood within the scope of a person's or a generation's lifespan, natural selection as a mechanism of evolution can therefore only serve as an analogue for human temporality in the social arena.

There are thus two incommensurable temporal gaps: on the one hand, the belated expression of change within the mechanism of evolution itself; on the other, the difference obtaining between evolution's dynamic process of change occurring over generations and human historical timekeeping of social transformation as an intragenerational phenomenon relevant only within the lifespan of historical actors. The appearance of the two within the general historical context of Darwin's assimilation therefore challenges the conventional wisdom concerning diachronic and synchronic modalities of time since the different orders of time cannot be said in any straightforward sense to be sequential or simultaneous. At the level of content, the confusion of evolutionary for human time leads in LVU to implausible conceits, such as the underground utopia in Bulwer-Lytton's *The Coming Race* that is inhabited by the Vril-ya, an orientalized humanlike race who have achieved social coherence after having followed an alternative evolutionary path, with their putative origin traceable to amphibians rather than primates. The success of the Vril-ya may well be due to their use of Vril, a miraculous source of energy with destructive as well as occult powers, but, in Bulwer-Lytton's telling, the threat this "coming race" poses to humans is rather more racial than military, as the odd marriage plot in which the human traveler becomes embroiled shows in its very implausibility. In H. G. Wells's *The Time Machine*, the Morlocks and the Eloi, the two human species the time traveler encounters in the future, represent different evolutionary lineages: the former are white, apelike creatures that have adapted to an underground existence, while the latter are "pretty little people" who, enfeebled and infantilized, merely serve to feed the Morlocks.[26] In this case, the branching out of humans into two distinct species represents a sort of devolution, as though humans had traveled backwards along the branches of the evolutionary tree and reverted to more primitive or less complex forms of animal existence.[27] The "Golden Age" that the Eloi inhabit constitutes a stage of arrested development in which human history exists only as a "natural" environment where huge buildings and other "vast shapes" erected by forgotten ancestors blend into the wooded hillsides as so many topographical landmarks with no cultural significance. The Eloi themselves, with their purple tunics and buskins, seem to be relics from an indeterminate past, a sort of preclassical or even prehistorical human infancy in which the symbolic order has yet to make itself available. But this future is posthistorical, and what at first glance appear to the time traveler to be aspects of a long-established utopia soon prove to be a projection of his own present since the human species of the future have foresworn intellect altogether ("I grieved to think how brief the dream of human intellect had been" [141], he muses at one point). Wells shows that adaptation is a value-neutral operation and evolution, as a whole, dysteleological. Far from being a paradise regained, the future for human descendants has little future; instead, it is a suicidal standoff in which the Morlocks end up feeding on the Eloi.

In terms of character, the traveler in LVU, while no doubt related to the figure of the enterprising navigator used to such good effect by early modern utopian writers, must also be understood to fit the model of the naturalist, a type of traveler whose discoveries, given the organization of knowledge in the nineteenth century, were of great public interest and whose cultural image, enhanced by the symbolic capital derived from Romanticism's rhetorical valorization of nature, gave his form of travel something of the aura of an heroic quest. The works of Darwin, to be sure, but also those of other naturalists who traveled in South America, such as Alexander von Humboldt, Alfred Russel Wallace, Henry Bates, William Henry Edwards, and William Henry Hudson, were widely disseminated, giving the figure of the scientific explorer who collected specimens a new cultural centrality. Butler's narrator in *Erewhon*, for instance, describes the flora and fauna he encounters with the eye of someone accustomed to observe nature: "And yet everything was slightly different. It was much the same with the birds and flowers on the other side, as compared with the English ones: thus there was a robin and a lark, and a wren, and daisies, and dandelion; not quite the same as the English, but still very like them—quite like enough to be called by the same name. . . . "[28] In addition, the fact that these naturalists were traveling to the *terra incognita* of South America made their quest a form of time travel in itself since they seemed to be traveling back in time to a prehistorical setting where nature had for long been untouched by humans.[29] Darwin opens the *Origin* with a reflection on this form of travel: "When on board H.M.S. 'Beagle,' as a naturalist, I was much struck with certain facts in the distribution of the inhabitants of South America, and in the geological relations of the present to the past inhabitants of that continent. These facts seemed to me to throw some light on the origin of species—that mystery of mysteries, as it has been called by one of our greatest philosophers" (1). The passage stages a scene of encounter between Darwin and the inhabitants of South America that is reminiscent of the first encounters between Europeans and Native Americans in the contact zone even as the inhabitants he does encounter in South America are for the most part themselves of European ancestry. The search for the origin of species, moreover, is framed as a quest for the solution to a "mystery of mysteries" that echoes earlier quests. Christopher Columbus's identification of the mouth of the Orinoco River as the common source of the Tigris, Euphrates, Ganges, and Nile rivers, for instance, was for him proof that he had found the Earthly Paradise (the origin of species, if you will) at the apex of a world shaped like a woman's breast.[30]

A scene in Butler's *Erewhon* provides an ironic staging of Darwinian time travel. Having long abandoned technology, the people of Erewhon live in a "natural" if highly ritualized state that has been purged of mechanical devices, which are now deemed dangerous and immoral. At one point, the King of Erewhon with some alarm asks Higgs, the protagonist, about his watch, which has inexplicably given offense to the people who have already seen it. Having been shown a pamphlet titled "The Book of the Machines" that gives an account of the country's history, Higgs later learns that approximately five hundred years before the present of the story the increasing sophistication of machines led the people of Erewhon to destroy them, fearing that they could eventually come to replace humans. The pamphlet contains this description of mechanical evolution: "'Take the watch, for example; examine its beautiful structure; observe the intelligent play of the minute members which compose it: yet this little creature is but a development of the cumbrous clocks that preceded it; it is no deterioration from them. A day may come when clocks, which certainly at the present time are not diminishing in bulk, will be superseded owing to the universal use of watches, in which case they will become as extinct as ichthyosauri, while the watch, whose tendency has for some years been to decrease the size rather than the contrary, will remain the only existing type of an extinct race'" (203). The watch here becomes a figure for the evolution of machinery and, since it is a timekeeping device, also for the way in which evolution occurs over or in time. The juxtaposition of zoomorphic elements ("creature," "race") with temporal markers ("A day may come . . . ," " . . . at the present time . . . ," " . . . for some years . . . ,") and the future tense ("will be," "will become," "will remain") colors the pamphlet's pseudo-Luddite extrapolation of Darwinian evolution with a sense of foreboding, as if the evolution of the watch were also a revolution in timekeeping, which is as much as to say that it is a revolution in time itself. But the watch, a mechanical device found quite commonly in LVU,[31] is not only a figure for time in a post-Darwinian world. Used most famously by William Paley in his work *Natural Theology* (1802), the watch was a privileged figure in the argument for design in that its complexity, akin to that of, say, the eye, implied, by analogy, a designer for the works of nature. Though Darwin does not directly address this teleological argument for the existence of God in the *Origin,* in his discussion of the complexity of the eye, he makes a point of stating unequivocally that his theory rests on the principle that an organ's design, however complex, can only have come about by means of natural selection: "If it could be demonstrated that any complex organ existed, which could not possibly have been formed by numerous, successive, slight modifications, my theory would absolutely break down. But I can find out no such case" (189).[32] Butler's conceit can thus be read as an endorsement of Darwinian evolution in a political context that would reject it on the grounds of its success, not of its implausibility.

It would be too neat (that is, clean) to suggest that the relation obtaining between Marxian and Darwinian forms of temporality was dialectical in nature. To be sure, the cultural contemporaneity of the two theories suggests that they both responded to, and assimilated, a similar sense of the Victorian present and its grand scale of possibility. It is not surprising, then, that the scope of their theories were similarly directed towards totality, nature in Darwin, history in Marx, and that their theoretical syntheses purported to be applicable universally. The question of "influence" is fraught, not least because they never met each other and their theories were already independently formulated by the time they read each other. Historically, at any rate, Marx seems to have been a better reader of Darwin than Darwin of Marx. Darwin famously thanked Marx for having sent him a copy of *Capital,* but he left no record of having read it. Of Darwin, Marx famously said: "Not only is a death blow dealt here for the first time to 'Teleology' in the natural sciences but their rational meaning is empirically explained."[33] And at Marx's graveside, Engels declared: "Just as Darwin discovered the law of development of organic nature, so Marx discovered the law of development of human history."[34] The intellectual history of the period is less important to the present argument, however, than the impact that their theories, together and in isolation, had on the cultural understanding of time and the specific ways in which this understanding made possible the temporal experimentation that characterizes LVU, to which I now turn.

A "River of Fire"

The nature of time travel in William Morris's *News from Nowhere* is at once proleptic and nostalgic. Waking up after a restless night, William Guest finds himself some two hundred years into the future in a world that resembles one that in his own childhood might at best have been a dimly remembered reality, "pleasanter, indeed, than the deep country was as he had known it" (54). The opening chapter, or, more precisely, the transition between the first two chapters, establishes this temporal dichotomy in formal as well as narrative terms. The world he imagines as a remote possibility in the present after attending a meeting at the Socialist League—a grim present in which he is "stewing discontentedly" as he travels in the London underground, that "vapour-bath of hurried humanity"—becomes actualized in the future, "a vague hope, that was now become a pleasure, for days of peace and rest, and cleanness and smiling goodwill" (55). Indeed, it is as though the vision that materialized before him were the fulfillment of a wish whose articulation is fully formed even as its content is initially obscure: "If I could but see a day of it" (54). But the act of wish fulfillment is not instantaneous: there is of course the time lapse inherent in the very notion of time travel that bridges present with future, but the duration of time travel is also registered in a subtle temporal shift that suggests traveling into the future is itself a time-consuming endeavor: "[I]t was winter when I went to bed the last night, and now, by witness of the river-side trees, it was summer, a beautiful bright morning seemingly of early June" (56). This shift corresponds, in formal terms, with a change in narrative voice as the present, narrated in the third person, becomes a first-person narrative in the future. The switch is self-consciously staged:

> Our friend says that from that sleep he awoke once more, and afterwards went through such surprising adventures that he thinks they should be told to our comrades, and indeed the public in general, and therefore proposes to tell them now. But, says he, I think it would be better if I told them in the first person, as if it were myself who had gone through them; which indeed, will be easier and more natural to me, since I understand the feelings and desires of the comrade of whom I am telling better than any one else in the world does. (55)

The conceit of making the narrative more intimate and personal by choosing first- over third-person narration is straightforward. But the grammatical structure of the second sentence seems to suggest that the shift is far from self-assured: "But, says he, I think it would be better if I told them in the first person. . . ." On the one hand, the subject pronoun "he" that stands in for "our friend" in this passage is given voice through the indirectly rendered locution "I think it would be better." On the other, the subject pronoun "I" that ventriloquizes the "he" by using the first-person "I" in indirect speech seems to occupy a different grammatical position in the phrase "if I told them" such that the "I" seems to refer to two different subjects at the same time. Whether taken in isolation, as I have done above, or together, following the grammatical logic of the sentence, the syntactical aberration becomes an instance of the rhetorical figure of anacoluthon. But insofar as this error is self-conscious, the positing of the "I" as a referential placeholder without definitive referent (a subject pronoun without a subject) signals or precipitates a different order of discourse. Indeed, the passage can be said to enact Benveniste's famous formulation of subjectivity in language: "Language is so organized that it permits each speaker to *appropriate to himself* an entire language by designating himself as *I*."[35] In the last clause of the passage (which is a subordinate clause even though it is grammatically rendered by the use of the semicolon as an independent clause), the "as if" becomes literalized and the distinction between the speaking "I" and the "I" that the "comrade" will now adopt comes undone as a narrative conceit and the direction of linguistic appropriation is reversed when the "I" designates himself as "I."

While the ostensible aim of the passage is to personalize the narrative by adopting a first-person narrative voice, the reverse is in fact the case, with the third-person narration of the first chapter having been deployed to create an effect of comradeship, since the "he" is already speaking in the first person. The further indirection of the pronoun "them," which stands in for "adventures" but whose referent can be easily read as "our comrades" by the juxtaposition of the subject pronoun and the verbal forms of "telling" in the sequence "told to our comrades," "to tell them," "if I told them," "the comrade of whom I am telling," suggests that the performative positing of the subject is an ongoing operation rather than a privative act. In the thematic context of the passage, the positing of the "I" as a multiple, ongoing event becomes a condition of possibility of time travel insofar as it stages the displacement of the present into a future as a sequence of always inaugural acts of subject constitution. The dream is only the narrative vehicle of a form of time travel that is discursive in nature, with the descriptive advantage that dreams, like grammar, stage multiple displacements of personality. Further, the shift in temporal registers accords well with the political objectives of the text insofar as the iterative positing of the "I" is also a collective positing, or better, the positing of the collective. The veiled anonymity of the narrator as a "guest" named Guest (of which more below) can be read in this context as the narrative elaboration of the discursive shifts that become the text's vehicle of time travel.

These shifts tend to go against the grain of the thematic and experiential stasis that Morris's novel both inhabits and seeks to promote (tellingly, the novel's alternative title is "An Epoch of Rest") as well as the peculiar tone of its discourse, which tends to be at once elegiac and apostrophic. But they correspond at the macronarrative level to the pattern of dissonance and interruption that characterizes the novel's temporal organization.[36] The voyage in the future can be divided into three parts, each of which has a different temporal orientation: the initial encounter with Dick and his rediscovery of London in the twenty-second century, which is dominated by the present (chapters two through seven); the interview with Hammond at the British Museum, which includes the historical reconstruction of the past as a way of accounting for how the "change" came to pass (chapters eight through twenty); and the trip upriver to participate in the hay-harvest, which faces towards the future even as it ends with Guest's return to the Victorian present (chapters twenty-one through thirty-two). The existence of different temporal vectors in the novel, however, is not limited to the narrative structure, since the temporality of each of the three sections is further divided into rhetorical, grammatical, and thematic registers characterized by the commingling of past, present, and future. Narrative continuity is achieved to some extent through Guest's voice, but his subject position, as we have seen, is unstable and, as a result, his development as a character remains indeterminate even as he experiences a potentially life-changing encounter with the world of the future. The obverse of this view is represented by the city of London, which seems to offer a sense of spatial continuity insofar as Guest's voyage is a displacement in time, not of place. But the city has undergone such drastic transformations in the interval between Guest's present and his visit to the future that it is characterized by its substitutability with, rather than by its contiguity to, the London he once knew (it is in this sense its metaphor rather than its metonymy). We are left with a narrative whose structure promises a sense of sequential coherence that it then fails to fulfill.

Nowhere is this pattern more clearly visible than in the novel's rhetorical treatment of the river Thames. First, it organizes time travel in two complementary senses: on the one hand, as a traditional figure for the passage of time (the same river never flows twice) as well as for travel itself (the river as corridor of global transport), the Thames, as its name might imply, is an apt rhetorical vehicle for Guest's voyage.[37] The particular attention the text pays to the bridges that span the two banks of the Thames serves as an index of the river's efficacy as a figure for time travel insofar as the river itself can be said to "bridge" the past to the present, which is the future: "Then the bridge! I had perhaps dreamed of such a bridge, but never seen such an one out of an illuminated manuscript; for not even the Ponte Vecchio at Florence came anywhere near it" (58). The fact that this particular bridge is "not very old . . . it was built or at least opened, in 2003," suggests that, at least from Guest's perspective, there are in fact several different bridges, each of which has spanned a different Thames: the bridge he is seeing, the bridge of which he has dreamed, the "plain timber bridge" the former has replaced, the bridge he crossed the night before he traveled into the future ("the ugly suspension bridge," whose historical counterpart, the Hammersmith suspension bridge, Morris is said to have loathed[38]), and the Ponte Vecchio, whose name suggests that there are ever newer ones that replace it or at least make it outdated. The pattern is again repeated, albeit in reverse, in the third part of the novel, when Guest, traveling upriver, is relieved to discover that "my old enemies the 'Gothic' cast-iron bridges had been replaced by handsome oak and stone ones" (201) and, further upstream, to reacquaint himself with Shillingford Bridge "new built, but somewhat on its old lines" (223) and New Bridge, which Ellen refers to correctly as an "old bridge" (228). We could describe the juxtaposition of old and new bridges at several points along the Thames as a form of anachronism (the bridges Guest sees, or no longer sees, in the present of the story do look out of place to him since they refer to his past), but the effect is one of timelessness or achrony, since the commingling of so many different temporal registers also does away with the ordering principle that would organize them in a logical sequence. The novel's title, *News from Nowhere,* captures the sense of timelessness achieved in utopia as a categorical absence of "news," or of history-in-the-making.[39]

On the other hand, the river is itself a stage for traveling in time insofar as Guest's voyage up the Thames in the last third of the novel is, with the notable exception of the train ride in the novel's opening chapter and the carriage ride that takes him to the British Museum, the only narrative action that involves spatial displacement, and, for that matter, the only narrative action in the novel as a whole. In the third part of the novel when Guest and his friends travel upstream, the Thames operates as a sort of Bakhtinian chronotope— the chronotope of the "river of time," perhaps—in that it gathers the various semantic and discursive currents of the novel into its flow.[40] But this spatial displacement is accompanied by temporal discontinuities, since Guest reads the Thames in historical terms by comparing, in however implicit a manner, what he sees with his experience of it in his own present. The effect is uncanny: the river, understood as a figure for the passage of time, seems to run both backwards and forwards at the same time as Guest and his friends paddle upriver in the utopian future while the past reappears in Guest's reminiscences of what the river had once been. The process, a sort of narrativization of the flood tide, is personally as well as politically rejuvenating:

> As we went higher up the river, there was less difference between the Thames of that day and Thames as I remember it; for setting aside the hideous vulgarity of the cockney villas of the well-to-do, stockbrokers and other such, which in older time marred the beauty of the bough-hung banks, even this beginning of the country Thames was always beautiful: and as we slipped between the lovely summer greenery, I almost felt my youth come back to me, and as if I were on one of those water excursions which I used to enjoy so much in the days when I was too happy to think that there could be much amiss anywhere. (186)

The convergence of present and future, which is here stylized as a return to the personal past, becomes, in political terms, the projection of utopian ideals as a concrete recuperation of a simpler social past before the vulgar excesses of capitalist prosperity ever "marred the beauty" of the river course itself. Time reversal is a shrewd ideological strategy for Morris in this regard since it renaturalizes (by returning to nature) what had already ceased to be historical. The point is as follows: ideology works by naturalizing what is in fact historical (the well-to-do as "naturally" predisposed to impose their "vulgar" taste on nature). By literalizing this process, by making nature itself stand in for what is natural and, therefore, beautiful ("this beginning of the country Thames was always beautiful"), Morris, who in this follows the Romantics, aestheticizes the experience of nature ("water excursions") rather than the things that are "amiss" (such as "cockney villas") and which need to be "set aside" before one can be "too happy." Against the blind valorization of the past, Guest chastises Ellen's grandfather, the "old grumbler," for defending the "damned flunkies" who "destroyed [the Thames's] beauty morally, and had almost destroyed it physically" (198). The beauty of the Thames is a recurring theme that, as we shall see in more detail below, carries ethical as well as political weight insofar as the river is made to stage in a figurative as well as literal manner the convergence or conciliation between the social and the natural that makes Morris's utopia an aesthetic experience.

Neither Morris nor the Romantics should be uncritically dismissed as ineffectual dreamers for taking this stance; it is a profoundly moral outlook with immediate practical implications. "As I strove to stir up people to this reform [to get rid of the "ugly disgraces of civilization"]," William Morris wrote in the preface to *Signs of Change,*

> I found that the causes of the vulgarities of civilization lay deeper than I had thought, and little by little I was driven to the conclusion that all these uglinesses are but the outward expression of the innate moral baseness into which we are forced by our present form of society . . . [41]

E. P. Thompson notes that Morris's revolutionary cast of mind was above all else practical, realizing that, even as the historical conditions in which he found himself were not ripe for revolution, one must nevertheless strive wholeheartedly towards making them so in the aesthetic as well as the political realm. Paraphrasing Morris in one of his last lectures, Thompson writes: "In True Society, the unit of administration must be small enough for every citizen to feel a personal responsibility. The community of Communism must be an organic growth of mutual obligations, of personal and social bonds, arising from a condition of practical equality. And between False and True Society there lay, like a 'river of fire,' the Revolution. It was the work of a realist to indicate where that river ran, and to hand down to us a 'tradition of hope' as to the lands beyond those deadly waters."[42] That Morris first used the phrase "river of fire" in a lecture on art (" . . . between us and that which is to be, if art is not to perish utterly, there is something alive and devouring; something as it were a river of fire that will put all that tries to swim across to a hard proof indeed . . . "[43]) suggests that politics and art become in practice indistinguishable. From this perspective, the genre of utopia, the one genre in the history of literature that makes thematically as well as rhetorically explicit the mutually constitutive relation obtaining between literary forms and social formations, fruitfully provides Morris with a ready-made convention for speculating on the future from a position "before the revolution." Moreover, by availing himself of the temporal plasticity of the genre, Morris is able to make this future come to life in the concrete detail of his realistic representation of nature. Morris is in this regard both a "revolutionary" and a "romantic."

Fredric Jameson writes on the temporality of utopia in a manner that accords well with this view of Morris: "It is in the context of the gradual reification of realism in late capitalism that romance once again comes to be felt as the place of narrative heterogeneity and of freedom from that reality principle to which a new oppressive realistic representation is the hostage. Romance now again seems to offer the possibility of sensing other historical rhythms, and of demonic or Utopian transformations of a real now unshakably set in place; and Frye is surely not wrong to assimilate the salvational perspective of romance to a reexpression of Utopian longings, a renewed meditation on the Utopian community, a re-conquest (but at what price?) of some feeling for a salvational future."[44] The recuperative logic of *News from Nowhere* centers on the aesthetic valorization of medieval art, less for its own sake than for the simplicity of its design and its relation to natural forms. Morris's medievalism, to be sure, is of a piece with the medieval revival in late-Victorian England (Tennyson, Swinburne, Ruskin, and, as their name plainly suggests, the Pre-Raphaelites, but also, in a second-order relay, the neo-Gothicism of Bram Stoker, Stevenson, and Wilde), but it also contributes in this particular novel to offer new "historical rhythms" to the complex temporal patterns it deploys in its "salvational" utopian project.

Which brings us to the second reason for why the river as a rhetorical device comes undone as a unitary image. As the principal topographical feature in the novel, the Thames seems to provide continuity between the Victorian present of the novel's opening and the utopian future. Yet, the novel remains, for most of its narrative, on the margins of its own central rhetorical flow. The middle section of the novel occurs at the British Museum and consists of a reconstruction of the historical past and a description of the present state of society, which bears the marks of the change that made it possible. At the level of structure, we can thus describe this middle section as an interruption in the flow of the narrative if we consider the third part as both motivated and conditioned by the initial boat ride during which Guest first meets Dick and which extends into the carriage ride from Hammersmith to Bloomsbury that follows it. The middle section is punctuated by references to the river trip (Hammond: "... I need not say much about all this, as you are going up the river with Dick, and will find out by experience how these matters are managed" [112]), but, in contrast to the first and third parts, it is almost devoid of narrative action and takes place almost entirely indoors. In keeping with the conventions of the genre, the middle section of *News from Nowhere*, like the middle of most utopian fictions before it from More to Bellamy, offers a static picture of "things as they are." In this case, however, it must be made to account for the difference between the state of things at "home" with the state of things in utopia in terms of historical time rather than in terms of rationality or national character.

Given the political stakes of the project, it is not surprising that the historical terms used by Morris to account for this difference accord well with the Marxian conception of temporality. As is well known, Morris's reading of *Capital* was a transformative experience that led him to become a socialist militant and, in 1884, to found the Socialist League, which features in the first sentence of the novel. The autobiographical elements in *News from Nowhere* remain implicit, however, and, though no secret is made of the author's aesthetic tastes and political sympathies, the ambiguity surrounding William Guest's true identity (not the least of which is that he is addressed indistinctly as "guest" and "Guest") invites the reader to speculate that the dream-narrative is in fact Morris's own. Similarly, the historical reconstruction provided by Hammond and, in the aesthetic realm, Morsom, makes oblique rather than direct references to historical materialism. The comparison Guest makes as a matter of course between the future he is visiting and his own present—Ellen calls it his "never-ending contrast between the past and this present" (242)—nevertheless has as one of its narrative aims the constatation of the sort of predictions that the science of history Marx founded would allow one to make. Conversely, the future Guest witnesses gives credence and support to the social projections he and his comrades could only have imagined or dreamed as a possible outcome to a historical situation that could not for long remain unchanged. Fittingly, it is through Ellen's voice that we get confirmation of history-made-material: "'It is true,' she said. 'It is true!' 'We have proved it true!'" (232).

The latent middle of the novel's narrative structure can be said in this regard to provide the proof, if proof be needed, that both Marxists and Guest's hosts in the future would need in order to show not only the adequacy but the justness and inevitability of utopia. The historical situation of Morris's own present, or his present as history already lived, thus becomes linked to the future as lived experience in the figure of G/guest, with the middle of the novel providing a narrative of historical development that is still latent in the Victorian present, "before the revolution." Hammond is a suitable "native informant" in that he occupies a "middle" position between the past and the present of utopia: he is old enough to have lived through a period of history that still resembles Guest's present or to at least have a sense of the culture's memory of it, and yet is still living in the present, involved with the lives of his relatives (he claims to have "managed" Dick and Clara's reconciliation [104]) even if he seems to have never left the library in which he's always worked. Hammond is thus able to decode the present for Guest, treating him as though he were "from another planet" (102). In doing so, however, he also corroborates what Guest, in his present, surmised. Those who worked for change, Hammond tells Guest, "because they could see further than other people went through all these phases of suffering; and doubtless all the time the most men looked on, not knowing what was doing, thinking it all a matter of course, like the rising and setting of the sun—and indeed it was so" (148). The result is that from Guest's perspective in the future, the change that has come about, regardless of the particulars, is seen as inevitable; that it came about through violence is not. Hammond offers the history of the period as a sequence of stages or confrontations between the bourgeoisie and the proletariat that go from State Socialism and the shortening of the working week together with the institution of the minimum wage in 1952 through the organization of labor into a Federation of Combined Workmen and a representative Committee of Public Safety. Civil war eventually breaks out after a peaceful meeting in Trafalgar Square turns into a massacre perpetrated by the army and the country begins a cycle of terror that does not end until a "system of life founded on equality and Communism" is founded (171).

There is nothing surprising or particularly new about the historical sequence Hammond offers, other than the length and detail in which he offers it, in that it follows, in broad strokes, the stages Marx and Engels had sketched in the *Communist Manifesto* for the future of the class struggle. What is surprising in Morris's narrative from this perspective, however, is that it offers an aesthetic vision of Communism. According to Hammond, the "new spirit of the time" was to be "delight in the life of the world" in which experience ruled over rationality and love over discord. It is a spirit that, in Hammond's own historical understanding, resembles a secular medieval spirit: "More akin to our way of looking at life was the spirit of the Middle Ages, to whom heaven and the life of the next world was such a reality, that it became to them a part of the life upon the earth; which accordingly they loved and adorned, in spite of the ascetic doctrines of their formal creed, which bade them contemn it" (175). The belief in heaven and hell has now of course "gone," but the view of a "continuous life of the world of men" has been preserved and a new form of art, no longer called art, but "a necessary part of the labour of every man who produces," now serves as a remedy for the onset of disappointment in the utilitarian comfort achieved (176).

But his meeting with Hammond reveals something else as well that escapes the historical account of the past and present. Upon first meeting Hammond, Guest experiences, quite literally, the uncanny: " . . . I was now looking at him harder than good manners allowed of, perhaps; for in truth his face, dried-apple-like as it was, seemed strangely familiar to me; as if I had seen it before—in a looking-glass, it might be, said I to myself" (101). It is here, with the suspicion that Dick's kinsman is also his own and that Dick is therefore his relative, that the sense of latency is most clearly expressed even as the genealogical connection is not explicitly made (and how could it?). The notion that utopia can only be achieved by violent revolutionary change, even as it is understood that, in Morris's present, revolutionary conditions are not yet in place, is very effectively illustrated by the generational conceit of having Guest find his own grandson in the future telling him how it is that the change he could not have lived to see finally came about. The latency of change can be read as forming part of the cultural legacy of Darwinian temporality in Morris's time even if there are no explicit references to Darwin in the novel. Darwin does not in fact appear in Morris's writings and there is no evidence that Morris ever read his work, but the retrospective description of utopia as a latent political solution to Guest's social present suggests that Morris did not see the gradualism associated with Darwinism as incompatible with the massive social mutations of revolutionary change.[45]

But in another sense, Darwinian temporality comes into play in utopia itself after the "river of fire" has been crossed insofar as it is nature, rather than history proper, that seems to prevail once social equality has been established. Hammond describes it in these terms: "The last harvest, the last baby, the last knot of carving in the market-place is history enough for them [Dick and Clara]. It was different, I think, when I was a lad, when we were not so assured of peace and continuous plenty as we are now . . . " (102). The return to nature signifies a slowing down of time when compared to the "hurried and discontented humanity" of Guest's Victorian present and suggests the social assimilation of biological rhythms. But nature also becomes an aesthetic principle in the future, not only in the sense of its valorization, as we saw in the context of Morris's medievalism; beauty in nature is considered biologically advantageous: "You must remember, also, that we are long-lived, and that therefore beauty both in man and woman is not so fleeting as it was in the days when we were burdened so heavily by self-inflicted diseases" (105). Indeed, the voyage up the river in the third part of the novel stages the narrative reconciliation of the social and the aesthetic in nature as Guest travels back into the future towards the hay-harvest accompanied by Dick (his future kinsman), Clara, and Ellen, a woman whose beauty is "strange and almost wild" (193). This reconciliation takes the form of a reconceptualization of nature, or rather its very negation, insofar as nature has become obsolete *as* a concept in the future. In their conversation with Morsom, which occurs on the third day of their voyage up the Thames, Clara makes this explicit: "Was not their mistake once more bred of the life of slavery that they had been living?—a life which was always looking upon everything, except mankind, animate and inanimate—'nature' as people used to call it—as one thing, and mankind as another? It was natural to people thinking in this way, that they should try to make 'nature' their slave, since they thought 'nature' was something outside of them" (219). The ideological uses to which the "people before our time" put nature so as to make its separation from humans seem "natural" have become superfluous, as did too, after the Great Change, the increasing mechanization of life to which the exploitation of nature once led. Work is not subject to factory time-management; rather it obeys biological cycles and individual choice. As Ellen puts it: "I work hard when I like it, because I like it, and think it does me good, and knits up my muscles, and makes me prettier to look at, and healthier and happier" (199). Dick too thinks of himself as forming "part of it all" and feels the "pain as well as the pleasure in my own person" of the seasons and their gains and their losses (245).

The mechanical production of goods has now been replaced by handicraft and the aesthetic pleasures one is able to derive from work: to handicraft, says Morsom, we "have added the utmost refinement of workmanship to the freedom of fancy and imagination" (220). By the time they reach the upper Thames, the social and the aesthetic, in the form of a dwelling, have become one with nature: "There was no garden between [a quite modern stone house] and the river, nothing but a row of pear-trees still quite young and slender; and though there did not seem to be much ornament about it, it had a sort of natural elegance, like that of the trees themselves" (231). And at the end of the journey, nature itself figures as a house: "Presently we saw before us a bank of elm-trees, which told us of a house amidst them, though I looked in vain for the grey walls that I expected to see there" (238). As Guest and Ellen disembark and approach the village, he feels the tug of the familiar ("almost without my will my feet moved on along the road they knew" [240]) and, when they reach the "many-gabled old house" that Ellen had all along wanted to see (a house whose historical counterpart is Morris's own Kelmscott Manor), she embraces it and cries: "O me! O me! How I love the earth, and the seasons, and weather, and all things that deal with it, and all that grows out of it, as this has done!" (241). The aesthetic experience of nature, or art experienced as nature, exemplified by Ellen's embrace of the house in this scene is further reinforced a few lines later by Guest's own description (or discursive "embrace") of Ellen herself: "Her exultation and pleasure were so keen and exquisite, and her beauty, so delicate, yet so interfused with energy, expressed it so fully, that any added word would have been commonplace and futile" (241). The unusual though deliberate use of the word "interfused" in this verbal description, reminiscent of Wordsworth's use of it in "Tintern Abbey" (" . . . a sense sublime / Of something far more deeply interfused, / Whose dwelling is the light of setting suns . . . " [96–98]), suggests that nature and art have become, from the perspective of experience, interchangeable, even as the words needed to express their relation remain necessary.

It is fitting that the journey should culminate with the history of the Thames and that it should be Ellen to whom Guest recounts it. Ellen is eager to learn about the past, not for herself alone, but for the many children she hopes one day to have and upon whom she wishes to impress "some part of my ways of thinking," the "essential part of myself" (233). When Guest tells her that the railroads actively prevented the country people from using the waterways as roads and that, as a consequence, the river ceased to have commercial value and became neglected, Ellen responds that this fact "is not stated clearly enough in our textbooks, and it is worth knowing" (235). A sentiment echoed at book's end by Guest himself, who, though now awake in his own present, ventriloquizes Ellen's last "mournful look" before he leaves the future: "Go back and be the happier for having seen us, for having added a little hope to your struggle" (249). The future has become history; a history to be disseminated and used to improve the present and impress upon it a "way of thinking" that might make it come to pass.

Frederic Jameson has argued that utopian fiction emerges at the "moment of the suspension of the political" during which institutions seem to be utterly unchangeable and, at the same time, infinitely modifiable.[46] A state of paralysis in which change is unfathomable, Jameson suggests, is also a precondition for intellectual freedom and imaginative play. Prerevolutionary conditions, in contrast, demand specific political attention and concrete intervention rather than wholesale reinvention. Utopian fiction is the calm before the storm, a moment of stillness that involves social ferment but systemic inertia. The situation of More, writing on the eve of capitalism, or of Francis Bacon, before the

English Civil War, is similar to that of the writers of LVU who wrote as the world was heading towards the October Revolution and the First World War. From this perspective, the latent middle of LVU can be said to also involve its own generic "middleness" as it comes to occupy a moment of political latency in which the distance marked from political institutions encourages imaginative play. The middleness of LVU can therefore be thought of as a historical condition of its own possibility. If we consider the emergence of LVU in the context of the literary production of the last three decades of the nineteenth century, this same point can be made from the perspective of literary history since it forms part of a veritable explosion of so-called paraliterary genres whose aesthetic, discursive, and imaginative bearings were no longer centered on the institutions of realism nor were they yet inexorably directed towards the revolutionary program of the modernist avant-gardes. LVU thus occupies a literary no-man's-land, a Nowhere without News, whose imaginative license is paradoxically granted by the suspension or latency of the literary itself. The literary formlessness of LVU is therefore a condition of possibility of its own formal inventiveness. The latent middle in LVU makes utopia possible on the principle of its antiliterary properties and, for the same reason, suspends it politically in the very middleness of a future always to come.

Notes

1. For the classic elaborations of desire as narrative logic, see Peter Brooks, *Reading for the Plot: Design and Intention in Narrative* (Cambridge: Harvard University Press, 1992) and Fredric Jameson, *The Political Unconscious: Narrative as a Socially Symbolic Act* (Ithaca: Cornell University Press, 1981).

2. The notion that narrative endows life with meaning by offering a retrospective perspective from a moment beyond death is common to models of narrative temporality that focus on the ending. See Peter Brooks, *Reading for the Plot* (Cambridge: Harvard Universuty Press, 1992) and Frank Kermode, *The Sense of an Ending* (Oxford: Oxford University Press, 1967).

3. This point is aptly illustrated by H. G. Wells, who, writing in 1905, explicitly calls for a "kinetic" modern utopia that "must shape not as a permanent state but as a hopeful stage leading to a long ascent of stages." See *A Modern Utopia* (London: Penguin Classics, 2005), 11.

4. See Fredric Jameson, "The Experiments of Time: Providence and Realism," in *The Novel*, vol. 1, ed. Franco Moretti (Princeton: Princeton University Press, 2006), 109.

5. Citing Lyman Tower Sargent's authoritative *British and American Utopian Literature, 1516–1985: An Annotated, Chronological Bibliography* (New York: Garland, 1988), Matthew Beaumont estimates that "hundreds of novels and short stories" were published in the United States and Britain during the last three decades of the nineteenth century. *Utopia, Ltd.: Ideologies of Social Dreaming in England 1870–1900* (Leiden: Brill, 2005), 1. By another estimate, nearly a hundred Utopian fictions were published between 1875 and 1905. See Francis Wheen, introduction to H. G. Wells, *A Modern Utopia* (New York: Penguin, 2005), xvi.

6. Edward Bellamy, *Looking Backward 2000–1887,* ed. Alex MacDonald (Toronto: Broadview, 2003), 77.

7. See Franco Moretti, "Serious Century," in *The Novel,* vol. 1, ed. Franco Moretti (Princeton: Princeton University Press, 2006), 364–400. For Moretti, the realist novel occupies an "intermediate" generic position between comedy and tragedy well suited to chronicle the "serious" middle class, intent on marking its distance from the "carnivalesque" laboring classes. The realist novel's greatest formal contribution, in this view, is the use of "fillers," rather than events, as the normative narrative principle of a form intent on representing the everyday *as* uneventful.

8. Eric Hobsbawm, *The Age of Empire 1875–1914* (New York: Vintage, 1989), 35.

9. For an account of the impact of Victorian "new media" and information technologies on fiction, see Richard Menke, *Telegraphic Realism: Victorian Fiction and Other Information Systems* (Stanford: Stanford University Press, 2008).

10. Hobsbawm, *The Age of Empire 1875–1914,* 13.

11. Wells, *A Modern Utopia,* 15. Hereafter cited parenthetically.

12. Eric Hobsbawm gives a detailed account of the publication history of *The Communist Manifesto* in his introduction to the 1998 edition. According to him, the Manifesto did not begin to be widely read until 1871, when the first of nine editions in six different languages that were to appear in the next two years was first distributed. See Eric Hobsbawm, "Introduction," *The Communist Manifesto,* by Karl Marx and Frederick Engels (London: Verso, 1998), 6.

13. See Northrop Frye, "Varieties of Literary Utopias," in Frank E. Manuel, ed., *Utopias and Utopian Thought* (Boston: Houghton Mifflin, 1965), 25.

14. See Frederick Engels, "Socialism: Utopian and Scientific," in Robert C. Tucker, ed., *The Marx-Engels Reader,* 2nd ed. (New York: W. W. Norton, 1978), 683–712.

15. Louis Althusser, "Preface to *Capital,*" in *Lenin and Philosophy,* trans. Ben Brewster (New York: Monthly Review Press, 1971), 72.

16. Karl Marx and Frederick Engels, *The Communist Manifesto* (London: Verso, 1998), 58.

17. Jacques Derrida, "Intellectual Courage: An Interview by Thomas Assheuer," trans. Peter Krapp, *Culture Machine* 2 (2000). http://www.culturemachine.net/index.php/cm/article/view/303/288.

18. Louis Althusser, "Ideology and Ideological State Apparatuses (Notes towards an Investigation)," in *Lenin and Philosophy,* 160–61. Hereafter cited parenthetically in text.

19. H. G. Wells's *A Modern Utopia* explicitly rejects this model, proposing instead a "kinetic" utopian scheme in which history does not stop: a "hopeful stage leading to a long ascent of stages" (11).

20. Fredric Jameson, "The Politics of Utopia," *New Left Review* 25 (January–February 2004): 40.

21. Gillian Beer, *Darwin's Plots: Evolutionary Narrative in Darwin, George Eliot and Nineteenth-Century Fiction* (Cambridge: Cambridge University Press, 1983).

22. George Eliot, *Middlemarch* (New York: W. W. Norton, 1977), 3.

23. Thomas S. Kuhn, *The Structure of Scientific Revolutions* (Chicago: University of Chicago Press, 1996), 172.

24. Charles Darwin, *On the Origin of Species, A Facsimile* (Cambridge, MA: Harvard University Press, 1964), 84. Hereafter cited parenthetically.

25. This is one of the key advances Darwin made over Lamarck, for whom inherited features expressed a concurrent rather than a latent form of adaptation in the absence of random mutations.

26. H. G. Wells, *The Time Machine,* ed. Nicholas Ruddick (Toronto: Broadview, 2001), 82.

27. For a structural description of the narrative consequences of devolution in the context of science fiction, see Darko Suvin, *Metamorphosis of Science Fiction* (New Haven: Yale University Press, 1979), 222–42.

28. Samuel Butler, *Erewhon,* ed. Peter Mudford (London: Penguin Classics, 1985), 75. Hereafter cited parenthetically in text.

29. A measure of this vision of South America as a laboratory in the British imaginary can be garnered from the monster's promise in Mary Shelley's *Frankenstein:* "If you consent [to create a mate], neither you nor any other human being shall ever see us again: I will go to the vast wilds of South America." Victor's incredulous response confirms it: "You propose . . . to fly the habitations of man, to dwell in those wilds where the beasts of the field will be your only companions." See Mary Shelley, *Frankenstein* (New York: W. W. Norton, 1996), 99.

30. See Beatriz Pastor, *Discurso narrativo de la conquista de América* (Habana: Casa de las Américas, 1983), 58.

31. In Bulwer-Lytton's *The Coming Race,* Aph-Lin's son rebuilds the protagonist's watch to make it keep both the time of the Vril-ya and that of the protagonist: "I have that watch still and it had been much admired by many among the most eminent watchmakers of London and Paris" (Toronto: Broadview, 2002), 149–50. Hereafter cited parenthetically in the body of the text.

32. For an account of Butler's views on the relation between Darwin's nonpurposive view of evolution and Paley's argument from design, see Hans Peter Breuer, "Samuel Butler's 'The Book of the Machines' and the Argument for Design," *Modern Philology* 72, no. 4 (May 1975): 365–83.

33. This quotation is from a letter Marx wrote to Lassalle dated January 16, 1861. Quoted in James Rachels, *Created from Animals: The Moral Implications of Darwinism* (Oxford: Oxford University Press), 110.

34. Karl Marx and Frederick Engels, *Selected Works* (London: Lawrence and Wishart, 1968), 435.

35. Emile Benveniste, "Subjectivity in Language," in *Problems in General Linguistics,* trans. Mary Elizabeth Meek (Coral Gables: University of Miami Press, 1971), 226. Emphases in original.

36. For a formal account of interruption in Morris's novel and its relation to the Victorian configuration of the autoethnographic imagination, see James Buzard, "Ethnography as Interruption: News from Nowhere, Narrative, and the Modern Romance of Authority," *Victorian Studies* (Spring 1997): 445–74.

37. Along with Mark Twain's Mississippi stories, Conrad's *Heart of Darkness,* Dickens's *Our Mutual Friend,* and Eliot's *The Mill on the Floss,* Morris's novel is one of the great "river narratives" of the nineteenth century.

38. See note 1 on page 54 in the Broadview edition.

39. For the obsolescence of "news" in utopia, see Buzard, "Ethnography as Interruption," 451.

40. For a Bakhtinian reading of Morris's novel, see Marcus Waithe, "*News from Nowhere,* Utopia and Bakhtin's Idyllic Chronotope," *Textual Practice* 16, no. 3 (2002): 459–72.

41. William Morris, *Signs of Change* (London: Reeves and Turner, 1888).

42. E. P. Thompson, *Persons and Polemics* (London: Merlin Press 1994), 66–76. This is the transcription of a lecture Thompson gave to the William Morris Society in 1959, some four years after his full-length study of Morris, *William Morris: Romantic to Revolutionary,* appeared

in Britain. Thompson uses the phrase "river of fire" as the title of the seventh chapter of the first part of this work.

43. William Morris, "The Prospects of Architecture," in *Collected Works*, vol. 22 (London: Longmans, 1910), 131. Quoted in Thompson, *William Morris: Romantic to Revolutionary* (Stanford: Stanford University Press, 1988), 244.

44. Fredric Jameson, *The Political Unconscious*, 104.

45. Gowan Dawson suggests that aesthetes such as Morris, Pater, and Swinburne formed something of a bond, or were at least part of a "concurrence," with Huxley, Tyndall, and other defenders of Darwin in the 1870s in the pages of the *Fortnightly Review* under John Morley's editorship, if only because both camps were attacked on similar grounds for blasphemy, paganism, and immorality. See Gowan Dawson, *Darwin, Literature and Victorian Respectability* (Cambridge: Cambridge University Press, 2007), 17–18.

46. Fredric Jameson, "The Politics of Utopia," 45.

SELECT BIBLIOGRAPHY

Bal, Mieke. *Narratology: Introduction to the Theory of Narrative,* trans. Christine van Boheemen. Toronto: University of Toronto Press, 1985.
Barthes, Roland. *S/Z,* trans. Richard Miller. New York: Hill and Wang, 1974.
Bivona, Dan, and Roger B. Henkle. *The Imagination of Class: Masculinity and the Victorian Urban Poor.* Columbus: The Ohio State University Press, 2006.
Brooks, Peter. *Reading for the Plot: Design and Intention in Narrative.* Cambridge, MA, and London: Harvard University Press, 1992.
Buzard, James. *Disorienting Fiction: The Autoethnographic Work of Nineteenth-Century British Novels.* Princeton: Princeton University Press, 2005.
Claybaugh, Amanda. *The Novel of Purpose: Literature and Social Reform in the Anglo-American World.* Ithaca: Cornell University Press, 2007.
Daly, Suzanne. *The Empire Inside: Indian Commodities in Victorian Domestic Novels.* Ann Arbor: University of Michigan Press, 2011.
Dames, Nicholas. *Amnesiac Selves: Nostalgia, Forgetting, and British Fiction, 1810–1870.* Oxford: Oxford University Press, 2001.
———. *The Physiology of the Novel: Reading, Neural Science, and the Form of Victorian Fiction.* Oxford: Oxford University Press, 2007.
Deleuze, Gilles. "He Stuttered." In *Essays Critical and Clinical.* Minneapolis: University of Minnesota Press, 1997. 107–14.
Freedgood, Elaine. *The Ideas in Things: Fugitive Meaning in the Victorian Novel.* Princeton: Princeton University Press, 2006.
Gallagher, Catherine. "Formalism and Time." *Modern Language Quarterly* 61, no. 1 (March 2000): 229–51.
Garcha, Amanpal. *From Sketch to Novel: The Development of Victorian Fiction.* Cambridge: Cambridge University Press, 2009.
Hughes, Linda K., and Michael Lund. *The Victorian Serial.* Charlottesville: University Press of Virginia, 1991.

Jameson, Fredric. "The Experiments of Time: Providence and Realism." In *The Novel.* Vol. 1, ed. Franco Moretti. Princeton: Princeton University Press, 2006. 95–127.

―――. *The Political Unconscious: Narrative as a Socially Symbolic Act.* Ithaca: Cornell University Press, 1981.

Kermode, Frank. *The Sense of an Ending.* Oxford: Oxford University Press, 1967.

King, Amy M. *Bloom: The Botanical Vernacular in the English Novel.* Oxford: Oxford University Press, 2003.

Laplanche, Jean. "Notes on Afterwardsness." In *Essays on Otherness.* London: Routledge, 1998. 264–69.

Laplanche, Jean, and J.-B. Pontalis. *The Language of Psychoanalysis,* trans. Donald Nicholson-Smith. New York: W. W. Norton & Co., 1973.

Lessing, Gotthold. *Laocoon: An Essay on the Limits of Painting and Poetry.* Baltimore: Johns Hopkins University Press, 1984.

Levine, Caroline. *The Serious Pleasures of Suspense: Victorian Realism and Narrative Doubt.* Charlottesville and London: University of Virginia Press, 2003.

Menke, Richard. *Telegraphic Realism: Victorian Fiction and Other Information Systems.* Stanford: Stanford University Press, 2008.

Miller, D. A. *Narrative and Its Discontents: Problems of Closure in the Traditional Novel.* Princeton: Princeton University Press, 1981.

―――. *The Novel and the Police.* Berkeley: University of California Press, 1988.

Miller, J. Hillis. *Fiction and Repetition: Seven English Novels.* Cambridge, MA: Harvard University Press, 1982.

―――. "Middles." In *Reading Narrative.* Norman: University of Oklahoma Press, 1998. 61–77.

Moretti, Franco. *Graphs, Maps, Trees: Abstract Models for a Literary Theory.* London: Verso, 2005.

―――. "Serious Century." In *The Novel.* Vol. 1, ed. Franco Moretti. Princeton: Princeton University Press, 2006. 364–400.

―――. *The Way of the World: The* Bildungsroman *in European Culture.* London and New York: Verso, 1987.

Ortiz-Robles, Mario. *The Novel as Event.* Ann Arbor: University of Michigan Press, 2010.

Puckett, Kent. *Bad Form: Social Mistakes and the Nineteenth-Century Novel.* Oxford: Oxford University Press, 2008.

Richardson, Brian. *Narrative Beginnings: Theories and Practices.* Lincoln and London: University of Nebraska Press, 2008.

―――. *Narrative Dynamics: Essays on Time, Plot, Closure, and Frame.* Columbus: The Ohio State University Press, 2002.

Said, Edward. *Beginnings: Intention and Method.* Baltimore and London: Johns Hopkins University Press, 1978.

Scarry, Elaine. *Resisting Representation.* Oxford: Oxford University Press, 1994.

Schor, Hilary. *Dickens and the Daughter of the House.* Cambridge: Cambridge University Press, 1999.

Thomas, Ronald R. *Detective Fiction and the Rise of Forensic Science.* Cambridge: Cambridge University Press, 2001.

Wahrman, Dror. *Imagining the Middle Class: The Political Representation of Class in Britain, 1780–1840.* Cambridge: Cambridge University Press, 1995.

Woloch, Alex. *The One vs the Many: Minor Characters and the Space of the Protagonist in the Novel.* Princeton: Princeton University Press, 2003.

CONTRIBUTORS

AMANDA CLAYBAUGH is professor in the Department of English at Harvard University. Her book, *The Novel of Purpose: Literary Ambition and Social Reform in the Anglo-American World* (Cornell University Press, 2007), won the Sonya Rudikoff Prize for Best First Book in Victorian Studies sponsored by the Northeast Victorian Studies Association. She has edited *Uncle Tom's Cabin* and *Mansfield Park*, published articles on Dickens and Howells, and written a number of reviews for the *London Review of Books*.

SUZANNE DALY is associate professor of English at the University of Massachusetts–Amherst. She is the author of *The Empire Inside: Indian Commodities in Victorian Domestic Novels* (University of Michigan Press, 2011). She is also co-editor with Ross G. Forman of a special issue of *Victorian Literature and Culture*, called "Food and the Victorians" (2007). Her published articles include "Spinning Cotton: Domestic and Industrial Novels" (*Victorian Studies*), "Indiscreet Jewels: The Eustace Diamonds" (*Nineteenth-Century Studies*), and "Kashmir Shawls in Mid-Victorian Novels" (*Victorian Literature and Culture*).

AMANPAL GARCHA is associate professor of English at The Ohio State University. He is author of *From Sketch to Novel: A Theory of Victorian Fiction* (Cambridge University Press, 2009). His work has appeared in *Dickens Studies Annual, Prose Studies, Connotations: A Journal of Scholarly Debate, Literature Compass, Nineteenth-Century Literature,* and *Victorian Literature and Culture*.

AMY M. KING is associate professor of English at St. John's University, in Queens NY, where she specializes in nineteenth-century British literature. She is the author of the book *Bloom: The Botanical Vernacular in the English Novel* (Oxford University Press, 2003) and articles that have appeared in *Victorian Studies, Novel, English Language*

Notes, and *Literature Compass.* She is currently at work on a book-project entitled *Reverent Form: Natural History and Natural Theology in the British Novel, 1789–1867.*

CAROLINE LEVINE is professor of English at the University of Wisconsin–Madison. She is the author of *Provoking Democracy: Why We Need the Arts* (Blackwell, 2007) and *The Serious Pleasures of Suspense: Victorian Realism and Narrative Doubt* (University of Virginia Press, 2003), winner of the Perkins Prize for the year's best book in narrative studies. She is at work on a book on form, and she is an editor of the *Norton Anthology of World Literature.*

MARIO ORTIZ-ROBLES is associate professor of English at the University of Wisconsin–Madison. His book, *The Novel as Event* (Michigan University Press, 2010), investigates the relation between language and action in the work of novelists such as Dickens, Thackeray, and George Eliot against the backdrop of Victorian ideologies of individualism. He has published articles in *Comparative Literature, Textual Practice,* and *ELH.* He is currently at work on a book-length project on the figure of the animal in late-Victorian fiction.

KENT PUCKETT is associate professor of English at the University of California at Berkeley. He is the author of *Bad Form: Social Mistakes and the Nineteenth-Century Novel* (Oxford University Press, 2008) and co-author, with Derek Nystrom, of *Against Oligarchies, Against Bosses: A Conversation with Richard Rorty* (Charlottesville: Prickly Pear Pamphlets, 1998). He is currently at work on two projects: an examination of the relation between close reading and psychoanalysis and a book-length reading of style in British war films.

HILARY M. SCHOR is professor of English at the University of Southern California. Her scholarship focuses on narrative theory; law, property and the nature of subjectivity in literature; popular culture and film. Her first book, *Scheherezade in the Marketplace: Elizabeth Gaskell and the Victorian Novel,* was published by Oxford in 1992. *Dickens and the Daughter of the House* appeared in Cambridge's series on Victorian literature and culture in 1999.

ALEX WOLOCH is associate professor of English at Stanford University. He works on the history of the novel and literary theory. He is the author of the *The One vs. the Many: Minor Characters and the Space of the Protagonist in the Novel* (Princeton University Press, 2004) and co-editor with Peter Brooks, of *Whose Freud?: The Place of Psychoanalysis in Contemporary Culture* (Yale University Press, 2000). He is currently at work on a book-length project on George Orwell and the problem of engaged writing.

INDEX

Abrams, M. H., 190n10
Adam Bede (Eliot), 15, 165, 188
Adorno, Theodor, 196, 212n4
aesthetics and politics, 91–92, 237–38
"Afterwardsness." See *Nachträglichkeit*
Agnes Grey (Brontë, A.), 13–14, 109–18, 122
Allen, David, 186, 190n19, 194n48
Althusser, Louis, 222, 224–25, 245n15, 245n18
Aristotle, 100n2
Arnold, Matthew, 91–92, 196, 212n2
Austen, Jane, 10–11, 25–46, 161, 164, 167

Bakhtin, Mikhail, 164, 189n9, 216, 236
Bakunin, Mikhail, 96–97, 104n51
Bal, Mieke, 46n17, 138–39, 141nn26–29, 163
Barthes, Roland, 6, 20n14, 140n4, 163, 172, 189n6, 191n26, 212n3, 214n24
Beaumont, Matthew, 244n5
Beer, Gillian, 226, 245n21
beginnings, 1–2, 48–49, 110
Bellamy, Edward, 218, 220

Benveniste, Émile, 233, 246n35
Bersani, Leo, 89, 103n39, 106n56
Bewell, Alan, 171, 191n23
Bhabha, Homi, 141n15
Bildungsroman, 110, 116, 145, 155, 217
Bivona, Dan and Henkle, Roger B., 136, 141nn22–23
Blackmur, R. P., 101n9
Blair, Sara, 103n33
Bleak House (Dickens), 10, 50
Bourdieu, Pierre, 146, 157n9
Bowler, Peter, 167, 190n14
Brontë, Anne, 13–14, 109–27
Brontë, Charlotte, 10, 109, 111, 113, 120–21
Brontë, Emily, 109, 115–16
Brooke, John H., 162, 189n4
Brooks, Peter, 6, 20n15, 48, 52, 73n3, 73n4, 90, 104n40, 104n48, 125, 126n22, 137, 141n24, 163, 189n6, 244nn1–2
Bruegel, Pieter, 26–27
Bruer, Hans Peter, 246n32
Bulwer-Lytton, Edward, 221, 229
Butler, Judith, 135
Butler, Marilyn, 29, 43n3, 43n4
Butler, Samuel, 221, 230–31

Buzard, James, 5, 20n12, 246n36, 246n39
Byerly, Alison, 154, 158n17

Cannon, Susan, 190n17
Case, Alison, 126n6
centers, 9–10, 12
characters: and ideology, 129; pairs, 10–11, 25–27, 42–43. *See also* repetition
Christmas Carol, A (Dickens), 131, 140n12
chronology: disruption, 49, 53, 55, 56–57, 63
clerks, 14, 129, 130–34
Collins, Wilkie, 10, 17, 196–214
Cook, Elizabeth Heckendorn, 191n24
Cooter, Roger, 193n42

Dames, Nicholas, 6–7, 21n20, 157n11
Daniel Deronda (Eliot), 11, 47–74
Darwin, Charles, 2, 9, 18, 167–68, 221–22, 226–28, 230–32, 241
Dawson, Gowan, 247n45
Deleuze, Gilles, 88, 103n34
Derrida, Jacques, 10, 19n1, 224, 245n17
Dever, Carolyn, 74n15
description, 16, 162–94
Dickens, Charles, 14, 128–41
digression, 55–56, 143, 148, 153
Dombey and Son (Dickens), 14, 128–41
Don Quixote (Cervantes), 26, 34, 39

Elfenbein, Andrew, 140n3
Eliot, George, 10, 11, 47–74, 134, 141n19
ellipsis, 83–84, 115
Emma (Austen), 25, 30, 161, 167
endings, 1–2, 52, 71, 139, 206
Engels, Friedrich, 223, 232, 245n14
epistemology, 197–98, 199–201
epistolary narratives, 165, 169, 174
Ermarth, Elizabeth Deeds, 213n8
Esch, Deborah, 79, 101nn11–12

Faraday, Michael, 198
Felix Holt, the Radical (Eliot), 50, 68, 165
Findlay, J. R., 157n2
Findley, J. M., 37, 45n14
focalization, 42, 58
François, Anne-Lise, 106n60
free indirect discourse, 10, 43
Freedgood, Elaine, 4, 20n6
Freud, Sigmund, 12, 80–82, 101n15
Frye, Northrop, 221, 245n13
Fukuyama, Francis, 1, 19n2
Fulford, Tim, 191n25
"Future of the Novel, The" (James), 77, 100n5, 101n21
Fyfe, Aileen, 164, 180, 190n10s, 192n37

Gallagher, Catherine, 6, 21n19, 163, 189n8
Garcha, Amanpal, 192n39
Gaskell, Elizabeth, 13, 164, 176
Genette, Gérard, 114–15, 126n8, 126n10, 189n7
Girard, René, 163, 189n6
Gissing, George, 140n3

Habermas, Jürgen, 144, 157n4
Harden, Edgar, 157n6
Hardy, Barbara, 69, 73n5
Hegel, G. W. F., 29, 37, 222
Helsinger, Elizabeth, 185, 192n39, 193n45, 194n46
Hertz, Neil, 97, 106n55
Hitchcock, Alfred, 198–99, 206, 213n21
Hobsbawm, Eric, 220, 245n8, 245n10, 245n12
Horne, Philip, 101n9
Houghton, Walter E., 139n1
Hughes, Linda K., 4, 20n8
Hunter, Shelagh, 192n39

identification, 51, 53
identity: formation, 38; and juxtaposition, 29, 31–32, 42–43
interiority, 41–43

Jager, Colin, 168, 174, 190n18, 191n28
James, Henry, 6, 11–12, 69, 71, 74n12, 75–106
Jameson, Fredric, 3, 20n5, 163, 189n6, 217, 225, 238, 243, 244n1, 244n4, 245n20, 247n44, 247n46
Jane Eyre (Brontë, C.), 10, 109, 111, 113, 115, 121, 196
Jevons, Stanley, 198, 201, 213n19
Johnson, Claudia, 50, 74n9
journalism, 14–15, 142–51

Kaplan, Fred, 128, 139n2, 140n9
Kellner, Douglas, 212n2
Kermode, Frank, 1, 2, 19n2, 20n4, 244n2
Knight, Deborah, 213n6, 213n9
Kropotkin, Peter, 96, 104n51, 105nn52–53
Kucich, John, 5, 20n13
Kuhn, Thomas, 227, 245n23

Lacan, Jacques, 81, 95, 101nn16–17
Laplanche, Jean, 80–82, 98, 101n14, 101nn18–20, 102n23
Lear, Jonathan, 97, 102n22, 106nn57–58
Leavis, F. R., 50, 70, 74n13
Lessing, Gotthold Ephraim, 12, 125, 126n22
Levine, Caroline, 213n12, 213n20
Levine, George, 157n11, 158n20
Life of Charles Dickens, The (Forster), 137–38
Lightman, Bernard, 167, 190nn14–15
literary form, 3–5, 7, 34–5, 52, 125, 147–48, 152, 163–64; experimentation, 109; organic form, 75–76
Litvak, Joseph, 100n7, 156, 157n11, 158n22
localism, 164, 171, 188
Lockwood, David, 132–33
Lubbock, Percy, 6
Lucas, John, 85
Lukács, Georg, 3, 8, 20n5
Lund, Michael, 4

Lynch, Deidre Shauna, 158n15, 192n39

Marx, Karl, 10, 18, 219, 232
Marxism, 3–4, 196, 221–22, 239
medievalism, 238, 240–41
Menely, Tobias, 191n24
Menke, Richard, 245n9
Michaels, Walter Benn, 88–89, 103nn37–38
middles, 2–3, 9–10, 71–72, 75–78, 82–86, 95, 112–25, 128–29, 155–57, 174–76, 203, 216, 238–39, 244; and stasis, 144, 148–49, 217
Middlemarch (Eliot), 51, 68, 72, 141n19, 226
middle class, 14, 128, 130
Mill, James, 147, 157n10
Miller, D. A., 6, 20n7, 20n16, 51, 74n10, 125, 127n23, 135, 152, 158n16, 167, 190n12, 213n7, 214n22
Miller, Hillis J., 2–3, 20n4, 125, 126n22, 141n29
Mitford, Mary Russell, 16, 161, 164, 179–94
More, Thomas, 215, 220, 226
Moretti, Franco, 3, 8–9, 20n5, 21nn21–22, 125, 127n23, 132, 137, 140n14, 181, 185, 192n39, 192n40, 194n47, 218, 245n7
Morgan, Susan, 43n4
Morris, William, 17–18, 215, 232–47

Nachträglichkeit, 12, 75, 80–83, 94–95
narrative theory, 5–7, 49, 125, 162–63
narrators, 154–55, 233
naturalism, 86–88
natural theology, 16, 162–94
News from Nowhere (Morris), 17–18, 215, 232–47
Nietzsche, Friedrich, 93, 104n44
North and South (Gaskell), 13

Our Mutual Friend (Dickens), 10

Paley, William, 231
Paris Sketch Book, The (Thackeray), 145, 147, 151, 154
Parrinder, Patrick, 141n20
Pastor, Beatriz, 246n30
Pendennis (Thackeray), 14–15, 142–58
Perec, George, 28
Perera, Suvendrini, 136, 141n21
Peterfreund, Stuart, 175–76, 190n21, 192n31
Picker, John, 74n16
plot: and change, 142, 225; courtship plot, 13–14, 38–39, 110, 117–19; and discourse, 34; double plot, 10–11, 25–26, 28, 37–38, 47, 52, 61, 63; plotlessness, 14–15, 17, 154–55, 218; temperance plot, 13–14, 118–24. *See also* Bildungsroman
Plotz, John, 4, 20n9
Poole, William, 131, 140n13
Poovey, Mary, 126n12, 194n49
Pratt, Mary Louise, 191n25
Price, Leah, 4, 20n9
Princess Casamassima, The (James), 12, 78–105
Professor, The (Brontë, C.), 109, 111–13

Rajan, Rajeswari Sunder, 136, 141n21
Rausing, Lisbet, 190n13, 192n30
Ray, Gordon, 156, 158n23
Ray, John, 166, 190n11
Raynor, John, 44n12
Reader, W. J., 158n21
repetition, 9, 12–15, 53, 58–59, 93–94, 114–17, 143–46; and characterization, 134–35, 139, 150, 154; and pulse, 97–98
Richardson, Brian, 19n3, 20n17
Rowe, John Carlos, 102n25
Ruth, Jennifer, 158n21

Said, Edward, 1, 19n1
Sales, Roger, 192n39
Scarry, Elaine, 13, 21n23, 111–12, 114, 126n3, 126n7
Secord, Anne, 193n41

Sedgwick, Eve Kosofsky, 76, 100n3, 101n9, 212n5
Sense and Sensibility (Austen), 10–11, 25–46
Shelley, Mary, 246n29
Shillingsburg, Peter, 157n3
Shirley (Brontë, C.), 111–12, 115, 121
siblings in fiction, 25–26, 30
Silverman, Kaja, 77, 100n4
sketch narratives, 146–47, 151–52, 154, 162
Stephen, Leslie, 69–70
Sternberg, Meir, 213n21
Sternlieb, Lisa, 210, 214nn25–26
Stewart, Garrett, 3, 20n5
story and discourse, 27–28, 34–36, 48
suspense, 9, 15–18, 196–212, 216
Sutherland, John, 143, 157n2
Suvin, Darko, 246n27
Sylvia's Lovers (Gaskell), 176–78, 188
Szondi, Peter, 104n46

teaching, 18–19; in fiction, 111–18
Teahan, Sheila, 104n47
Tenant of Wildfell Hall, The (Brontë, A.) 13–14, 109, 118–24
textual objects, 4, 61–66
Thackeray, W. M., 10, 14–15, 142–58
Thomas, Ronald R., 4, 20n10, 212n3
Thompson, E. P., 237–38, 246n42
Tillotson, Kathleen, 140n3
Todorov, Tzvetan, 74n8
Tolstoy, Leo, 34, 195
Topham, Jonathan, 164
Torgovnik, Marianna, 6, 20n18
Tragic Muse, The (James), 75–78, 85
Trilling, Lionel, 32, 85–86, 92, 103nn28–29
Trollope, Anthony, 13, 164, 188
Turner, Frank, 167–68, 190n14, 190n16
Tyndall, John, 198

utopia, 17–18, 215–247

Villette (Brontë, C.), 111, 113, 115, 121

Virginians, The (Thackeray), 143

Wahrman, Dror, 44n12
Waithe, Marcus, 246n40
Wallace, Anne D., 192n39
Ward, Mary (Mrs. Humphry), 120, 126n16
Wells, H. G., 215, 220, 229, 244n3
West, Rebecca, 85
Whewell, William, 201
White, Gilbert, 16, 162, 164, 167–79
Winnett, Susan, 189n6
Wives and Daughters (Gaskell), 176, 178–79
Wolfson, Susan J., 5, 20n11

Woloch, Alex, 129, 140n5
Woman in White, The (Collins), 17, 196–214
work in fiction, 111–15, 242; and alienation, 155–56
Wulff, Hans J., 197, 213n10
Wuthering Heights (Brontë, E.), 109, 115–16, 122

Yeats, W. B., 9
Young, Arlene, 130–31, 133, 140nn10–11

Žižek, Slavoj, 104nn49–50

THEORY AND INTERPRETATION OF NARRATIVE
James Phelan, Peter J. Rabinowitz, and Robyn Warhol, Series Editors

Because the series editors believe that the most significant work in narrative studies today contributes both to our knowledge of specific narratives and to our understanding of narrative in general, studies in the series typically offer interpretations of individual narratives and address significant theoretical issues underlying those interpretations. The series does not privilege one critical perspective but is open to work from any strong theoretical position.

The Real, the True, and the Told: Postmodern Historical Narrative and the Ethics of Representation
  ERIC L. BERLATSKY

Franz Kafka: Narration, Rhetoric, and Reading
  EDITED BY JAKOB LOTHE, BEATRICE SANDBERG, AND RONALD SPEIRS

Social Minds in the Novel
  ALAN PALMER

Narrative Structures and the Language of the Self
  MATTHEW CLARK

Imagining Minds: The Neuro-Aesthetics of Austen, Eliot, and Hardy
  KAY YOUNG

Postclassical Narratology: Approaches and Analyses
  EDITED BY JAN ALBER AND MONIKA FLUDERNIK

Techniques for Living: Fiction and Theory in the Work of Christine Brooke-Rose
  KAREN R. LAWRENCE

Towards the Ethics of Form in Fiction: Narratives of Cultural Remission
  LEONA TOKER

Tabloid, Inc.: Crimes, Newspapers, Narratives
  V. PENELOPE PELIZZON AND NANCY M. WEST

Narrative Means, Lyric Ends: Temporality in the Nineteenth-Century British Long Poem
  MONIQUE R. MORGAN

Joseph Conrad: Voice, Sequence, History, Genre
  EDITED BY JAKOB LOTHE, JEREMY HAWTHORN, JAMES PHELAN

Understanding Nationalism: On Narrative, Cognitive Science, and Identity
  PATRICK COLM HOGAN

Joseph Conrad: Voice, Sequence, History, Genre
  EDITED BY JAKOB LOTHE, JEREMY HAWTHORN, JAMES PHELAN

The Rhetoric of Fictionality: Narrative Theory and the Idea of Fiction
  RICHARD WALSH

Experiencing Fiction: Judgments, Progressions, and the Rhetorical Theory of Narrative
  JAMES PHELAN

Unnatural Voices: Extreme Narration in Modern and Contemporary Fiction
  BRIAN RICHARDSON

Narrative Causalities
  EMMA KAFALENOS

Why We Read Fiction: Theory of Mind and the Novel
  LISA ZUNSHINE

I Know That You Know That I Know: Narrating Subjects from Moll Flanders to Marnie
GEORGE BUTTE

Bloodscripts: Writing the Violent Subject
ELANA GOMEL

Surprised by Shame: Dostoevsky's Liars and Narrative Exposure
DEBORAH A. MARTINSEN

Having a Good Cry: Effeminate Feelings and Pop-Culture Forms
ROBYN R. WARHOL

Politics, Persuasion, and Pragmatism: A Rhetoric of Feminist Utopian Fiction
ELLEN PEEL

Telling Tales: Gender and Narrative Form in Victorian Literature and Culture
ELIZABETH LANGLAND

Narrative Dynamics: Essays on Time, Plot, Closure, and Frames
EDITED BY BRIAN RICHARDSON

Breaking the Frame: Metalepsis and the Construction of the Subject
DEBRA MALINA

Invisible Author: Last Essays
CHRISTINE BROOKE-ROSE

Ordinary Pleasures: Couples, Conversation, and Comedy
KAY YOUNG

Narratologies: New Perspectives on Narrative Analysis
EDITED BY DAVID HERMAN

Before Reading: Narrative Conventions and the Politics of Interpretation
PETER J. RABINOWITZ

Matters of Fact: Reading Nonfiction over the Edge
DANIEL W. LEHMAN

The Progress of Romance: Literary Historiography and the Gothic Novel
DAVID H. RICHTER

A Glance Beyond Doubt: Narration, Representation, Subjectivity
SHLOMITH RIMMON-KENAN

Narrative as Rhetoric: Technique, Audiences, Ethics, Ideology
JAMES PHELAN

Misreading Jane Eyre: A Postformalist Paradigm
JEROME BEATY

Psychological Politics of the American Dream: The Commodification of Subjectivity in Twentieth-Century American Literature
LOIS TYSON

Understanding Narrative
EDITED BY JAMES PHELAN AND PETER J. RABINOWITZ

Framing Anna Karenina: Tolstoy, the Woman Question, and the Victorian Novel
AMY MANDELKER

Gendered Interventions: Narrative Discourse in the Victorian Novel
ROBYN R. WARHOL

Reading People, Reading Plots: Character, Progression, and the Interpretation of Narrative
JAMES PHELAN

www.ingramcontent.com/pod-product-compliance
Lightning Source LLC
Chambersburg PA
CBHW030132240426
43672CB00005B/113